The Myth
of the
Liberal Media

MEDIA & CULTURE

Sut Jhally & Justin Lewis
General Editors

Vol. 2

PETER LANG
New York · Washington, D.C./Baltimore · Boston · Bern
Frankfurt am Main · Berlin · Brussels · Vienna · Canterbury

Edward S. Herman

The Myth of the Liberal Media

An Edward Herman Reader
With a Preface by Noam Chomsky

PETER LANG
New York · Washington, D.C./Baltimore · Boston · Bern
Frankfurt am Main · Berlin · Brussels · Vienna · Canterbury

LIBRARY OF CONGRESS CATALOGING-IN-PUBLICATION DATA

Herman, Edward S.
The myth of the liberal media:
an Edward Herman reader / Edward S. Herman.
p. cm. — (media and culture; vol. 2)
Includes bibliographical references and index.
1. Mass media—Political aspects. 2. Mass media—Economic aspects.
3. Mass media—United States. 4. Liberalism. I. Title. II. Series.
P95.8.H475   302.23—dc21   99-35205
ISBN 0-8204-4186-4
ISSN 1098-4208

DIE DEUTSCHE BIBLIOTHEK-CIP-EINHEITSAUFNAHME

Herman, Edward S.:
The myth of the liberal media: an Edward Herman reader /
Edward S. Herman. –New York; Washington, D.C./Baltimore; Boston; Bern;
Frankfurt am Main; Berlin; Brussels; Vienna; Canterbury: Lang.
(Media & culture; vol. 2)
ISBN 0-8204-4186-4
NE: GT

Cover design by Lisa Dillon

The paper in this book meets the guidelines for permanence and durability
of the Committee on Production Guidelines for Book Longevity
of the Council of Library Resources.

Printed in the United States of America

Acknowledgments

I want to thank first Christopher Myers of Peter Lang Publishing, and Sut Jhally and Justin Lewis, editors of the new Peter Lang series on Mass Communication, for inviting my participation with this collection of papers on the media. Sut Jhally and Justin Lewis were also very helpful in the selection and organization of the materials included in this volume.

The collection here reproduces and sometimes expands on and updates articles and papers published earlier in *Z Magazine, EXTRA!, Dollars & Sense, Monthly Review, CovertAction Quarterly, Journal of International Affairs, La Revue Communication, Journal of Communication Inquiry*, and in Robert Babe's edited volume *Information and Communication in Economics*. Thanks are due these journals and publishers for permission to use these writings here.

I also want to express my thanks to Noam Chomsky for his contributions to this volume through co-authored studies, the long-term stimulus of his criticisms and insights, and the Preface he has written here. Richard DuBoff, Robert McChesney, and Herbert Schiller have also been important sources of encouragement, ideas, and effective criticism over the years. My friend and ally David Peterson has been a great help in the updating and verification of documentation for this book. Bob Walther, a reference librarian at the University of Pennsylvania's Van Pelt library, was also very helpful in this documentation process. Kathleen Babbitt's copyediting was ruthless but painfully useful in strengthening the text and making it more readable. Any remaining deficiencies are to the account of the author.

Table of Contents

Preface

Noam Chomsky

Edward Herman's invaluable studies of the media in market-oriented democracies find their natural place in the broader sweep of contemporary history.

From the earliest modern democratic revolutions of seventeenth-century England, one leading theme has been the concerted effort of dominant economic and political elites to keep privilege and power from the "rascal multitude" that sought to enter the public arena, and sometimes succeeded. "The men of best quality," as they called themselves, expressed their willingness to grant the people rights, but only within limits, and on the principle that by "the people" they did not mean the confused and ignorant rabble. The founding fathers of American democracy faced similar problems and discussed them in almost the same words. As one put it, "when I mention the public, I mean to include only the rational part of it. The ignorant vulgar are as unfit to judge of the modes [of government], as they are unable to manage [its] reins." The people are a "great beast" that must be tamed, Alexander Hamilton exclaimed. In more nuanced tones, the leading framer of the constitutional order, James Madison, lucidly elaborated the reasons why that order must be designed to ensure that authentic power remained in the hands of "the wealth of the nation," "the more capable set of men," who could be "expected to sympathize sufficiently with [the] rights [of property]"—meaning the right *to* property, which the founding fathers needed to privilege above all other rights.

The concerns of the "responsible men" only heightened as popular struggle extended the opportunities for meaningful public participation in policymaking. Early in this century, corporate leaders recognized that "the public mind" was "the only serious danger" that confronted their domination of the social order. By the roaring twenties, business leaders confidently assumed that labor had been tamed for good. But order had been restored in "a most undemocratic America" that was "created over its workers' protests," as Yale University labor historian David Montgomery describes the process. A few years later, the great beast once again escaped its cage. Popular mobilization and struggle at last brought the U.S. closer to the mainstream of industrial society with regard to the rights of poor and working people.

The "more capable set of men" reacted in the standard way, and warned of the "hazard facing industrialists in the newly realized political power of the masses," which had to be beaten back. Corporate propaganda offensives in the postwar era reached an extraordinary scale, targeting captive audiences in factories, schools, churches, and even sports leagues. And of course these efforts used corporate media as a major instrument of their campaign to wage and win "the everlasting battle for the minds of men" and to "indoctrinate citizens with the capitalist story" until "they [were] able to play back the story with remarkable fidelity." That "story" also includes what leaders in the corporate-state nexus required to ensure passive obedience to, if not active participation in, the domestic and international programs they designed.

The "bewildered herd," as Walter Lippmann described the great beast in his influential essays on democratic theory, are to be "spectators" but not "participants" in the political system. Their role is limited to periodic choice among selected members of the "specialized class" of "responsible men"—who, it is unnecessary to observe, typically serve the interests of "the wealth of the nation" if they are to retain their status. They intend that the herd perceive few real options in life beyond their "function" as atomized consumers who are granted "consumer choice" but not "consumer sovereignty," as Herman explains.

In the United States, the power of the state to coerce is limited by comparative standards, at least for those with some share in privilege—which is a large part of the population in a very rich society. Not surprisingly, control of opinion and attitudes has been honed to a high art, particularly because civil and political rights were won in this country—not granted. The interplay between freedom and thought control is clearly understood by the "experts in manipulation," to borrow Gramsci's phrase. One of the founders and leading figures of the huge public relations industry, Edward Bernays, reminded his colleagues that with "universal suffrage and universal schooling . . . even the bourgeoisie stood in fear of the common people. For the masses promised to become king." That unfortunate tendency could be contained and reversed, he urged, by new methods of "propaganda" that could be used by "intelligent minorities" to "[regiment] the public mind every bit as much as an army regiments the bodies of its soldiers." Bernays had in mind the dramatic successes of Anglo-American propaganda, which enabled the Wilson administration to whip up jingoist war hysteria among a generally pacifist population. As a member of Wilson's state propaganda agency, Bernays was well-placed to observe the operation and draw lessons from it. So was Walter Lippmann, another participant, who perceived a "revolution" in "the practice of democracy" as "the manufacture of consent" became "a self-conscious art and a regular organ of popular government."

Reasoning along similar lines in the second leading Western democracy, the chair of the British Conservative Party, who recognized the threat that the extension of the franchise posed to party dominance, advised his associates of the need to "apply the lessons" of wartime propaganda "to the organization of political warfare." So the party did with much success, drawing on the ample resources provided by the business world. The founders of modern political science were also impressed by these successes, as were others, among them Adolf Hitler, who determined that next time Germany would forge its own propaganda tools to combat those of the Western democracies.

It would be close to a miracle if the practices of corporate and state media shapers were not influenced significantly by their institutional structure and position within power systems. The critical question is to discover how these insitutional factors operate in the context of many other tendencies and influences, some convergent and others discordant. These are among the topics that are addressed in the essays that follow, which review and advance Herman's work of the past thirty years in these domains. His incisive case studies have lent powerful empirical support to his theses about market control of media, "the triumph and consolidation of market failure" that for systemic reasons is rooted in prevailing institutional structures and power relations, and the ways the media shapes the picture of the world that reaches the general public—the audiences who are, in effect, the "product" that is sold by the owners and managers to their market (other businesses, advertisers), all of which are closely linked to state power. The essays proceed beyond analysis to constructive proposals to democratize the media, in both the short and the longer term, with a realistic and instructive review of prospects and opportunities.

Herman quotes James Madison's observation in later life that "a popular government without popular information, or the means of acquiring it, is but a prologue to a farce or tragedy, or perhaps both." The observation is apt; formal guarantees of personal freedom do not suffice to prevent the farce or the tragedy, even if the guarantees are observed. These issues, explored and illuminated in the essays that follow, should be at the center of the concerns of those who seek to create a society that is more free and more just.

The Illiberal Media

Claims of a pervasive "liberal" or "left" media bias are heard repeatedly in the allegedly liberal/left media, but counterclaims of exceptional "illiberal" or "conservative" bias and power in the media are exceedingly rare. This is hardly a reflection of reality: there is a huge right-wing Christian radio and TV system; the right-wing Rupert Murdoch owns a TV network, a movie studio, 132 newspapers, book publishers (including HarperCollins), and 25 magazines, among other holdings; Rush Limbaugh admirer John Malone's Tele-Communications Inc. is the largest cable system in the United States (14 million subscribers) and has interests in 91 U.S. cable content services;[1] the editorial page of the largest circulation national newspaper, the *Wall Street Journal*, is aggressively reactionary; the talk show world on radio and TV is dominated by the likes of Robert Novak (CrossFire), the McLaughlin Group, and Rush Limbaugh and Limbaugh clones; and even PBS is saturated with right-wing regulars (William Buckley Jr., Tony Brown, John McLaughlin, Ben Wattenberg).

The Pitiful Giant Syndrome

Fairness and Accuracy in Reporting (FAIR) recently listed 40 national right-wing commentators and pundits, from Michael Barone to Armstrong Williams, most of whom have proclaimed the media's liberal bias from positions of access and power that few liberals have attained.[2] Leftists are an extinct species in the mainstream media; the firing of Jim Hightower by ABC, immediately following its 1995 acquisition by Disney, was like the passing of the last carrier pigeon. This doesn't prevent the pundits, and even the media moguls, from making bitter complaints about the power of the "left." In 1996, Rupert Murdoch and John Malone announced that they were jointly planning a news channel in order to combat the "left bias" of the media. The right-wing Canadian mogul Conrad Black, who owns more than half the daily newspapers in Canada and over 100 newspapers in this country (including the *Chicago Sun Times*), also constantly whines about the liberal-left bias of the press.

The reason we only hear plaints of a "liberal" media is that the right-wing is so well entrenched and aggressive that its members can pretend that their own potent selves don't exist when they speak of media bias. Just as power allowed the right-wing and a complicit "liberal media" to label university dissidents a "political correctness" threat, while ignoring the massive right-wing attempt to impose its own political agenda on the university,[3] so in the case of the media, views disapproved by the powerful are "liberal" or "left." The views of the numerous right-wing moguls and pundits are portrayed as implicitly unbiased or merely counters to those of the omnipresent, subversive, but elusive liberals and leftists. We can call this the "pitiful giant syndrome," harking back to Nixon-era claims that the poor United States was a pitiful giant being pushed around by Third World upstarts.

The pitiful moguls are of course in the supremely privileged position of being able to create their own right-wing news and commentary operations and exclude those that don't meet their political standards. Murdoch personally funded the new conservative magazine *The Weekly Standard* in 1995, and he has placed Roger Ailes in charge of his new cable news services. Ailes, who came to the Murdoch news operation after a stint as Rush Limbaugh's producer, is a veteran Republican specialist in media dirty tactics, famous for his role in the Willie Horton ploy used in the 1988 presidential election. Malone has created his own new talk-commentary program, "Damn Right!," hosted by David Asman, the *Wall Street Journal* editorial page's noted apologist for state terrorism in Central America, along with another "citizen education" show, "The Race for the Presidency," put under partisan Republican management. He has also welcomed to TCI cable Pat Robertson's Family Channel and the new, exclusively right-wing, Empowerment Channel. At the same time, Malone succeeded in killing The 90s Channel, that rare (and now approaching the extinct) entity called a "liberal" channel, by raising its entry rates to his cable system to prohibitive levels. The pitiful giant exercised raw economic power in pursuit of his political agenda, but the liberal media didn't notice or complain. And the Clinton Federal Communications Commission (FCC), while sanctioning one giant monopoly power-enhancing merger after another, refused to intervene.

Flabby Centrists versus Aggressive Right

In the real world, the resurgent power of corporate and financial interests, an increasingly concentrated media ever more closely integrated with advertisers, who now spend over $75 billion each year on the media, the proliferation of corporate-funded think tanks, and the corporate "leasing" of the ivory tower,[4] has shifted political power and media opinion sharply to the right. At this point, "left" in the media is conservative, centrist, and in a defensive mode, accepting without question the premises of corporate capitalism and the imperial state, and only weakly defending an eroding welfare state. The older liberalism of Louis Brandeis (*The Curse of Bigness*) and John Dewey (*Reconstruction in Philosophy*), with its powerful strain of equalitarianism and opposition to concentrated economic power, is still deeply rooted in the consciousness of the public, but is hard to find in mainstream media and politics.

The media "left" is epitomized by syndicated columnist David Broder, although Mark Shields, Roger Rosenblatt, or Jack Germond would do just as well. Broder's views are strictly conventional, and he either evades tough issues or joins the establishment mob, as he did in dealing with the North America Free Trade Agreement (NAFTA), the Persian Gulf war, the Soviet Threat and U.S. military buildup, and the more recent claim that welfare and other noncorporate entitlements are out of control. Devoting maximum attention to election horse-racing, and never challenging the real power centers, David Broder is the ideal liberal/leftist for an era of right-wing advance and agenda-setting.[5]

Just as Broder and his fellow media leftists are really centrist and conservative, the more numerous and aggressive forces of the right—George Will, Charles Krauthammer, Robert Bartley, Fred Barnes, William Buckley, Mona Charren, Irving and William Kristol, John Leo, and dozens more—are not properly labelled conservatives; they are, in fact, statist reactionaries. They have been serving the corporate community's quarter-century-long struggle to remove all obstacles to corporate growth and profitability. These obstacles include the welfare state, regulation of corporate practices, and an effective labor movement. Removing or severely weakening these obstructions and returning us to nineteenth century socioeconomic conditions is not "conservative," it is a reactionary project. So is the support of the "strong state" in the Pinochet-Reagan-Thatcher modes, which feature ruthless law and order regimes, imperial aggressiveness, and high-riding military-industrial and prison-industrial complexes.

Rightwing Echo Chamber

With centrists like Broder as the left, and even these in small numbers, the large array of aggressive right-wing pundits, and supportive editors like the *Wall Street Journal*'s Robert Bartley, can significantly influence the national agenda. The right-wingers are sufficiently numerous to be able to constitute an "echo chamber," in which favored charges are repeated, with great indignation, each small elaboration used to keep the subject on the agenda, and the agenda pushed relentlessly. They are able to elevate sleazy trash with a suitable message (Gary Aldrich's *Unlimited Access*) into national prominence, turn the relatively trivial "filegate" scandal into the equivalent of Watergate,[6] and make President Clinton's sex life into an urgent national issue. They can even make genuine contributions to war hysteria and the militarization of foreign policy, with their steady pressure to drop bombs as the first order of business during international crises. In the Persian Gulf crisis of 1990-1991, their demonization of the enemy and misreading of the military threat helped stoke a war fever.[7]

The overmatched and spineless political and media liberals not only don't set agendas, they regularly get on the right-wing bandwagons themselves. They quickly accepted the claim of a serious military threat from Nicaragua in the 1980s, and in the phony MIG crisis of 1984 they competed with one another in urging an aggressive U.S. response.[8] In the Iran-contra crisis of the mid-1980s, which followed the disclosure that the Reagan-Bush administration had secretly supplied arms to Iran—despite President Reagan's highly publicized promise that "America will never make concessions to terrorists"—and had also engaged in a massive effort to raise funds from U.S. client states—using persuasion, bribery, and threats—to support the Nicaraguan contras, despite an explicit congressional prohibition of such actions,[9] the Democrats and the liberal media were remarkably uncritical and sought neither reforms nor punishment for serious law violations.[10]

The right-wing media maintained a ferocious attack on Iran-contra Special Prosecutor Lawrence Walsh,[11] whose work was vastly more relevant to substantive issues—as well as less politically motivated and tainted—than Kenneth Starr's inquiries into Whitewater and President Clinton's sexual escapades. The liberal media, which failed to defend Walsh and give his investigation major attention, have cooperated with the members of the right-wing echo chamber to elevate and honor Starr and help forward his Whitewater-Lewinsky investigation.

In fact, although the right-wing echo chamber has been important in pushing numerous nasty policy trends, its claims would not echo without liberal media cooperation. In addition to giving massive and largely un-critical attention to the Starr investigation, *Newsweek* and the *New York Times* were major participants in the "political correctness" propaganda wave of the early 1990s; they gave prominence and generous treatment to *The Bell Curve*; they both swallowed the claim that the KGB had organized the assassination attempt against the Pope in 1981; they sup-ported the Reaganite arms race and wars of the 1980s; and they and their media confreres are virtually all now in the Concord Coalition camp that elevates the threat of entitlement costs into a crisis and sets the stage for the further erosion of the welfare state.[12]

Proving Liberal Domination

Just as money and power allow the dominant illiberals to call the media liberal and left, so money and power allow them to study and "prove" media bias. S. Robert Lichter, Linda Lichter, and Stanley Rothman have been the most prominent rightists who have engaged in this "scientific" effort. The Lichters organized their Center for Media and Public Affairs in 1985, with accolades from Reagan and Pat Buchanan; Rothman, a long-time member of the Smith College faculty, has received generous right-wing foundation support for his research program. In an article on "Me-dia and Business Elites" (*Public Opinion*, October/November 1981), Robert Lichter and Rothman tried to prove the liberal bias of the media by showing that the "media elite" votes Democratic and has opinions more liberal than that of mainstream America.

The Lichter-Rothman study violated every scientific standard one could name. They claimed to be studying a "media elite," but actually sampled media personnel who had anything to do with media "content," including ordinary reporters (they failed to disclose the composition of their sample). Lichter and Rothman compared their "media elite" with a sample of middle and upper level corporate managers, not with comparable professionals such as teachers, let alone nonprofessional "middle Americans." Their questions were ambiguous and loaded,[13] making one wonder why anyone would participate in this survey. And in fact, Ben Bradlee, the top editor of the *Washington Post*—one of the papers allegedly sampled by Lichter and Rothman—claimed that he couldn't locate a single employee who had participated in their survey.

One key technique of right-wing proofs of liberal bias is to focus on social issues, because the affluent and urban media journalists and editors do tend to be more liberal than blue collar workers on issues such as abortion-choice, gay rights, and the handling of drug problems, as are urban professionals across the board. On the other hand, on matters like government regulation, distrust of big business, trade agreements, income distribution, and jobs policies, "middle America" is to the left of the business and media elite.[14] Rightwingers like Lichter and Rothman handle this by bypassing the problematic areas and focusing on social issues, where the media elite are more liberal and Lichter and Rothman can score points.

Right-wing proofs of a liberal media also focus on voting patterns. The 1981 Lichter and Rothman piece featured the pro-Democrat voting records of the media elite in the four elections between 1964 and 1976. In April 1996 a similar finding was published by the Roper Center and Gannett Freedom Forum; 89 percent of a sample of 139 Washington journalists allegedly voted for Clinton in 1992.[15] The inference drawn from this, as from the Lichter and Rothman study, was that the media has a liberal bias. But the true media elite are the owners, such as John Malone and Rupert Murdoch, who have legal control of the media companies, can hire, promote, and fire their employees, and can and do shape policy. Lichter and Rothman and their allies never poll owners.[16] There are other problems with these conservative polls. Why don't they ever ask questions on the attitudes of the elite versus those of middle America toward trade agreements such as NAFTA and the power of big business? How can we explain the mainstream media's failure to focus on the declining economic position and the insecurity of middle Americans as news and election issues? How is it that a majority of newspapers came out editorially for Bob Dole with the "liberals" controlling the media? How can we reconcile the steady attacks on Clinton's character and the focus on Whitewater and the more cursory treatment of Iran-contra with a pro-Democrat bias? In what sense is Clinton a "liberal" anyway?

Many of these and other questions can be answered by media analyses that focus on the control, funding, structure, and performance of the media, rather than on reporter opinions and voting patterns. For example, the "propaganda model" spelled out in *Manufacturing Consent*,[17] describes the working of the mainstream media in terms of underlying structural factors and "filters" that define the parameters within which media underlings work. These constraints and filters include ownership and the financial pressures for bottom-line performance; the need to adapt to the interests of advertisers, who pay the media bills; sourcing processes that cause journalists to depend heavily on government and business newsmakers; the threat of flak, which keeps the journalists under pressure and in line; and anticommunist and market-supportive premises that journalists internalize. The right-wing pundits and their echo chamber, which are funded by General Electric and other large corporate advertisers, but which complain bitterly about liberal and left domination of the media, fit into this model quite nicely.

It should be noted that FAIR, in its bimonthly publication *EXTRA!*, has published numerous studies that provide compelling evidence of right-wing domination of talk shows and public broadcasting.[18] With the exception of their study of the bias in the selection of guests on Nightline,[19] their efforts have been given much less attention in the mainstream media than right-wing claims of liberal media bias as pronounced by Lichter and Rothman and the recent Roper-Gannett study. This is a reflection of genuine media bias; the right-wing network is always able to push congenial findings into the echo chamber and give themselves and their principals a boost. But this publicity and neglect of the critical FAIR offerings are living proof that the claim of "liberal bias" is false and that the reality is one of illiberal domination.

Notes

1   TCI agreed to a merger into AT&T during 1998; Malone is to become the largest AT&T stockholder and in charge of the AT&T subsidiary that owns and manages the TCI cable channels. Geraldine Fabrikant, "Tracking the Rich Deals of TCI's Chairman Is No Easy Job, *New York Times*, 27 July 1998.

2   "Conservative Top 40," *EXTRA!* (July/August 1998), 25.

3   See John Wilson, *The Myth of Political Correctness* (Durham: Duke University Press, 1995), chap. 2.

4   Lawrence Soley, *Leasing the Ivory Tower: The Corporate Takeover of Academia* (Boston: South End Press, 1996).

5   For a fuller treatment of Broder, see chapter 11 below.

6   See Jeff Cohen, "'Filegate Equals Watergate': The Conservative Echo Chamber Circulates a Myth," *EXTRA!* (October 1996).

7   See Eric Alterman's *Sound and Fury* (New York: Harper-Perennial, 1992), chap. 12.

8   In early November 1984, U.S. officials claimed that the Sandinista government of Nicaragua was importing a shipload of MIG airplanes from the Soviet Union. This was not true, but the mainstream media, by featuring this piece of disinformation heavily, helped drive out of public view the Nicaraguan election, which the Reagan administration was eager to discredit. See Edward Herman and Noam Chomsky, *Manufacturing Consent* (New York: Pantheon, 1988), 137–39.

9   See especially, Peter Kornbluh and Malcolm Byrne, *The Iran-Contra Scandal: The Classified History* (New York: The New Press, 1993); also, Lawrence Walsh, *Firewall: The Iran-Contra Conspiracy and Cover-up* (New York: Norton, 1997).

10 See John Canham-Clyne, "Iran-Contra Revisionism," *Lies of Our Times* (June 1994), 6–8; Robert Parry, "Bipartisan Geo-Politics," *The Consortium* (March 16, 1998), 6–7.

11 See Walsh, *Firewall*.

12 The Concord Coalition, led by investment banker and former Nixon administration official Peter Peterson, claims that Social Security is in crisis and needs "reform" by scaling back, means testing, and privatization. But Social Security is still in surplus, and even on conservative assumptions will not exhaust its resources for another generation (2032). Even on those assumptions small tax increases would keep the system viable; and on less conservative assumptions as to productivity growth the "crisis" disappears. The right-wing does not like a well-functioning government operation, with administrative costs far below those of private insurance companies; and the securities industry is eager to get its hands on

those large cash flows out of elemental self-interest. For effective critiques of the alleged crisis, see Robert McIntyre, "Pete Peterson, False Messiah," *The American Prospect* (Summer 1994); Robert Dreyfuss, "Raid of the Privateers," *The American Prospect* (May/June 1996); Dean Baker, "Robbing the Cradle: A Critical Assessment of Generational Accounting" (Economic Policy Institute, 1995).

13   For a good analysis, see Herbert Gans, "Are U.S. Journalists Dangerously Liberal?," *Columbia Journalism Review* (November/December 1985).

14   For solid documentation of this difference between the media elite and general public on social and economic issues, see David Croteau, "Challenging the 'Liberal Media' Claim," *EXTRA!* (July/August, 1998).

15   For a critique of the sampling methods in the Roper study, see Robert Parry, "Media Mythology: Is the Press Liberal?," *The Consortium* (February 17, 1997). For a more general critique, see "'The 89 Percent Liberal Media'," *EXTRA!* (July/August, 1998), 10.

16   On the importance and politics of owners, see chapter 5 below; also, Jim Naureckas, "From the Top," EXTRA! (July/Aug. 1998), 21–22.

17   Herman and Chomsky, *Manufacturing Consent*.

18   "PBS Tilts Toward Conservatives, Not the Left, *Extra!* (June 1992); "The Broken Promises of Public Television: A Special Edition of EXTRA!," *EXTRA!* (September/October 1993); "The Right-Wing Media Machine," Special issue of *EXTRA!* (March/April 1996).

19   "Are you on the Nightline Guest List?," *EXTRA!* (January/February 1989).

Part 1

THE MARKET SYSTEM VERSUS FREEDOM OF EXPRESSION

Chapter 1

Market System Constraints on Freedom of Expression

The Hyde Park Soapbox Model

The U.S. tradition of freedom of expression has focused heavily on the need for protection from governmental encroachments and restrictions. It rests on what we may call the Hyde Park Soapbox (HPS) model of freedom of expression, according to which the condition of freedom of expression is met if people are permitted to speak and pass out handbills to passersby in the streets and other public places without interference.[1] The U.S. tradition (and application of the HPS model) has never considered positive government acts and policies necessary to make free expression a reality, except possibly for public education needed to foster a literate and minimally knowledgeable populace.

It is also assumed in the HPS model that no threat to freedom of expression can arise from private sector developments and policies. This assumption reflects both the classic liberal faith in free competition and the market and a preoccupation with the threat of government. The lack of concern over private restraints on freedom of expression also manifests the class bias of constitution makers and legislators, who often owned (and own) property and represented (and represent) property interests. In James Madison's Federalist Paper Number X, the class bias was clear: majority rule threatened the "permanent interests" of society (i.e., property), but fortunately the pursuit of majority interests was encumbered by fragmentation and geographic dispersion.[2] That Madison viewed effective majority rule as a threat and welcomed structural impediments suggests that inequality of access to and control over the means of communication would not have bothered him, and would in fact have been seen as another valuable protection against the leveling tendencies of the general population.[3]

Acceptance of the HPS model and its assumptions, along with the evolution of the structure of the communications industries, has yielded a system in which private rights of free expression are protected, but rights to public access, insofar as they entail outreach through privately owned communications facilities, are not. Decisions about access are left to the marketplace and those who control it. This means that individuals with facts, ideas, and proposals important to the public interest may be effectively ignored (or relegated to marginal forums) if the controllers of the marketplace disapprove of and refuse to disseminate their messages. But in the framework of free market thought and ideology, competition among the existing media, and freedom of entry, assure that all views that are important to substantial numbers—and to the truth—will be heard. In A.J. Liebling's famous irony: We are all free to start our own newspaper if we don't like those available to us.[4]

The Free Market Model

A free market model can readily be constructed, however, that shows how market processes naturally constrain free expression and marginalize dissent. And there is evidence that such constraints and processes are operative and have significant effects. It is well known that the market rations goods by price, and that people without "effective demand"—that is, wants backed up by money—will be excluded from, or priced out of, the market. The point is not often applied to the media and to freedom of expression, possibly because those who might make the point have already been priced out of the market and denied access!

Access is restricted, first, by the requirement that one have capital to enter the media industries.[5] From the earliest times, capital requirements have ensured that the media gatekeepers are members of the economic elite, with associated class biases; other interest groups, some with enormous constituencies but without substantial capital, such as trade unions, racial and ethnic minorities, environmentalists, and consumer organizations, have to depend on the elite gatekeepers for access to the general public.[6]

This control mechanism has been strengthened over the years as the scale of production and capital requirements have steadily enlarged, the wealth of mass media owners has greatly increased,[7] newspaper chains and television and cable networks have grown in importance, the media have become parts of conglomerates, and the media industries have spread beyond single country borders. The media have been further integrated into the market by increasing competition and an active takeover market. The result of all this has been both delocalization and steadily greater pressure to focus on profitability.

The bias of the media toward the status quo and the interests of the corporate system is assured by this set of considerations alone.[8] But beyond this, profit-oriented media are extremely sensitive to advertiser, governmental, and other powerful interest group desires, needs, and pressures, and tend to avoid controversy and oppositional views even more comprehensively than government-funded media enterprises.[9]

Although the owners of the media are wealthy individuals and companies, their operations are funded mainly by advertisers; that is, by business firms trying to sell goods and corporate messages. These have a powerful impact on the media, especially on television but also on the print media.[10] Their influence is exercised within a competitive system mainly by advertisers' demands for a suitable program environment for their commercial messages, and their power to choose among stations and programs according to these preferences.[11] The biases of corporate advertisers, whose ideological assumptions and fondness for the status quo are similar to that of the media's owners, should reinforce establishment positions and tend to marginalize dissent.

A third factor that causes market forces to limit free expression arises from the media's quest for cheap, regular, and credible sources of information. Dissident sources are expensive to locate and their claims must be checked out carefully. Claims of the secretary of state and other high officials, or police officers in charge of investigating an act of violence, are readily available, are newsworthy in themselves, are supplied by credible sources, and do not require careful checking (although media concerned seriously with truth and *substantive* objectivity would treat all sources with the same degree of scrutiny). A symbiotic relationship commonly develops between dominant sources and the media that makes the latter more reluctant to transmit dissident claims, which would embarrass and annoy the media's primary sources.

The dominant sources within the government and corporate system also finance and otherwise support quasi-private institutes and think tanks, where experts who will preempt further space in the mass media for proponents of establishment views are funded and accredited.[12] Dissidents have no comparable endowed funding and accrediting agencies. The largest of the dissident think tanks, the Institute for Policy Studies, had a 1997 budget of $1.4 million, which was between 6 and 8 percent of the budgets of the Heritage Foundation ($25.9 million), the Hoover

Institution ($22.3 million), and the American Enterprise Institute ($18.6 million). This funding differential and lack of well-publicized accredited expertise contributes heavily to dissidents' limited access to the mass media.

A fourth route through which the market limits free expression is by the generation and use of flak. Flak is negative feedback that threatens, imposes costs upon, and therefore constrains the media. The importance of flak to the media is a function of money and power, which allow monitoring and serious media challenges that include advertising boycotts, threats of libel suits, congressional hearings, and FCC and antitrust actions. Just as the American Enterprise Institute, Hoover Institution, and Georgetown Center for Strategic and International Studies serve the establishment by providing accredited experts, so Accuracy in Media, the American Legal Foundation, and Capital Foundation are funded to discipline the media by systematic challenges to "liberal bias," unfairness, and libel.

A final factor in media control by market forces is the ideological premises of the system, which reflect a culture centered in private property. Central components of this ideology are the belief in the merits of free enterprise, the threat of state ownership and intervention, the benevolent role of the government in international affairs, and anticommunism. Anticommunism has been especially strategic as a disciplinary device, keeping the media and Democratic Party in line by their fear of being tagged unfaithful to the national religion, when they might otherwise be inclined to respond to mass demands by raising questions about tax equity, the size of the military budget, and the propriety of destabilizing and attacking countries not governed in accord with U.S. establishment interests and demands.[13]

These free market mechanisms work in concert, and on foreign policy matters are usually geared closely to a government agenda. They provide a powerful means of filtering out dissident and inconvenient information and opinion. One of the great merits of this system of control is that it operates so naturally, without collusion or explicit censorship, merely by the decentralized pursuit of a set of micro-interests. It "just works out that way." If Poland, a Communist power aligned with a then-hostile Soviet Union, cracks down on the Solidarity union in the early 1980s, this is deemed extremely newsworthy, whereas if at the very same time Turkey, a U.S. client state, is cracking down on its trade unions, the filters work to keep this out of the news. Similarly, if Yugoslavia brutally pacifies its Albanian population in Kosovo in 1998, this is treated with close attention and indignation, whereas Turkey's equally ruthless treatment of its Kurds in the same time frame is treated in low key and without the slightest indignation.

When it was serviceable to the Reagan administration to inflate the Libyan menace, the market caused Khadaffi to become a featured "terrorist." At the same time, when state policy toward South Africa and Guatemala was one of accommodation and "constructive engagement," their far more severe terrorism was not found newsworthy, was largely suppressed, and the word terrorism was not applied to these states and their leaders.[14] When it served state propaganda needs to focus on the abuses of the Khmer Rouge in Cambodia, the market did so energetically and with great indignation; at the same time when client state Indonesia invaded East Timor and decimated its population with at least equal ferocity, the market-based media averted their eyes.[15] The ease and naturalness with which this is done by uncoordinated self-censorship makes for extremely effective propaganda as free market processes create and maintain a virtually Orwellian world of doublespeak.

A second great merit of the evolving market system of control is that it is not total and responds with some flexibility to the differences that frequently crop up among elite groups. This allows controversy to rage within the mass media, but confined almost entirely to tactical matters that do not challenge fundamental premises. Thus, during the Vietnam War, it was fiercely debated whether we could win, how this could be done, and whether the costs (to us) were too great. The premises that we had a right to be there, that we were not invaders and aggressors, and that we were seeking self-determination and "protecting South Vietnam" were rarely questioned in the mainstream media.[16]

Similarly, in the case of the subversion and proxy warfare against Nicaragua in the 1980s, the view that this was plain aggression and international terrorism and that the U.S. design was to oppose independence, self-determination, and the pursuit of the "logic of the majority" was simply not addressed in the mainstream media. The access to the mass media by individuals and groups anxious to make such points, in both news columns and opinion pages, was so low as to approach total exclusion.[17] The mainstream "left" lauded our benevolent ends and the eventual achievement of a "democratic election" through "patience" (that is, not invading Nicaragua with large U.S. forces).[18] This view ignored the fact that the United States had virtually destroyed the Nicaraguan economy by boycott and terror, and that the election was held under the ongoing threat of more of the same in the absence of a U.S.-approved outcome.[19] In short, the market system of control performed here a propaganda feat that a system of state censorship could hardly improve upon.

A third merit of the market-based system is that a dissident media is allowed to function, but without the capacity to reach large numbers. This is interpreted in the mainstream as evidence that the public does not want the excluded products. But their producers can rarely raise the capital or attract advertising support sufficient to allow a valid product test. For those products that do come into existence, advertiser disinterest, and the benefits of advertiser support for rival publications in price charged, promotion, technical quality, etc., make the survival of dissident media difficult. In Great Britain, the *Daily Herald*, which had a large working class audience, failed in the 1960s despite a circulation larger than *The Times, Financial Times,* and *Guardian* combined; but its 8.1 percent of national circulation yielded it only 3.5 percent of advertising revenue.[20]

It should be emphasized that the excluded dissident product often includes facts and perspectives that bear on the issues, but which the mainstream media simply filter out. They can ignore or downplay unpalatable matters and feature facts and claims (including fabrications and myths) that support the status quo and ongoing policy, leaving inconvenient truths and corrections of lies and myths to the marginalized press.[21] Meanwhile, establishment pundits can argue that the public is free to choose, and simply doesn't want the messages offered by the marginalized press.

Concluding Note

In sum, a market system of control limits free expression by market processes that are highly effective. Dissident ideas are not legally banned, they are simply unable to reach mass audiences, which are monopolized by large profit-seeking corporations that offer programs supported by advertising, from which dissent is quietly and unobtrusively filtered out. Excluded individuals are free to say what they want, and may have access to a marginalized media, but they do not have the power to contest the market-dominated mass media's selectivity and propaganda in communication to the larger public.

This system is extremely difficult to attack and dislodge because the gatekeepers naturally do not allow challenges to their own direct interests to reach the public consciousness. Nonetheless, structural change is imperative if freedom of expression is be increased in the United States. This will only happen with greater public understanding of the stakes and massive grassroots support for a democratic media.[22]

Notes

1   Hyde Park in London is the most famous of these public places, where cranks and dissident speakers are free to get up on soap boxes and speak out.

2   Henry Cabot Lodge, ed., *The Federalist* (London: G. P. Putnam, 1888), 51–60.

3   In 1822, an older and apparently more democratically inclined Madison wrote that "a popular government without popular information, or the means of acquiring it, is but a prologue to a farce or a tragedy, or perhaps both." Letter to W.T. Barry, Aug. 4, 1822, in *Letters and Other Writings of James Madison* vol. 3 (New York: R. Worthington, 1844), 276.

4   A.J. Liebling, *The Press* (New York: Ballantine, 1964), 15.

5   The five factors to be discussed here are elements of the "propaganda model," spelled out in greater detail in Edward Herman and Noam Chomsky, *Manufacturing Consent: The Political Economy of the Mass Media* (New York: Pantheon, 1988).

6   Back in 1947, A.J. Liebling said that "I cannot believe that labor leaders are so stupid they will let the other side monopolize the press indefinitely." (*The Press*, 23). Liebling was not thought to have been an optimist or to underestimate human stupidity. He may have underrated the economic costs of starting and maintaining a newspaper, however.

7   The median value of the wealth of the control groups of the largest media corporations in the mid-1980s, as measured by the value of stock they owned in the controlled mass media corporation alone, was approximately $450 million. (See Herman and Chomsky, *Manufacturing Consent*, 8–10.) This value had more than doubled by 1998, with the great increase in stock market values and the market's fondness for media stocks. The value of the Sulzberger family's controlling stock interest in the *New York Times*, which happened to be the median value in the mid-1980s, rose from $450 million to $1.2 billion in 1998.

8   As noted in the Introduction, those expounding the view that the mass media have a liberal bias always avoid the question of ownership and control and imply that lower echelon personnel set their own agendas without rules from above. The massive historic evidence that key owners like Henry Luce, DeWitt Wallace (*Reader's Digest*), Katherine Graham, Arthur Hays Sulzberger, Robert Sarnoff, and Rubert Murdoch have had definite policy agendas that they enforced in their organizations is simply not discussed. The effects of profitability rules and policies based on advertiser interests and sensitivity is not discussed either. The neoconservative analysts also don't do much in the way of analyzing actual news and opinion outputs. Their main focus is on whether the reporters and copy editors vote Republican or Democratic.

9   See Erik Barnouw's discussion of the evidence for this in the media's coverage of the Vietnam War, quoted here in chapter 3, 5–6.

10   On the huge impact of advertisers on the editorial content of women's magazines, see Gloria Steinem's account of her experiences with *Ms. Magazine* during the years that it depended on advertising. "Sex, Lies and Advertising," *Ms Magazine* (July/August 1990).

11   See Erik Barnouw, *The Sponsor* (New York: Oxford University Press, 1978), 79–121. The finding that advertisers don't very often actively intervene in programming misses the point: the main route through which advertisers intervene is by the mere exercise of their demand and their ability to choose among a number of alternative programs.

12   For an examination of how this has been done on the subject of terrorism, see Edward Herman and Gerry O'Sullivan, *The "Terrorism" Industry: The Experts and Institutions That Shape Our View of Terror* (New York: Pantheon, 1990).

13   Declaring that the Sandinista government of Nicaragua was "Marxist-Leninist" played an important role in obtaining mass media and Democratic Party cooperation in the economic and military warfare carried out against Nicaragua in the years 1981–1989. As in the case of the overthrow of the democratically elected government of Guatemala by proxy invasion in 1954, both the press and Democrats accepted the false claim that the objective of U.S. government actions was to bring about "democracy." See Peter Kornbluh, *Nicaragua: The Price of Intervention* (Washington, D.C.: Institute for Policy Studies, 1987), chap. 4; Herman and Chomsky, *Manufacturing Consent*, xii–xiii.

14   See Herman and O'Sullivan, *The "Terrorism" Industry*, Preface, chaps. 1–3, and 8.

15   These two cases are discussed in detail in chapter 16.

16   Herman and Chomsky, *Manufacturing Consent*, chap. 5. The fit of this analysis to the *New York Times'* coverage of the Vietnam war is described in chapter 8.

17   For details, see Herman and Chomsky, *Manufacturing Consent*, xii–xiii and 116–42; Noam Chomsky, *The Culture of Terrorism* (Boston: South End Press, 1988), 39–61, 203–211; Jack Spence, "The U.S. Media: Covering (Over) Nicaragua," in Thomas Walker, ed., *Reagan Versus the Sandinistas* (Boulder, CO: Westview, 1987), 182–201.

18   David Shipler, "Nicaragua, Victory for U.S. Fair Play," *New York Times*, 1 March 1990; Anthony Lewis, "Out of This Nettle," *New York Times*, 2 March 1990.

19   At a press conference with Violetta Chamorro in Washington, D.C., in early November 1989, President Bush stated explicitly that the U.S. embargo would be lifted only if her UNO party won the election. See Lauter, "Nicaragua's Opposition Candidate at White House," *Los Angeles Times*, 9 November 1989.

20   James Curran, "Advertising and the Press," in Curran, ed., *The British Press: A Manifesto* (London: Macmillan, 1978), 252–55.

21   Sometimes these lies are corrected belatedly and in muted fashion in the mainstream press. See chapter 5, under "Unwillingness to correct error."

22   For a further discussion of the conditions and prospects of democratic media, see chapter 21.

Chapter 2

A Propaganda Model

In countries where the levers of power are in the hands of a state bureaucracy, monopolistic control over the media, often supplemented by official censorship, makes it clear that the media serve the ends of a dominant elite. It is much more difficult to see a propaganda system at work when the media are private and formal censorship is absent. This is especially true when the media actively compete, periodically attack and expose corporate and governmental malfeasance, and aggressively portray themselves as spokespersons for free speech and the general community interest. What is not evident (and remains undiscussed in the media) is the limited nature of such critiques, the huge inequality in ability to command resources, and the effects of such limitations both on access to a private media system and on its behavior and performance.

A propaganda model focuses on this inequality of wealth and power and its multilevel effects on mass media interests and choices. It traces the routes by which money and power are able to filter out the news fit to print, marginalize dissent, and allow the government and dominant private interests to get their messages across to the public. The essential ingredients of the propaganda model, or set of news "filters," fall under the following headings: (1) the size, concentrated ownership, owner wealth, and profit orientation of the dominant mass media firms; (2) advertising as the primary income source of the mass media; (3) the reliance of the media on information provided by government, business, and "experts" who are funded and approved by the primary sources and agents of power; (4) "flak" (negative and constraining feedback) as a means of disciplining the media; and (5) anticommunism as a national religion and control mechanism.[1] These elements interact with and reinforce one another. The raw material of news must pass through successive filters, leaving only the cleansed residue fit to print. The filters fix the premises of discourse and interpretation and the definition of what is newsworthy in the first place, and they explain the basis and operations of what amount to propaganda campaigns.

The First Filter: Size, Ownership, and Profit Orientation of the Mass Media

In their analysis of the evolution of the media in Great Britain, James Curran and Jean Seaton describe how a radical press emerged in the first half of the nineteenth century that reached a national working-class audience. This alternative press was effective in reinforcing class consciousness: it unified the workers because it fostered an alternative value system and framework for looking at the world and because it "promoted a greater collective confidence by repeatedly emphasizing the potential power of working people to effect social change through the force of 'combination' and organized action."[2] This was deemed a major threat by the ruling elites. One member of Parliament asserted that the working-class newspapers "inflame[d] passions and awaken[d] their selfishness, contrasting their current condition with what they contend to be their future condition—a condition incompatible with human nature, and those immutable laws which Providence has established for the regulation of civil society."[3] The result was an attempt to squelch the working-class media by using libel laws and prosecutions, by requiring an expensive security bond as a condition for publication, and by imposing various taxes designed to drive out radical media by raising their costs. These coercive efforts were not effective, and by midcentury they had been abandoned in favor of the liberal view that the market would enforce responsibility.

Curran and Seaton show that the market did successfully accomplish what state intervention failed to do. Following the repeal of the punitive taxes on newspapers between 1853 and 1869, a new daily local press came into existence, but not one new local working-class daily was established through the rest of the nineteenth century. Curran and Seaton note that

> Indeed, the eclipse of the national radical press was so total that when the Labour Party developed out of the working-class movement in the first decade of the twentieth century, it did not obtain the exclusive backing of a single national daily or Sunday paper.[4]

One important reason for this was the increase in scale of newspaper enterprise and the associated growth in capital costs from the mid-nineteenth century onward, which were based on technological improvements and owners' increased stress on reaching large audiences.

Thus the first filter—the ownership of media with any substantial outreach limited by the requisite large size of investment—was applicable a century or more ago, and has become increasingly effective over time.

The Second Filter: The Advertising License to do Business

In arguing for the benefits of the free market as a means of controlling dissident opinion in the mid-nineteenth century, the Liberal Chancellor of the British Exchequer, Sir George Lewis, noted that the market would promote those papers "enjoying the preference of the advertising public."[5] Advertising did, in fact, serve as a powerful mechanism that weakened the working-class press. Curran and Seaton give the growth of advertising a status comparable with the increase in capital costs as a factor that allowed the market to accomplish what state taxes and harassment failed to do. They note that these "advertisers thus acquired a de facto licensing authority since, without their support, newspapers ceased to be economically viable."[6]

Before advertising became prominent, the price of a newspaper had to cover the costs of doing business. As advertising grew, papers that attracted ads could afford a copy price well below production costs. This put papers that lacked advertising at a serious disadvantage: their prices would tend to be higher, which would curtail sales, and they would have less surplus to invest in changes that would improve the salability of the paper (features, an attractive format, promotion, etc.). For this reason, along with the economies of scale based on high first-copy costs,[7] an advertising-based system tends to drive out of existence or into marginality the media companies and types that depend on revenue from sales alone. With advertising, the free market does not yield a neutral system in which final buyer choice decides. The advertisers' choices influence media prosperity and survival.

The Third Filter: Sourcing Mass-Media News

The mass media are drawn into a symbiotic relationship with powerful sources of information by economic necessity and reciprocity of interest. The media need a steady, reliable flow of the raw material of news. Economics dictates that they concentrate their resources where significant news often occurs, where important rumors and leaks abound, and where regular press conferences are held. The White House, the Pentagon, and the State Department in Washington, D.C. are central nodes of such news activity. On a local basis, city hall and the police department are the subject of regular news beats for reporters. Business corporations and trade groups are also regular and credible purveyors of stories that are deemed newsworthy. These bureaucracies turn out a large volume of material that meets the demands of news organizations for reliable, scheduled flows. Mark Fishman calls this "the principle of bureaucratic affinity: only other bureaucracies can satisfy the input needs of a news bureaucracy."[8]

Government and corporate officials are also credible sources by virtue of their status and prestige. This is important to the mass media. As Fishman notes,

> Newsworkers are predisposed to treat bureaucratic accounts as factual because news personnel participate in upholding a normative order of authorized knowers in the society. Reporters operate with the attitude that officials ought to know what it is their job to know... In particular, a newsworker will recognize an official's claim to knowledge not merely as a claim, but as a credible, competent piece of knowledge. This amounts to a moral division of labor: officials have and give the facts; reporters merely get them.[9]

Another reason for the heavy weight given to official sources is that the mass media claim to be "objective" dispensers of the news. Partly to maintain the image of objectivity, but also to protect themselves from criticisms of bias and the threat of libel suits, they need material that can be portrayed as presumptively accurate. This is also partly a matter of cost: taking information from sources that may be presumed to be credible reduces investigative expense, whereas material from sources that are not prima facie credible, or that will elicit criticism and threats, requires careful checking and costly research.

The Fourth Filter: Flak and the Enforcers

Flak refers to negative responses to a media statement or program. It may take the form of letters, telegrams, phone calls, petitions, lawsuits, speeches and bills before Congress, and other modes of complaint, threat, and punitive action. It may be organized centrally or locally, or it may consist of the entirely independent actions of individuals.

If flak is produced on a large scale, or by individuals or groups with substantial resources, it can be both uncomfortable and costly to the media. Positions have to be defended both inside and outside the organization, sometimes before legislatures and possibly even in courts. Advertisers may withdraw patronage. If certain kinds of fact, position, or program are thought likely to elicit flak, this prospect can be a deterrent.

Freedom House, an example of a well-funded flak organization that dates back to the early 1940s, has had interlocks with Accuracy in Media (AIM), the World Anti-Communist League, Resistance International, and U.S. government bodies such as Radio Free Europe and the CIA, and has long served as a virtual propaganda arm of the government and international right wing. It has expended substantial resources to criticize the media for insufficient sympathy with U.S. client states. Its most notable publication of this genre was Peter Braestrup's *Big Story*, which contended that the media's negative portrayal of the Tet Offensive helped lose the Vietnam war. The work is a travesty of scholarship, but more interesting is its premise: that the mass media not only should support any national venture abroad, but should do so with enthusiasm, as such enterprises are by definition noble.

The Fifth Filter: Anticommunism as a Control Mechanism

A final filter is the ideology of anticommunism.[10] Communism as the ultimate evil has always been the specter that haunts property owners, as it threatens the very root of their class position and superior status. The Soviet, Chinese, and Cuban revolutions were traumas to Western elites, and the ongoing conflicts and the well-publicized abuses of communist states have contributed to the elevation of opposition to communism to a first principle of Western ideology and politics. This ideology helps mobilize the populace against an enemy, and because the concept is fuzzy it can be used against anybody who advocates policies that threaten property interests or supports accommodation with communist states and radicalism. It therefore helps fragment the left and labor movements and serves as a political control mechanism. If the triumph of communism is the worst imaginable evil, then the support of fascism abroad can be justified as a lesser evil. Opposition to social democrats who are too soft on communists and "play into their hands" is rationalized in similar terms.

Liberals at home, often accused of being procommunist or insufficiently anticommunist, are kept continuously on the defensive in a cultural milieu in which anticommunism is the dominant religion. If they allow communism, or something that can be labeled communism, to triumph in the U.S. sphere of influence while they are in office, the political costs are heavy. Most of them have fully internalized the religion anyway, but they are all under great pressure to demonstrate their anticommunist credentials.

Conclusion

The five filters narrow the range of news that passes through the gates, and even more sharply limit what can become "big news" that is subject to sustained news campaigns. By definition, news from primary establishment sources meets one major filter requirement and is readily accommodated by the mass media. Messages from and about dissidents and weak, unorganized individuals and groups, both domestic and foreign, are at an initial disadvantage in terms of sourcing costs and credibility, and they often do not comport with the ideology or interests of the gatekeepers and other powerful parties that influence the filtering process.

Notes

1   For an extension of this ideological control mechanism to a faith in the market, see "The Propaganda Model Revisited," chapter 18.

2   James Curran and Jean Seaton, *Power Without Responsibility: The Press and Broadcasting in Britain*, 2nd ed. (London: Methuen, 1985), 24.

3   Ibid., 23.

4   Ibid., 34.

5   Ibid., 31.

6   Ibid., 41.

7   This factor is stressed in C. Edwin Baker, *Advertising and a Democratic Press* (Princeton: Princeton University Press, 1994), 21–22.

8   Mark Fishman, *Manufacturing the News* (Austin: University of Texas Press, 1980), 143.

9   Ibid., 144–45.

10 As I pointed out earlier, this final filter is readily extended to include belief in the "miracle of the market" as an ideological control mechanism, as I describe in chapter 18.

Chapter 3

The Deepening Market in the West: Commercial Broadcasting of the March

The balance between commercial and public broadcasting in the West shifted steadily, and perhaps decisively, in favor of the former in the 1970s and after. Public broadcasting was under siege from commercial interests and conservative governments throughout this period, and the tempo of attack stepped up in the 1980s and 1990s. Public broadcasting monopolies have been broken in Belgium, France, Italy, Norway, Portugal, Spain, Switzerland, and elsewhere. Commercial broadcasters have been rapidly enlarging their domains, encroaching on public system advertising, putting public broadcasters' state funding under further pressure by reducing their audience shares, and forcing them to alter their programs to compete for audiences.

In the United States, public broadcasting was marginalized in the early 1930s; the defeat of an amendment to the Communications Act of 1934 that would have reserved 25 percent of broadcasting space for educational and nonprofit operations confirmed the triumph of commercial broadcasting,[1] and its power was steadily enlarged thereafter. A small place was carved out for educational and other nonprofit broadcasting in the 1950s and after, but federal sponsorship and funding of public broadcasting did not come about until 1967. One of the functions of public broadcasting was to relieve commercial broadcasters of a public service obligation that they did not want and were sloughing off. Even in the small niche reserved for it, public broadcasting has been a target of steady conservative attack for its excessive preoccupation with public affairs, and was subjected to a further financial crunch and politicization in the Reagan era.

Although many democratic and progressive critics of the media have been harsh in their assessment of public broadcasting, most of them have looked upon its decline as a distinctly adverse and threatening development. The most common view is that although public broadcasting has never realized its potential, it has nevertheless contributed modestly to a public sphere of debate and critical discourse and has provided information and viewpoints essential to the citizenship role. By contrast, media critics view commercial broadcasting as an entertainment vehicle that tends to marginalize the public sphere in direct proportion to its increasing dominance and profitability.[2]

Commercial Broadcasting and "Market Failure"

Commercial broadcasting, in fact, offers a model case of "market failure" in both theory and practice, although you will rarely see this point discussed in the mainstream media. But broadcasting has important "public goods" properties, with a potentially important yield of positive externalities; and negative externalities, such as the effects of the exploitation of sex and violence to build audiences are a likely (and observable) consequence of commercialization. Externalities are, by definition, things that the market does not take into account, such as pollution or worker injuries (when the employer can escape liability). On the positive side, externalities include the benefits to passersby of the beauties of well planned and maintained private gardens and buildings, and greater productivity resulting from technological advances that serve industry in general.

Broadcasting can be an important generator of positive externalities because it is a potentially powerful educational tool and contributor to democratic participation and citizenship. From the time of the Communications Act of 1934, and even earlier, the "public service" possibilities of broadcasting were widely recognized in the United States, and it was accepted even by the broadcasters that their grant of rights to use public air channels was in exchange for their serving "the public convenience, interest and necessity." In the 1934 hearings, the National Association of Broadcasters acknowledged that it is the "manifest duty" of the Federal Communications Commission (FCC) to assure an "adequate public service," which "necessarily includes broadcasting of a considerable proportion of programs devoted to education, religion, labor, agricultural and similar activities concerned with human betterment."[3] The 1946 FCC report, *Public Service Responsibilities of Broadcast Licensees*, contended that "sustaining programs" (that is, those aired at the station's expense, unsupported by advertising) are the "balance wheel" whereby "the imbalance of a station's or network's program structure, which might otherwise result from commercial decisions concerning program struc-ture, can be redressed." The report referred to sustaining programs as an "irreplaceable" part of broadcasting, and public service performance in the interest of "all substantial groups among the hearing public" as a fundamental standard and test for the approval and renewal of licenses.[4]

Commercialization and the Decline of Public Service

But a funny thing happened as the commercial system matured. It be-came possible to sell time to advertisers for all hours of the day, and the price at which time could be sold depended on "ratings," which measure the audience size (and from 1970, its "demographics"). As time became saleable and its price rose, the pressure for high ratings increased; and as Erik Barnouw noted in *The Sponsor*, "The preemption of the schedule for commercial ends has put lethal pressure on other values and inter-ests."[5] One effect was the steady trend away from "controversial" and modestly rated public service programs and toward entertainment. Rich-ard Bunce found that by 1970 public affairs coverage had fallen to 2 percent of programming time, and the entire spectrum of public interest programming was far below that provided by public broadcasting systems in Canada, Great Britain, and elsewhere in the West.[6]

The decline in public service performance of the U.S. commercial broad-casters paralleled a steady increase in broadcasting station and network profitability. By 1970 the profits of major station owners was in the range of 30–50 percent of revenues, and the profit rate was even higher on invested capital. Bunce estimated that for the period 1960–72, the ratio of pretax income to depreciated tangible investments for the broadcast networks never fell below 100 percent a year.[7] These staggering profits did not alleviate broadcaster pressure for additional profits because the workings of the market cause profits to be capitalized into higher stock values, which become the basis of calculation of rates of return for both old and new owners.

The force of competition and stress on the rate of return on capital, which comes to prevail in a free market, compels firms to focus with increasing intensity on enlarging audience size and improving its "qual-ity," as these will determine advertising rates. A recent audience decline for NBC's morning "Today Show" that moved it a full rating point behind ABC's "Good Morning America" was reportedly the basis of a $280,000-

a-day advertising income differential between the shows. Managements that fail to respond to market opportunities of this magnitude will be under pressure from owners and may be ousted by internal processes or takeovers. There will be no room for softheaded "socially responsible" managers in a mature system, and in the United States the four top networks have come under the control of strongly market-driven corporate owners.[8]

The maturing of commercial broadcasting not only steadily reduces public service programming, the U.S. experience suggests that maturation also brings a decline in variety of viewpoints and an increased protection of establishment interests. The handling of the Vietnam war provided a telling illustration of this. As Erik Barnouw notes, "The Vietnam escalation of 1965–67 found commercial network television hewing fairly steadily to the administration line. Newscasts often seemed to be pipelines for government rationales and declarations. . . . Though a groundswell of opposition to the war was building at home and throughout much of the world, network television seemed at pains to insulate viewers from its impact. . . . Much sponsored entertainment was jingoistic." The U.S. networks made none of the seriously critical documentaries on the war, and during the early war years they barred access to outside documentaries. As Barnouw points out, "this policy constituted de facto national censorship, though privately operated."[9]

But although the mass protest against the war rarely found outlets in commercial TV, it "began to find occasional expression in NET programming in such series as Black Journal, NET Journal, The Creative Person, and—explosively—in the film *Inside North Vietnam*, a British documentarist's report on his 1967 visit to 'the enemy.'"[10] This pattern helps explain why Presidents Johnson and Nixon fought to rein in public broadcasting; Nixon quite openly sought to force it to deemphasize public affairs. The commercial systems did this naturally.

In-depth news presentations reached their pinnacle with Edward R. Murrow's "See It Now" programs in the mid-1950s. There was a resurgence of news documentaries in the early 1960s in the wake of the quiz scandals of 1959, but subsequently the decline continued, despite occasional notable productions. Sponsors don't like controversy and depth—in entertainment as well as nonfiction. In the years when environmental issues first became of national concern, NBC dropped the environmental series "In Which We Live" for want of sponsorship, although the major companies were all busily putting up commercials and other materials about the environment. Corporate materials, however, reassured, and did not explore the issue in depth and with any balance, as the NBC series did. More recently, a program with Barbara Walters on the abortion issue was unable to obtain sponsors, who openly rejected participation for fear of controversy.

Fear of Fairness Doctrine requirements of balance also made serious programs that took a stand on an issue a threat to broadcasters; and watering them down to obviate challenges over lack of balance made them lifeless. Documentaries that appealed to sponsors were about travel, dining, dogs, flower shows, lifestyles of the rich, and personalities past and present. In short, under the system of commercial sponsorship, the documentary was reduced to "a small and largely neutralized fragment of network television, one that can scarely rival the formative influence of 'entertainment' and 'commercials.'" The form survived mainly in an aborted quasi-entertainment form called "pop doc" that specializes in brief vignettes featuring villains pursued by superstar entertainers, and settling "for relatively superficial triumphs."[11] "Infotainment" has also come to the fore, in which entertainers titillate audiences with "information" about other entertainers.

Other public affairs programs with lower ratings, such as discussion panels, were placed in weekend ghetto slots, and consisted mainly of unthreatening panels that asked unchallenging questions of officials. In the years before the death of the Fairness Doctrine, the "public service" obligation was met largely by public service announcements cleared through the Advertising Council, which provided a further means for broadcasters to establish a record of public service without addressing any serious issue.

Public broadcasting, by contrast with commercial broadcasting, is likely to give substantial weight to positive externalities. This is because the broadcasting media were recognized from the beginning as potentially valuable tools of education and citizen training, capable of universal outreach and service to both mass audiences and minorities. Public broadcasting took an early responsibility for realizing this potential. Most important, public broadcasting has not been driven by the profit motive or funded primarily by advertising, so that its functional role has not been incompatible with its funding source or institutional linkage, as the market-tied and profit-oriented commercial systems have been. It should be noted, however, that insofar as public broadcasting is forced to compete with growing commercial systems for a mass audience, with limited funding, there will be an erosion of original purpose and quality.

The evidence from Western Europe on the treatment of public service and positive externalities by commercial and public broadcasters is similar to that from the United States. European public broadcasting systems offer wider ranges of choice and significantly more national news, discussion programs, documentaries, and cultural and minority programs than do commercial systems in the United States or those in Europe.[12] The spread of commercial systems in Europe has not increased diversity and in fact threatens it through its damaging effects on the capabilities of public broadcasters. The first commercial broadcast channel in Italy offered literally zero news and public affairs programming, and Murdoch's British-based Sky Channel provided 95.6 percent entertainment and under 1 percent information.[13] French commercial TV has been notable for "the lack of variety . . . the tendency of the stations to align their programming on each other; the excessive screening of films and the neglect of the documentary; and . . . the haziness of the frontier between the commercial and the programme."[14]

Children's Programming

Broadcasting offers a potentially major and efficient vehicle for educating and entertaining children. Children, however, are not very important buyers of goods, especially small children, and are therefore of modest interest to advertisers. The positive social benefits of quality children's radio and TV are externalities, and the U.S. experience demonstrates that they will be ignored or marginalized by commercial broadcasters.

As in the case of public affairs programming, the U.S. commercial system eventually ghettoized children's programming to Saturday and Sunday morning, providing largely cartoon entertainment saturated with commercials. Between 1955 and 1970, weekday programming for children on network-affiliated TV stations in New York City fell from 33 to 5 hours. Only on Saturday did children continue to get substantial time, but not with any new or nonentertainment programs.[15] A major FCC study of children's TV published in 1979 concluded that children are "dramatically underserved."[16]

The failure of commercial TV in children's programming was so severe that a number of citizens groups were formed during the 1960s to fight the commercial system. One, Action for Children's Television (ACT), formed in 1968, lodged a protest with the FCC in 1970 that demanded reform. The FCC response in 1974 admitted the industry's failures and responsibilities, but left the resolution to the voluntary actions of the broadcasters. In 1983, the Reagan-era FCC, in a further response to the ACT petition, declared that the broadcasters had *no* responsibility to children. The situation deteriorated after 1983. Children's programming of substance was left to public broadcasting, but there was no national policy or regular funding of children's programs. The poor performance of U.S. schoolchildren is often noted in the mass media, and is sometimes attributed in part to the underfunding of schools, but the foregone potential of TV broadcasting is never mentioned.

Negative Externalities

Although the failure of commercial broadcasting to produce public affairs, cultural, and children's programs that promise important positive externalities has been subject to only modest study and even less publicity, its exploitation of the audience-enlarging vehicles of sex and violence has aroused important elements of the mainstream and has received greater attention. The aggressive use of themes of sex and violence, often in combination, can produce externalities in the form of distorted human and sexual attitudes, insecurity and a reduced ability to function in a social order, and aggressive and violent behavior.

TV violence builds audiences. It therefore makes its way onto the screen under the growing pressure of commercial imperatives. Professor George Gerbner and his associates have compiled since 1967 an annual television program Violence Profile and Violence Index. They have found that on average 7 of 10 prime time programs use violence, and that the rate of violent acts runs between 5 and 6 per hour. Some half of prime time dramatic characters engage in violence and about 10 percent kill, as they have since 1967. Children's weekend programming "remains saturated with violence," with more than 25 acts of violence per hour, as it has for many years.[17]

Violence programming has grown in Western Europe, along with the new surge in commercialization, and in direct relation to the shift to action-adventure films. With the proliferation of commercial channels and the high cost of original programming, there has been a heavy European demand for foreign movies and series to fill the program gap.[18] Preben Sepstrup contends that the great increase in the use of U.S. movies and serials is not based on a special preference for U.S. products, it is grounded in commercialization.[19] With market-based imperatives in place, violence as an important ingredient of programming follows. Citing their transnational study of TV violence, Huesmann and Eron state that "of the violent programs evaluated in the first wave of the study in Finland, Poland, and Israel, about 60% have been imported from the United States."[20]

Although there has been little dispute that commercial broadcasting has been associated with a large diet of violence, there are ongoing debates over the effects of violent programs. There are problems of causality: does alienation and aggression come from watching violence on TV, or do alienated and violence-prone people tend to watch programs that express their world view? Is TV violence an incitement and stimulus to violence or a catharsis? Despite continuing debate, the overwhelming consensus of experts and studies over several decades, covering a number of countries, and supported by a variety of models of behavior and controlled experiments, is that TV violence makes a significant contribution to real world violence by desensitizing; making people insecure and fearful; and habituating, modeling, and sometimes inciting people to violence.[21]

Commercial Broadcasting and Antidemocratic Power

The threat of a centralized, monolithic, state-controlled broadcasting system is well understood and feared in the West. What is little recognized or understood is the centralizing, ideologically monolithic, and self-protecting properties of an increasingly powerful commercial broadcasting system. The U.S. experience suggests that once a commercial system is firmly in place it becomes difficult to challenge, and that as its economic power increases so does its ability to keep threats at bay and to gradually remove all obstacles to commercial exploitation of the public airwaves. There is competition between members of a commercial system, but it is for large audiences through offering entertainment fare under the constraint of advertisers, and it ignores externalities as a matter of structural necessity and the force of competition.

As one illustration of the power of the industry to fend off virtually any threats, in the liberal environment of 1963 the FCC leadership decided to try to impose a formal restraint on commercial advertising, but only to the extent of making the limits suggested by the broadcasters' own trade association as the regulatory standard. This enraged the industry, which quickly went to work on Congress, and the FCC quickly backed down.[22]

Another important illustration of the commercial broadcasting industry's self-protective power is found in the area of children's television. The country claims to revere children, and child abuse is given frequent and indignant attention. But although the erosion of children's programming and the commercial exploitation of the residual ghettoized programs occurred as the commercial networks were making record-breaking profits, and although substantial numbers of adults have been angered by this programming, it has taken place with only a muted outcry. The FCC has been pressed hard to do something about the situation by organized groups like ACT, but the mass media have not allowed this matter to become a serious issue. When, after a 13 year delay in dealing with an ACT petition to constrain abuses in children's television, the FCC decided in December 1983 that commercial broadcasters had no obligation to serve children, the decision was not even mentioned in the *New York Times*. In fact, during the years 1979 through 1989, although many important petitions were submitted by ACT and decisions were made by the FCC that bore significantly on the neglect and abuse of children by commercial broadcasters, the *New York Times*, *Washington Post*, and *Los Angeles Times* had neither a front-page article nor an editorial on the subject. The dominant members of the press, most of them with substantial broadcasting interests of their own, simply refused to make the huge failure of commercial broadcasters in children's programming a serious issue.

It is also enlightening to see how the principles of public service responsibility of the broadcasters were gradually amended to accommodate broadcaster interests, without discussion or debate. As advertised programs displaced sustaining programs, and the "balance wheel" envisioned by the FCC in 1946 disappeared, what gave way was any public interest standard. The industry defense was in terms of "free speech" and the Alice-in-Wonderland principle that if the audience watches then the public interest is served. But the industry hardly needed a defense: raw power allowed the public interest standard to erode quietly, the issues undiscussed in any open debate.

Notes

1   Robert McChesney, *Telecommunications, Mass Media & Democracy* (New York: Oxford, 1993).

2   See Philip Elliott, "Intellectuals, the 'information society' and the disappearance of the public sphere," *Media Culture & Society* (July 1982); Preben Sepstrup, "Implications of Current Developments in West European Broadcasting," *Media Culture & Society* (January 1989); G. Patrick Scannell, "Public Service Broadcasting and Modern Public Life," *Media Culture & Society* (April 1989).

3   Quoted in Federal Communications Commission, *Public Service Responsibilities of Broadcast Licensees* (Washington: FCC, 1946), 10.

4   Ibid., 12–13.

5   Erik Barnouw, *The Sponsor* (New York: Oxford University Press, 1978), 95.

6   Richard Bunce, *Television in the Corporate Interest* (New York: Praeger, 1976), 27–31. On the superior performance of foreign public broadcasting systems, see Jay Blumler et al., "Broadcasting Finance and Programme Quality: An International Review," *European Journal of Communication* (September 1986), 348–50.

7   Bunce, *Television in The Corporate Interest*, 97.

8   In the first half of the 1980s, NBC was taken over by General Electric Company, a huge multinational manufacturer of weapons and nuclear reactors; ABC was acquired by Capital Cities, a media conglomerate famous for its bottom-line orientation; and control of CBS was assumed by Lawrence Tisch of Loews, a large conglomerate in the cigarette, hotel, and other businesses. Control over ABC and CBS was shifted once again in the 1990s, to Disney (ABC) and Westinghouse (CBS), as described in chapter 4. A fourth network that emerged in the 1980s and 1990s, Fox, is controlled by Rupert Murdoch, owner of a global media empire not known for its socially forward-looking policies.

9   Barnouw, *Sponsor*, 138.

10 Ibid., 63. NET, or National Educational Television, was a precursor of the larger public broadcasting system that was organized in 1967 and absorbed NET.

11 Ibid., 138.

12 Blumler et al., "Broadcasting Finance and Programme Quality: An International Review," 348–50.

13 Andrew Pragnell, *Television in Europe: Quality and Values in Times of Change* (Media Monograph No. 5, Manchester: European Institute for Media, 1987), 6.

14 Statement of Gabriel de Broglie, the departing head of the national supervisory organization CNCL, in January 1989, quoted in G. Graham, "Never mind the quality," *Financial Times*, 28 June 1989.

15 Edward Palmer, *Television and America's Children: A Crisis of Neglect* (New York: Oxford University Press, 1988).

16 Quoted in ibid., 5.

17 George Gerbner and Nancy Signorielli, "Violence Profile 1967 through 1988–89: enduring patterns," (Mimeo: Jan. 1990).

18 This is an important reason for the surge in cross-border and vertical mergers in the communications business, as the value and importance to broadcasters of gaining access to old stocks of movies and TV series, and to the ongoing production of such programs, has risen sharply.

19 Sepstrup, "Implications of Current Developments in Western European Broadcasting."

20 L. Rowell Huesmann and Leonard D. Eron, *Television and the Aggressive Child: A Cross-National Comparison* (Hillsdale, N.J.: Erlbaum Associates, 1986), 47.

21 George Gerbner and Nancy Signorielli, "Violence Profile 1967 through 1988–89: enduring patterns"; L. Rowell Huesmann and Leonard Eron, *Television and the Aggressive Child*; Frank Mankiewicz and Joel Swerdlow, *Remote Control* (New York: Ballantine, 1979); Geoffrey Barlow and Alison Hill, *Video Violence and Children* (New York: St. Martin's, 1985); National Institute of Mental Health, *Television and Behavior: Ten Years of Scientific Progress and Implications for the Eighties*, vol 2: Technical Reviews (Washington: Department of Health and Public Services, 1982).

22 Edwin Krasnow, Lawrence Longley and Herbert Terry, *The Politics of Broadcast Regulation* (New York: St. Martin's, 1982), 194–96.

Chapter 4

The Media Megamergers

The recent wave of giant mergers has sharply increased media concentration in the United States, and with merger opportunities significantly enlarged by the 1996 Telecommunications Reform Bill, we can anticipate further merger activity and concentration. The current wave may be dated back to the 1989 merger of Time and Warner, which created the world's largest media complex. After several years' lull, the cable power Viacom acquired Paramount Communications in 1994 and Blockbuster Video in January 1995; the merger wave then accelerated with the almost simultaneous July 1995 announcements of merger agreements between Disney and Capital Cities/ABC, and between Westinghouse and CBS. Also in July, Viacom agreed to sell its sizable cable system (1.1 million subscribers) to Tele-Communications Inc. (TCI), the largest cable company, for $2.3 billion. Only a month or so later, Time Warner offered to acquire Turner Broadcast Systems for $8.5 billion, a transaction that was completed shortly thereafter.

A notable feature of the biggest recent mergers is that the firms dominating this process are not media companies in a strict sense: Disney is avowedly a "family entertainment communication company" in the business of selling theme parks, toys, movies, videos, and associated commodities and services. Its focus, in the words of CEO Michael Eisner, is the provision of "non-political entertainment and sports."[1] Time Warner has a similarly wide spectrum of business interests and a comparable marketing orientation. Disney and Time Warner are what Herbert Schiller calls "pop cultural corporate behemoths."[2] Westinghouse, by contrast, has long been primarily a nuclear power and weapons producer; its media interests represented a small proportion of the corporation's activities (accounting for 10 percent of sales revenue) and were not a major preoccupation of its leaders before the merger. With the Westinghouse takeover of CBS, two of the three top networks are now controlled by large firms in the politically sensitive nuclear power/weapons industries (the other, General Electric Company [GE], which owns NBC, is, along with Westinghouse, one of the top 15 defense contractors). These developments suggest obvious questions about how news, public affairs, and public service will fare, and whether any independent and critical programming can survive in marginalized positions in entertainment and weapons-seller complexes.[3]

Business Opportunities

The economic underpinning of the recent megamergers has been the rapid growth of the entertainment business at home and abroad and the new global horizons of media entrepreneurs. *Business Week* noted in 1994 that "Europe and Japan used to mock America by calling it a 'Mickey Mouse` economy. Well, they're right. By any yardstick Mickey and his friends have become a major engine for U.S. economic growth. Since the economy turned up in 1991, entertainment and recreation—not health care or autos—have provided the biggest boost to consumer spending. . ."[4] Forecasters are predicting continued relatively high growth rates in entertainment, recreation, and communication outlays over the next five years.

TV advertising revenues recovered in 1994 and revived the bottom line of TV stations and networks; one financial analyst noted in 1995 that "the advertising market is so frenzied" that even CBS was witnessing an increase in cash flow despite its declining ratings.[5] Rupert Murdoch's aggressive bidding away of stations from CBS and NBC for his Fox network in 1995 helped cause TV station prices to soar.

Global entertainment and media markets have been growing even faster than domestic markets, and companies like Disney and Time Warner have huge stakes in foreign markets and plan to use their larger assets and linkages to increase their reach overseas. The European motion picture industry, for example, is suddenly reviving, but "what is sparking the growth is investment by the big American film studios like Walt Disney and Warner Brothers," who are behaving, according to Jeremy Thomas, chairman of the British Film Institute, "like when you have a predator fish in a pond."[6] Murdoch and his rivals are enthralled with the prospects of the newly opening Chinese market, and are aggressively positioning themselves with alliances, mergers, and satellite stations in pursuit of this and other Asian markets.

The growing global market for entertainment has been a huge windfall for U.S. "content" producers of movies, TV shows, popular music, videotapes and cassettes, and owners of old movies and cartoons (for example, Ted Turner) have seen the market value of their properties rise accordingly. Owners of cable channels with access to growing foreign audiences have been anxious to affiliate with content suppliers, especially producers or owners of films, syndicated TV shows, and cartoons. And the owners of content have been eager to gain assured access to the means of reaching audiences, such as TV channels, stations, and distribution networks. Disney wanted Capital Cities/ABC in good part for the assured access that Capital Cities could provide to its content. Time Warner wanted Turner Broadcast Systems in large measure for its marketable content supplied by CNN, its Cartoon Channel and cartoon stocks, and its current producing capacity.

Beyond security of access, the vertical mergers (Disney—Cap Cities; Time Warner—Turner) allow what is euphemistically called "synergies," which in practice means cross-selling. The merger participants have been quite open and enthusiastic over the prospect that, for example, Disney could not only show its films and TV programs on ABC, but that Disney theme parks and toys could be promoted on ABC and on the Cap Cities ESPN (sports channel), and that ABC's and ESPN's programs could be promoted in Disney theme parks, and that the entire system could buy advertising globally on favorable terms. According to the *Wall Street Journal*, Disney head Eisner and Cap Cities head Thomas Murphy anticipated other synergies, such as "promotion of the Disney Channel during Disney-produced Saturday morning cartoon shows and the use of Disney's syndication muscle to sell ABC-owned and produced programs."[7] Viacom has successfully used its Blockbuster video stores to push Paramount movies, and in the summer of 1995, Time Warner mobilized its Six Flags theme park and its Warner retail store system to promote its movie *Batman Forever*. ABC's news magazine program "Prime Time Live" has several times profiled personalities and stars on other ABC programs—cross-selling under the guise of infotainment. Financial analyst John Reidy notes that Murdoch "had set a standard that other studios now want to follow by using his network to create value for shows Fox owned. . . . Only a network can create value by making a program a hit. Even if you don't have very good ratings, you can still showcase a program and then sell it in Bulgaria or some place."[8] Jerome Dominus of the J. Walter Thompson ad agency agrees: the "promotional capabilities of a network" can build audiences for new shows by plugging them during existing hits or "events" programming such as the Olympics.[9]

All of these "synergies" provide what economists call "pecuniary" as opposed to "real" economies; that is, they involve financial and strategic advantages to the private firm, but no real cost reductions that would benefit society. There is also an exclusionary and monopolistic aspect to cross-selling synergies: a book that Time Warner publishes because of its synergistic potential as a movie that will yield spinoff toy and video sales not only receives massive advertising, it also benefits from promotion on Time Warner TV shows and in its magazines, at the expense of possibly superior books that don't meet the synergistic standard. The reviewing process may be compromised in favor of the privileged books. It is of course not openly acknowledged, but Westinghouse or GE might regard their power to suppress or edit programs critical of nuclear power or the military budget as one of the "synergistic" merits of network control.[10]

Real economies are hard to locate in the giant mergers, and most of the claims of advantage are of the cross-selling and strategic-complementarity variety. A possible exception is Westinghouse's acquisition of CBS, as Westinghouse's only media holdings are TV and radio stations, a number of which are in the same market as stations held by CBS. This horizontal merger might afford some small potential real economies in the sharing of services like news reporters (or the closing of overlapping stations) in common markets—but these small hypothetical economies have to be weighed against the reduction in competition in these markets. The other major mergers provide interesting testimony to the state of dominant political and economic opinion as substantial increases in the centralization of power in a strategic industry don't even require a supporting case for real economies and improved *social* efficiency.

Regulatory Cave-in

The Disney-Capital Cities merger was made possible by the ending of the so-called "fin-syn" rules, which for several decades have barred the networks from owning program producers (and cutting themselves into syndication profits) and have prevented Hollywood studios from owning networks. As one commentator noted: "Hollywood's titans seem to be trying to buy broadcast outlets for one major reason: They can."[11]

But the megamergers also rest on a broader collapse of political and regulatory opposition to increased media concentration. This reflects in part the changing political climate of increased business hegemony and deference to the demands of business and "competitiveness." The media are substantial political funders, but a more important consideration is the politicos' fear of the raw propaganda power of media barons. In Great Britain, Rupert Murdoch's role in causing Labour's past electoral defeats led the new Labour Party leader Tony Blair to abandon Labour's 1992 campaign pledge of a Monopoly Commission investigation of Murdoch's "unacceptable concentration of power" (he holds a 35 percent share of weekday newspaper circulation, among other interests); instead, Blair traveled to Australia to meet with Murdoch to persuade him of his credentials for office. In the United States, Murdoch's book deal with Newt Gingrich, which was preceded by a discussion of Murdoch's media regulatory problems, merely added icing to an already rich cake of Republican-megamedia solidarity. Equally interesting was the ease with which Murdoch got the Clinton-era FCC to allow him to retain his Fox network in 1995, despite Murdoch's admission that his 1986 application for the right to own TV stations failed to make clear de facto (and illegal) foreign ownership.

The Reagan-Bush years witnessed a steady erosion of both antitrust limits on mergers and FCC concern over issues of market power. The new laxity was intellectually grounded in the new faith that the market automatically serves the public interest. This was reinforced by the claims that new media forms like cable, direct satellite-based TV transmissions, and videotapes were breaking down any monopoly power of broadcast stations and networks. It also rested on the fact of increased globalization and the alleged need to allow U.S. media enterprises to get large and exploit "synergies" to meet the new global competition. The argument was further reinforced by the fact that media and other communications industries make a strong positive contribution to the U.S. balance of payments. For the Clinton administration, with its heavy emphasis on trade expansion, the media giants represented the national interest and were to be encouraged and given support.

The FCC has never been been a forceful defender of the public interest; no station has ever been deprived of its license for low-quality programming, and the FCC has gradually adapted its policies to broadcaster demands. On the degradation of children's programming under the commercial system, the appeals for improvement by Action for Children's Television from 1968 onward were not met under either Democratic or Republican rule—the differences have been that the "liberal" FCC acknowledges a problem, carries out studies that confirm the problem's severity, and sometimes asks the broadcasters to voluntarily do something about it; whereas in 1983 the Republican controlled FCC found that the broadcasters had *no* responsibility whatsoever to children.[12]

During the Reagan-Bush years the Fairness Doctrine was ended, the time between broadcast station license renewals was increased to five years, and ownership rules were amended to allow more concentrated holdings and cross-ownership. From 1953 into the Reagan years ownership limits were fixed by the 7-7-7 rule (7 AM, 7 FM, and 7 TV stations per owner), and cross-ownership of newspapers and broadcasting stations within the same market was barred (although over a hundred exceptions were grandfathered). These limits were raised to 12-12-12 in 1985, with TV station owners allowed to reach up to 25 percent of the national population. The ownership limits for radio were raised to 24–24 in 1992 and owners were given the right to acquire multiple stations in each market. The 1996 Telecommunications Reform Act removed the national ceiling on radio station ownership and allowed as many as eight stations to be acquired by a single owner in the largest markets. The ceiling on TV station ownership was raised to allow a single owner to reach 35 percent of the national audience.

Merger guidelines have also been softened, and giant mergers have been approved as a matter of course. GE was allowed to acquire NBC in 1986, in a regression from the 1967 decision that prevented International Telephone and Telegraph (ITT) from buying ABC on grounds of serious potential conflict of interest between ITT's international business interests and the objective performance of the news media.

In 1948, Paramount was forced to divest itself of its system of movie theatres on the ground that this gave the moviemaker an unfair advantage over its rivals, who could be excluded from Paramount's distribution network. These same underlying issues are present now; potential cable entrants sued Time Warner and Turner for fear of exclusion from program supply, and independent program makers worry about access to Time Warner-Turner and affiliated TCI cable channels and networks. But the climate of opinion and law has changed to such a degree that the Disney-Capital Cities merger breezed through the FCC, with seven waivers for combinations of media properties in single markets. "I think its great that a major network like ABC would be thinking of combining resources with a family-oriented company like Disney," said Republican Commissioner Rochelle Chong.[13] The vertical monopoly power implicit in such a marriage doesn't occur to her, nor did it influence the FCC as a whole.

The new political warmth toward giant mergers is reflected in the fact that the Justice Department gave the Westinghouse-CBS merger quick approval, and the FCC gave Westinghouse 19 permanent or temporary waivers of agency rules that limit broadcaster concentration.[14] This was done despite Westinghouse management's lack of experience relevant to CBS's managerial problems, a conflict of interest similar to the one that halted ITT's attempt to acquire ABC in 1967, and serious liberal advocacy group criticisms of Westinghouse's poor record in children's educational programming. Then chairman Reed Hundt expressed great pleasure that as part of the merger deal Westinghouse had agreed to serve as a children's "trustee" in "correcting the disappointing performance of its stations and the CBS stations in terms of educating children."[15] The FCC claimed in a news release of November 22, 1995, that "the overall public interest benefit of the transaction [confined to possible cost reductions in combined operations, perhaps helped along by station closure] outweigh any diminution in diversity and competition." So much for diversity and competition.

Bigness and Monopoly Power

Limiting the size of businesses in order to preserve the social and economic basis of a political democracy was considered to be one of the main purposes of antitrust laws for many years. That notion is no longer operative for liberals like former FCC head Reed Hundt as well as for conservatives. On the basis of the old democratic standard, bigness, especially when obtained by merger rather than internal growth, should require proof of real economic advantage to society, not merely corporate pecuniary advantage based on cross-selling. None of the great media mergers that took place from 1989 to 1996 met this standard.

On more conventional antitrust principles, mergers should not be allowed when they enhance market power and reduce competition, actual or potential, in already concentrated markets. The giant mergers of 1989–1996 also fail this test, in one or more of three ways. First, some degree of competition existed among these media corporations before the mergers, which will necessarily be reduced as tighter oligopolies are created by the megamergers. For example, the Time Warner/Turner merger, with Malone's TCI a closer partner with a large ownership interest transferred from Turner to the enlarged Time Warner, will tighten the bonds between the two top cable powerhouses (TCI and Time Warner), and between them and a leading cable channel supplier (Turner). Second, the mergers remove major rivals who were well-positioned to compete and enter into the niches filled by the merger itself; that is, Capital Cities was in a strong position to enlarge its production of content to compete with Disney, as Capital City head Murphy acknowledged in pre-merger days ("The only thing the studios bring to the creative process is money, and we've got that too");[16] and Disney was strong enough to enter the distribution field de novo by building up its own network of stations. The merger ended this strong basis of potential competition.

Third, the mergers weaken the position of outsiders who want to sell programs, introduce new channels, and enter the distribution field. John Malone of TCI was able to prevent a company as powerful as GE from starting a 24-hour news channel by refusing to carry it on his cable system; he has been able to favor rightwing cable channels like Paul Weyrich's Empowerment Channel, and the large number in which he has a financial interest, while literally destroying the liberal The 90s Channel by limiting its exposure and imposing discriminatorily high prices for admission. Only the phone companies are serious potential rivals to cable companies and over-the-air broadcasters, and they are likely to enter very slowly and in alliances with existing oligopolists. As noted, even these powerful companies were worried enough about access to programming from the Time Warner-Turner combine to sue to prevent the merger or assure protection against exclusion. The recent mergers are almost certain to elicit further defensive mergers, which will result in a tightened oligopoly of very large firms with great market power.

Entertainment and the Public Sphere

Companies like Disney, Time Warner, and Viacom openly proclaim themselves to be first and foremost, bottom-line-oriented *entertainment* companies. They are selling movies, TV shows, books, magazines, theme parks, and toys to the public, searching for "added value" in cross-selling among these marketed products. For these companies "creativity" is producing books, movies, videos, and spin-off toys based on the saleable qualities of movies such as *Forest Gump, Dumb and Dumber*, and *The Lion King*. Disney's *Lion King* represents the ideal toward which the entertainment complexes aspire: the movie was the centerpiece of a marketing program that linked Disney's book, movie, recording, and theme park subdivisions; one million books were quickly shipped to retailers; hundreds of thousands of sound tracks were issued that pushed *Lion King* to the top of the Billboard charts; there were tie-ins with Toys "R" Us and Kodak and special Disneyland and Disney retail store promotions—all of which produced an estimated $1 billion in profits over a short time span.

In contrast with *The Lion King* and the Cartoon Channel, news, public interest documentaries and debates, and public interest programs in general have little "synergistic" potential and do not sell well abroad. With each major merger, from the Time Warner merger in 1989 to the present, there have been sharp cutbacks in news bureau staff, partly reflecting the pressure from heavy debts to cut costs, but also reflecting the priorities of the bottom-line-oriented entertainment complexes.

When broadcasting began in the 1920s, and in subsequent years when rights to the public airwaves were being debated, both broadcasters and politicians claimed that radio and TV would not merely amuse and divert, but would also serve a very important public service function, educating, providing quality children's programs, and playing a citizenship-enhancing role as a forum for news and debates on public issues. With the growth of advertising, however, the commercial media gradually sloughed off public service in favor of the more saleable entertainment. The triumph of the entertainment complexes represents the culmination of this process of displacing public service with mainly light entertainment.

If entertainment complexes find that the public sphere is unprofitable whereas audience-generating programs that feature sex and violence are profitable, we can express this in terms of "externalities" effects (and market failure): the positive externalities of public service programming will be neglected because the benefits cannot be captured in revenue; the negative externalities associated with sex and violence will be pursued as audience- and profit-enlarging. Thus, a cultivation of antisocial and mindless distraction and the systematic neglect of educational and citizenship-enhancing programming is built-in to the system that is advanced in the ongoing merger movement. We are witnessing the triumph and consolidation of market failure!

Who Owns the Airwaves?

The profit-making companies that are licensed to use the airwaves were given those rights in exchange for a commitment to serve the "public interest, convenience, and necessity." The quoted phrase did *not* mean serving up entertainment programs to pull in large audiences for advertisers. Nevertheless, although the broadcasters have successfully rid themselves of any public service responsibilities they maintain free access to the airwaves, even while the remaining airspace is auctioned off at skyrocketing prices. The broadcasters are even now obtaining from Congress and the Clinton administration additional digital channels without charge as supposed compensation for their costs in moving to digitalized

TV. These free channels are estimated to have a market value of as much as $70 billion.

The market value of the airwaves that are now used for cellular, phone, broadcast, and satellite transmission is estimated to be in the order of $100 to 300 billion.[17] Were these public assets to be taxed or leased at the moderate rate of 5 percent of market value they would yield a government revenue stream of 5 to 15 billion dollars per year. If this revenue was turned over to an authority that would distribute it to nonprofit community and public broadcasting stations, the public service function of the media could be revived and a public sphere could be rehabilitated.

But an adequate policy response to ongoing trends that sought to make possible a genuinely democratic society would entail an even more far reaching effort to democratize the media. Not only would the megamergers be disallowed, the existing structures of power would also be attacked, global combines would be dismantled, and the system would be biased toward local control. It will be very difficult to maintain a democratic political order with an increasingly concentrated, centralized mass media buried within global entertainment complexes.

Notes

1   Quoted in Lawrence Grossman, "Reshaping political values in the information age: the power of the media," *Vital Speeches of the Day*, January 15, 1997, City News Publishing Company, 1997, vol. 63. no. 7.

2   Herbert Schiller, "United States (1)," in *Media Ownership and Control In An Age of Convergence*, Global Report Series (London: International Institute of Communications, 1996), 254.

3   Since this was written in 1996, Westinghouse has divested itself of most of its non-media holdings and has become a mainly media entity, but retaining the top management of the earlier regime.

4   "The Entertainment Economy," *Business Week* (March 14, 1994), 58.

5   Bill Carter, "Broadcast Networks Come Back Strong," *New York Times*, 2 August 1995.

6   Bill Carter, "Film Redux in Europe: Action; New Signs of Life After a Long Decline," *New York Times*, 24 February 1996.

7   Laura Landro and Elizabeth Jensen, "All Ears: Disney Deal for ABC Makes Show Business a Whole New World," *Wall Street Journal*, 1 August 1995.

8   Bill Carter, "Broadcast Networks Come Back Strong," *New York Times*, 2 August 1995.

9   Elizabeth Jensen, "Entertaining Talks: Major TV Networks, Dinosaurs No More, Tune in to New Deals," *Wall Street Journal*, 17 March 1994.

10 For some evidence of GE's exercise of its power in its political interest, see "In The Belly of G.E.," *Extra!* (January/February 1991); "GE Flexes Its Media Muscle," *EXTRA! Update* (August 1994).

11 Laura Landro, "Morning After: It May Be Hollywood, But Happy Endings Are Unusual in Mergers," *Wall Street Journal*, 2 August 1995.

12 See the discussion of Children's Programming in chapter 3.

13 Daniel Pearl, "Regulators See Results of Their Work in Mergers Between Networks, Producers," *Wall Street Journal*, 1 August 1995.

14 "CBS Now Reports to Westinghouse Electric's Jordan," *Television Digest* (November 27, 1995).

15 "Hundt, Quello News Conference," *Communications Daily*, 24 November 1995.

16 Jensen, "Entertaining Talks: Major TV Networks, Dinosaurs No More, Tune in to New Deals."

17   See Lawrence Grossman, "Cut the Public In on the Mega-Mergers," *New York Times*, 21 August 1995; Peter Huber, "The FCC could have a going-out-of-business sale," *Forbes* (May 8, 1995), 142.

Part 2

NEWS VALUES, NEWS PAPERS, NEWS SHAPERS

Chapter 5

The Politics of "Newsworthiness"

In his article "Are U.S. Journalists Dangerously Liberal?," Herbert J. Gans claims that mass media news choices rest on a foundation of "professional values" and rules of news judgment that "call for ignoring story implications." Thus, although extremists of the right and left may complain about news bias against themselves, their complaints are largely sour grapes.[1] Insofar as there is bias in news selection, Gans contends that it is mainly because of the nature of sourcing and related efficiency considerations,[2] with the result that non-standard and dissident suppliers tend to be excluded. His policy recommendations are thus oriented mainly toward strengthening such sources and encouraging the media to be receptive to their messages.[3]

Warren Breed offered an alternative view of news choices in his article "Social Control in the Newsroom: A Functional Analysis," in which he contended that newspapers generally have a "policy" about a number of strategic issues that reporters must learn and apply in order to prosper and even survive in their jobs. This policy is determined, in Breed's view, by the proprietors, and reflects their values and weighting of the factors that affect the newspaper's success.[4] The implication is that the news is skewed by a combination of economic factors and political judgments that are imposed from above and that override professional values.

In the tradition of the Breed approach, Noam Chomsky and I have put forward a "propaganda model," which spells out a number of market and structural factors that, in our view, powerfully shape the U.S. mass media's treatment of news and opinion. Proprietary interests are among those factors that define the framework within which journalists operate. But we also include the role of advertisers, sourcing, flak, and anticommunist and free market ideology as constraining forces. These may operate in part by influencing proprietary choices, in part through their effects on the overall intellectual and news environment within which journalists operate.

In this chapter, I will argue in support of the view that there is a dominant policy and/or ideological basis for decisions about newsworthiness in a number of areas of newsmaking in the U.S. mass media, and that these often overwhelm professional values. In the next section, I will discuss briefly "professional values," "policy," and "ideology," and then describe and illustrate the ways in which policy and ideological bias manifest themselves and can provide the materials for testing.

Professional Values Versus Ideology and Policy

I interpret "professional values" to encompass two things: First, it implies "objectivity" in the sense of presenting a variety of sides to a story, searching out facts without political constraint, and presenting these fairly and impartially. It is, of course, important to distinguish between *nominal* and *substantive* objectivity. The latter refers to the attempt to meet the objectivity standard in substance, not just in form. Nominal objectivity refers to the use of the forms of objectivity alone, sometimes as a cover for de facto bias, as in citing two sides of a story, but giving a preferred side prominence and space for a full argument and allowing the other side only a feeble and empty riposte.[5] Another important mode of nominal objectivity is quoting officials on a point, but failing to provide historical or other context that would enable a reader/listener/watcher to understand the purpose and evaluate the truthfulness of the statement. Adherence to nominal objectivity facilitates news management by the government and other powerful sources. This may be understood and approved by journalists and media officials as they work with government officials toward a common end (see my discussion below of The Gullibility Quotient).

A second element of professional values is deciding what is newsworthy on the basis of consistently applied news values and not in pursuit of a policy agenda that is biased by ideological premises or compromised by strategic or profitability considerations. "Policy" means that a line or newsgathering procedure is imposed by proprietors and editors that predetermines news choices, emphases, framing, tone, and investigative zeal in accord with a political agenda or in response to the influences of power or profit. This would include allowing oneself to be used by a source to get over its line, as well as fixing a policy position from within. Policy may extend to few or many topics, leaving professional values intact in the residual areas. It may be tightly or loosely enforced and it can change over time.

Ideological assumptions are implicit value judgments, or premises about facts that are debatable and rest on value judgments. The assumptions that national leaders have benevolent intentions and speak the truth, whereas leaders of hostile states have ill- or self-serving motives and are not truthful, are ideological. The assumptions that free enterprise and free trade are good and government enterprise and regulation, and constraints on free trade, are bad, are ideological. Herbert Gans lists a number of assumptions, such as "ethnocentrism," "altruistic democracy," and "responsible capitalism," that he also calls "enduring values," that are taken for granted by U.S. journalists.[6] He gives them the term "paraideology," but he contends that their presence as an underpinning of newswork does not constitute a violation of objectivity. Because they are already built into news judgments "they do not conflict with objectivity—in fact, they make it possible. Being part of news judgment, the enduring values are those of journalism rather than of journalists; consequently, journalists can feel detached and need not bring in their personal values."[7] But if premises that reflect the dominant ideology are already incorporated into news judgments, objectivity is compromised in advance and Gans's journalists don't have to introduce "personal values" because this is already done for them. He salvages journalistic objectivity by the semantic shift of the ideological bias and nonobjectivity toward "journalism" and away from journalists.[8] But the penetration of ideology, including "paraideology," into the newsmaking process at any stage is incompatible with meaningful conceptions of objectivity and professional values.

It is well established that important media proprietors have had definite, strong political views that they have imposed on their media outlets,[9] and there is episodic evidence that a great many less strongly ideological proprietors have had a distinct and well understood ongoing influence on media policy choices.[10] Close connections and reciprocal service between top media owners and executives, on the one hand, and U.S. presidents and State Department, CIA, and Pentagon officials on the other hand, are also easily documented.[11] For some reason these cases, though numerous and applicable to many important media institutions, are given little weight and are rarely mentioned in discussions of the sources and direction of media bias.[12]

Although there is extensive evidence of proprietary influence, it is often difficult to prove on an ongoing basis. It is frequently only for the past that compelling documentation is accessible. Policy is likely to be transmitted to the lower echelons in subtle ways: By the hiring of top-level editors known to fit the owner's "general outlook" and to be sensitive to proprietary demands; by politically biased reporter selection, promotion, and dismissal;[13] and by editorial instruction on story selection, emphases, and tone that guide underlings as to what is expected of them.[14]

Equally important, it is difficult to distinguish between proprietor-editor policy and mere profit-seeking. It should be recognized, however, that a decision to focus strictly on profitability, which calls for sticking closely to establishment sources and avoiding disturbing advertisers and other powerful constituencies, is a major and conservative policy decision in its own right. We may distinguish between an explicit and intended policy line, and a policy by default, whereby a proprietor who is trying to maximize profits follows the line dictated by dominant sources, which will be cheap ("efficient") and will not offend the powerful. Those proprietors who fit the latter category and are unwilling to absorb the costs necessary to provide more accurate and balanced news have a policy by default that conflicts with "professional values."

Dominant ideologies reflect the interests of the powerful. Thus, policies imposed by proprietors often incorporate dominant ideologies as suitable premises and frames of reference. Reporters who treat these uncritically are hired and rewarded; those that do not are either not hired, adapt, or fall by the wayside.

Whatever the evidence of "smoking guns" that point to high level intervention, and despite the problem of separating out intended policy bias from mere profitmaking, it is still possible to test the relative strength of policy and ideology, on the one hand, and professional values, on the other, by examining their effects on news outputs. Whether the bias is planned or based on too ready dependence on official sources and uncritical acceptance of ideological assumptions, there would be sharp limits to such bias if professional values were operative.

Manifestations of Policy Bias

Let me enumerate and illustrate briefly a number of ways in which policy and ideological bias may be manifested and how professional values play a correspondingly limited role. More detailed illustrations are given in the chapters that follow.

Differential Tone and Language

It is elemental that professional values should not permit a dichotomous use of language, in which "snarl" words are applied to disfavored people, groups, and countries, whereas "purr" or neutral language is applied to those looked upon with favor.[15] For example, when the United States was withdrawing from UNESCO in 1983–1984, editorial opinion in the U.S. mass media was uniformly hostile to UNESCO and its head Amadou M'Bow. This was reflected in a spectacular dichotomization of language, both in news and editorials, with M'Bow portrayed as "autocratic," "ripping off" the Third World, "wily," "evasive," UNESCO described as "wasteful," "totally deformed," "scandalous," "abominably managed," "corrupt," etc. On the other hand, the U.S. officials engineering the withdrawal and their allies were treated with wholly neutral language, and the United States was portrayed as a benevolent parent "goaded beyond endurance."[16]

In another enlightening case, when the Soviet Union shot down Korean airliner 007 in 1983, the U.S. media freely used words like "atrocity," "deliberate," "wanton," "barbarian," "criminal," and "murder," whereas when the Israelis shot down a Libyan civilian airliner with 110 civilian casualties in 1973, the dominant phrase was "tragic error," and the word "criminal" was used only in citations from the Arab press.[17] That "policy" underlay this word usage was suggested explicitly in a New York Times editorial of March 1, 1973, that discussed the tragic error: "No useful purpose is served by an acrimonious debate over the assignment of blame for the downing of a Libyan airliner in the Sinai peninsula last week."[18] That is, the "useful purpose" of news was acknowledged to influence the paper's coverage; it was not "ignoring story implications."

Double Standard in Intensity of Coverage

Just as the New York Times found it not "useful" to focus heavily on the Israeli shootdown, so by contrast it cooperated enthusiastically with the Reagan administration by giving intensive coverage to the Soviet downing of KAL 007; the ratio of column inch space in the two cases was 5.7 to 1.[19] This was a politically congenial story, and although it was newsworthy by standard rules, the frenetic play it eventually received had little or nothing to do with efficiency or professional news values.

The same point may be made for innumerable other cases of dichotomization between what I refer to as "worthy" and "unworthy" victims, a division based on political preference and serviceability in politically motivated propaganda campaigns. For example, of 22 cases in which human rights victims were given intensive news coverage in the New York Times between 1976 and 1981, 21 involved victims in the Soviet sphere of influence; only one was a victim of a Western state.[20] As there was a plentiful supply of human rights abuses in the West during this period,[21] this selectivity was clearly a product of ideological preference and policy, not the application of professional news values.

Double Standard in the Application of Relevant Principles

The selectivity in the coverage of terrorism and human rights violations by ourselves and our clients, on the one hand, and declared enemies on the other, entails a double standard in application of principles that is extremely common in media practice. The cases just discussed involve such a double standard—shooting down civilian airliners by hostile states is "inexcusable" and criminal, but when it is done by us or our allies it becomes a tragic error or is perhaps even provoked by the victims.[22] Further illustrations are spelled out later in detail in connection with terrorism and human rights violations (chapters 15 and 16) and in connection with media coverage of foreign elections (chapter 13). In the latter case, it is shown that the media regularly follow a government line, finding client state elections "encouraging" whereas the elections held in disfavored states are a "sham." This is accomplished in part by applying different criteria of evaluation in the two sets of cases.

Politically Biased Selection of Facts

The biased use of criteria for evaluating elections necessarily entails a biased choice of facts about those elections. In the U.S. government-supported elections, U.S. officials have played down the inability of alternative candidates to qualify and compete, whereas such difficulties in "enemy" elections have been given prominence. The mainstream media have followed this line, aggressively pursuing and suppressing facts in the different cases in accord with the official double standard. This was dramatically evident in their coverage of the elections in El Salvador and Nicaragua in the 1980s, but it has been equally true of more recent election coverage in Mexico and Russia.[23]

In the 1982 Salvadoran election, no leftist candidate could run because, among other reasons, they were all on a list of 138 "traitors" that the army had issued in March 1981. In none of its many articles dealing with the 1982 and 1984 elections did the *New York Times* ever mention this death list. But on March 17, 1989, in an article devoted to a tentative leftwing electoral bid, reporter Lindsey Gruson pointed out that "in 1981 . . . the armed forces put a bounty on the heads of 138 leftists by publishing a list of their names and describing them as wanted traitors."[24] This belated disclosure served to add credibility to the 1989 election in El Salvador, when a leftist finally felt able to run, just as the paper's failure to mention this fact earlier helped support the U.S. government's effort to legitimize those prior elections when leftists were excluded.

Selectivity based on framing merges indistinguishably into selectivity based on prior belief and simple correspondence with policy. For example, once the U.S. news establishment had adopted the idea that the Bulgarians and KGB were behind the shooting of the Pope in May 1981, events and facts that would cast doubts on this idea were regularly found to be unnewsworthy.[25] The evidence for a tie-in of the shooting with Bulgaria and the KGB was based entirely on the confessions of the Turkish rightist, Mehmet Ali Agca, who had done the shooting, made in an Italian prison many months after his incarceration. He confessed after lengthy interviews with members of the Italian secret service agency (SISMI) and the investigating magistrate, Ilario Martella.

There were numerous reports in the Italian press in 1982–1984 that Agca had been coerced, threatened, and bribed to implicate the Eastern Bloc. None of these reports made it into the *New York Times* or network television. The *Times* was lavish with details of the investigating magistrate's visits to sites where Agca claimed to have visited Bulgarians, and they assiduously searched out the opinion of notables such as Zbigniew Brzezinski and Italian prosecutors about whether the Bulgarians and Soviets would do this sort of thing. But documents and opinions that pointed to possible manipulation of Agca in prison were ignored.

The Gullibility Quotient and the Transmission of Lies

A closely related test of policy and ideology versus professional values may be called the "gullibility quotient." The hypothesis is that when official handouts or media-generated themes like the Bulgarian Connection are congenial to ideological biases and media policy, the media news managers will often be extremely gullible and will accept dubious stories without feeling any obligation to verify them. Professional values, if they were operative, would call for caution and insistence on evidence. The mass media's handling of the 1981 shooting of the Pope falls into this high gullibility quotient class.[26] In the case of the Libyan "hit squad" allegedly sent to the United States to kill President Reagan in 1981, the U.S. mainstream press jumped on this bandwagon with enthusiasm despite the convenience of the claim to ongoing government strategies, its implausibility, and the absence of evidence.[27] The alleged shipment of MIG airplanes to the Nicaraguan government in early November 1984, an Office of Public Diplomacy tactic designed to push the Nicaraguan election out of the headlines, was taken at face value.[28]

Another important illustration is the U.S. mass media's receptivity to the official claim that in client states in which the government is killing large numbers of civilians, the killing is being done by extremists of the right and left who the moderates in the government are allegedly unable to control. This view of the Argentine military regime's holocaust of 1976–

1983 was faithfully transmitted to readers of the *New York Times* by its reporter, Juan De Onis: "The military junta headed by Lieutenant General Jorge Raphael Videla, Commander in Chief of the army, has been unable to control the rightwing extremists, who are clearly linked to the military and police, . . ."[29]

Likewise, the official view of El Salvador in the 1980s was that the moderate government was having difficulty containing the extremists. John Bushnell of the State Department told Congress in 1980 that "there is some misperception by those that follow the press that the government is itself repressive in El Salvador" when in fact the violence is "from the extreme right and extreme left" and "the smallest part" of the killings come from the army and security forces."[30] On September 27, 1981, Alan Riding wrote in the *New York Times* that "under the Carter administration, United States officials said security forces were responsible for 90 percent of the atrocities," not "uncontrollable rightwing bands."[31] Nevertheless, despite this isolated admission, widely confirmed by independent sources, *Times* editorials and virtually all of its news articles from 1980 to the present have maintained the distinction between the government and the people on the extreme right and left who kill. In 1987, for example, *Times* reporter Lindsey Gruson wrote that "Today, death squads of the right and left no longer terrorize the population into submission and silence."[32] In 1990, the paper still had the president of El Salvador "bravely" pressing criminal charges against the killers of the six Jesuits. "By so doing, he defied the zealots in his own rightist camp."[33] In other words, there was still a moderate in command who deserved support as he fought extremists of the right and left.

When the priest Jerzy Popieluszko was murdered by the Polish police in 1984, the *Times* never suggested that it was a killing by police extremists whom the government must bring to justice. *Times* coverage took it for granted that this was the Polish *government* in action. The consistent distancing of agents of the government who murder from the government itself in Argentina, Guatemala, and El Salvador is an expression of ideology and policy that flies in the face of professional values.

Lack of Investigative Zeal
Professional values would call for a determined search for confirmation or disproof when propaganda agencies make convenient but implausible claims. The failure to ask questions and seek evidence is the corollary of a high gullibility quotient. This failure is applicable to all the cases mentioned earlier. For example, in the instance of the disclosure that the

administration had lied in the case of KAL 007 when it claimed that the Soviets knew they were shooting down a civilian plane, years later the *Times* acknowledged editorially that it had been taken in,[34] but the editorial neglected to point out the paper's own failure to question and investigate from the beginning. The information that contradicted the lie was provided by Congressman Lee Hamilton, who used Freedom of Information Act procedures that the *Times* and other mass media organizations had neglected to tap.

Unwillingness to Correct Error

Another possible check on the force of policy or ideology versus professional values is the willingness of the media to correct error. In principle, if a paper or broadcast station transmits a lie, it should be anxious to clear the matter up and straighten out the record. The cost of admitting gullibility should be more or less offset by a desire to get back at the victimizer. True integrity would demand that the correction be featured at least as prominently as the original lie, and that the media explain who was responsible for the deception.

On the other hand, if the errors reflect a politically based gullibility and bias, then the points scored against enemies (the Soviet Union and Libya), and the protection afforded allies (pre-1983 Argentina, El Salvador) are desirable and correcting error would cancel out some or all of the benefits of policy. Although professional values would call for assiduity in correction, ideological and policy bias would militate against it.

The U.S. mass media almost never give corrections equal prominence with original fabrications, and often don't admit error at all.[35] In the case of the Bulgarian Connection, the media never admitted error after the case against the Bulgarians was lost in an Italian court in 1986, but blamed the loss on peculiarities of the Italian legal system or on Italian politics, although that legal system and political order was biased, if at all, *against* the Bulgarians.

Five years after the event, when the *New York Times* did admit it had transmitted a lie claiming Soviet knowledge of the fact that KAL 007 was a civilian plane, the editors blamed it on the government, and gave the news correction only back-page treatment under the heading "Reagan Said to Ignore Data on Downing of Jet." The *Times* has never acknowledged error in reference to the Libyan hit squad story of 1981. Although the hit squad never surfaced, the mainstream U.S. press simply dropped the story. It was revealed in the British *New Statesman* of August 16, 1985, that the source for the claim of a hit squad—about which the president of the United States had said "we have the evidence and [Khadaffi] knows it"—was Manucher Ghorbanifar, an individual linked to Israeli intelligence, whose hit squad list was of a Lebanese group strongly hostile to Khadaffi.[36]

In the case of the U.S. withdrawal from UNESCO in the years 1983–1984, and up to the present, the *New York Times* has repeatedly asserted that UNESCO favored a New World Information and Communication Order (NWICO) that would license journalists and allow governments to control the media.[37] UNESCO officials kept writing to the *Times* (and other papers as well) to point out that UNESCO had never even voted on, let alone passed, proposals approving the licensing of journalists or a NWICO; that UNESCO officials had varying opinions on the subject; and that it was entirely improper to say that UNESCO favored these things. In one reply to such a UNESCO complaint, the foreign editor of the *Times* acknowledged that this mode of expression was not "fully fair," but the *Times* did not publish the letter and, most important, continued to make the same error in later years.[38] This reflected a clear *Times* policy of hostility to UNESCO that led to manifestations of bias at many levels.

Notes

1 "The beliefs that make it into the news are *professional* values that are intrinsic to national journalism and that journalists learn on the job . . . .People with a strong interest in ideological matters have often been dissatisfied with the news media, but their dissatisfaction is also the product of certain rules of news judgment . . . .The rules of news judgment call for ignoring story implications [except for libel and national security matters]." Herbert J. Gans, *Columbia Journalism Review* (November/December 1985), 32–33.

2 This point is developed in his book *Deciding What's News* (New York: Vintage Books, 1979), where he says that "The considerations [of journalists in choosing among sources] are interrelated because they have one overriding aim: efficiency" (128; see also 281–82). In this complex and detailed work, Gans also brings in other factors, including the *power* of dominant sources, but the main thrust of his argument is the dominance of the efficiency factor.

3 Ibid., 313ff, 328ff.

4 Warren Breed, "Social Control in the Newsroom: A Functional Analysis," *Social Control* (May 1955), 326.

5 This distinction is implicit in Gaye Tuchman's discussion of the rules of objectivity in "Objectivity as Strategic Ritual: An Examination of Newsmen's Notions of Objectivity," *American Journal of Sociology* (January, 1972), which stresses that while the media's rules of objectivity could provide the basis for a serious approximation to true objectivity, their primary role is ritualistic and formal, to protect the media from complaints of unfairness and libel suits.

6 Gans, *Deciding What's News*, 42–55.

7 Ibid., 196–97.

8 Gans also contends that paraideology is less biasing than other ideologies: "in the final analysis it encourages them [reporters] to be somewhat more open-minded than would an integrated ideology" (Ibid., 277–78). This claim is unconvincing. A journalist who doesn't even recognize his bias is hardly likely to be more objective than one who does. The former need not makes any concessions for balance as the truth is entirely clear.

9 Famous cases are those of Henry Luce and his *Time-Life-Fortune* empire, the Hearst press, Colonel Robert McCormick and the *Chicago Tribune*, the Wallace family's *Reader's Digest*, William Knowland's *Oakland Tribune*, Rupert Murdoch's papers, the Moon-sponsored *Washington Times*, Walter Annenberg's *Philadelphia Inquirer*, and the Copley papers. There are many others.

10 Turner Catledge, the top *New York Times* editor for 17 years, noted that the paper's chief owner, Arthur Hays Sulzberger, was in the habit of "making his likes

and dislikes known," and that "he sought executives who shared his general outlook, and he tried, by word and deed, to set a tone for the paper." Catledge, *My Life and the Times* (New York: Harper and Row, 1971), 189. It is clear that during the later era, when A. M. Rosenthal was managing editor of the *Times* and imposed a distinct structure of policies on the paper, that this was in accord with the political preferences of the publisher Arthur Ochs Sulzberger (see chapters 6–8 below). Similar conclusions can be drawn from histories of the *Washington Post*, CBS, and the *Los Angeles Times*. For the *Post*, see Deborah Davis, *Katherine the Great* (Bethesda, MD: National Press, Inc., 1984) and David Halberstam, *The Powers That Be* (New York: Alfred Knopf, 1981). On CBS, see Halberstam and Lewis J. Paper, *Empire: William S. Paley and the Making of CBS* (New York: St. Martin's Press, 1987). On the *Los Angeles Times*, see Halberstam.

11   On the links of the *New York Times* and *Wall Street Journal*, see below, chapters 6–9. David Sarnoff, head of RCA and NBC, received the title of Brigadier General during World War II for his armed services propaganda effort. In the late 1940s he chaired an organization called the "Armed Forces Communication Association," where he pressed numerous Cold War propaganda themes. See *Broadcasting*, 1950 [1], 21, and *Broadcasting*, 1950 [2], 21. On the extensive connections of Paley and CBS to the government and CIA, see Paper, *Empire*, 303–4; Daniel Schorr, *Clearing the Air* (New York: Berkeley Medallion Books, 1978), 204, 275ff. The revolving door between top level government and media officials has been extremely active. James Hagerty went from President Eisenhower's press secretary to chief of ABC News. David Gergen went from Reagan's White House media staff to a high editorial position at *U.S. News and World Report*. Edward W. Barrett resigned as Under Secretary of State for Public Affairs to work for NBC. Before he went to State he was editorial director of *Newsweek*. On the *Washington Post*'s official links to government and CIA, see Davis, *Katherine the Great*.

12   In the numerous neoconservative tracts on media bias, I believe this point is never brought up and evaluated. In other instances, cases of strenuous proprietor intervention are dismissed as reflecting a distant past, before the rise of professional management, etc. Many great media firms, however, are still owner controlled, and in the instance of the Murdoch empire the intrusion of the proprietor's political views into the newsmaking process is as blatant as in the classic Luce, Hearst, and Wallace cases (see Thomas Kiernan, *Citizen Murdoch* [New York: Dodd, Mead & Co., 1986], 198–322).

13   According to Deborah Davis, at Ben Bradlee's interview for a top job at the *Washington Post*, Katherine Graham asked him how he planned to cover the Vietnam war, which she consistently supported. "Bradlee said he didn't know, but that he'd hire no 'son-of-a-bitch' reporter who was not a patriot." Davis, *Katherine the Great*, 302.

14   See Breed, "Social Control in the Newsroom"; John Soloski, "News Reporting and Professionalism: Some Constraints on the Reporting of News," *Media Culture & Society* (April 1989), 207–28.

15   See further, chapter 22, "Word Tricks and Propaganda."

16   This dichotomization of language is described in detail in William Preston, Jr.,
     Edward S. Herman, and Herbert Schiller, *Hope and Folly: The United States
     and UNESCO 1945–1985* (Minneapolis: University of Minnesota Press, 1989),
     Tables 5 and 6, 248–50.

17   On the differential use of language, see Table 9.3 in Edward S. Herman,
     "Gatekeeper Versus Propaganda Models," in Peter Golding et al., *Communicat-
     ing Politics* (Leicester: Leicester University Press, 1986), 192.

18   Editorial, "After Sinai," *New York Times*, 1 March 1973.

19   Herman, "Gatekeeper Versus Propaganda Models," 189.

20   See Table 4.1 in Edward S. Herman, *The Real Terror Network* (Boston: South
     End Press, 1982), 197. "Intensive coverage" is defined there as a case where an
     individual received attention in the news columns six or more times in any con-
     secutive 30-day period, as recorded in the *New York Times Index*.

21   In its *Annual Report for 1975–76*, Amnesty International noted that "more than
     80 percent" of the urgent appeals involving torture were coming out of Latin
     America [p. 84].

22   The *Times* suggested as much in its editorial on the U.S. navy shootdown of an
     Iranian civilian airliner in 1988, which killed 290 people. The editorial argued
     that "blame may be with the Iran Air pilot for failing to acknowledge the ship's
     warnings . . . Iran, too, may bear responsibility for failing to warn civilian planes
     away from the combat zone of the action it had initiated" (ed., July 5, 1988). In
     fact, the Iranian airliner was in its proper civilian airliner corridor, and Iran had
     not initiated any combat action—it had been attacked by Iraq, then a U.S. ally,
     and the U.S. ship was on duty supporting Saddam Hussein. See further, chapter
     7, under "Shooting down 007."

23   For a detailed analysis of the dichotomous treatment of the El Salvadoran and
     Nicaraguan elections, Edward Herman and Noam Chomsky, *Manufacturing
     Consent* (New York: Pantheon, 1988), chap. 3; on media treatment of more
     recent elections, see chapter 13.

24   Lindsey Gruson, "Fingerhold for Dissent in El Salvador," *New York Times*, 17
     March 1989.

25   This statement and the account that follows are based on Herman and Chomsky,
     Manufacturing Consent, 154–67; Edward Herman and Frank Brodhead, *The
     Rise and Fall of the Bulgarian Connection* (New York: Sheridan Square Press,
     1986), chap. 7.

26   This propaganda campaign was to a considerable extent media rather than gov-
     ernment sponsored, with the *Reader's Digest*, NBC-TV, and the *New York Times*
     playing especially important roles. See Herman and Brodhead, *Rise and Fall of
     the Bulgarian Connection*, 174–81.

27   For a good discussion, William Perdue, *Terrorism and the State* (New York: Praeger, 1989), 50–57.

28   Herman and Chomsky, *Manufacturing Consent*, 137–39.

29   De Onis, "Rightist Terror Stirs Argentina," *New York Times*, 29 August 1976.

30   Quoted in Raymond Bonner, *Weakness and Deceit* (New York: Times Books, 1984), 172.

31   Alan Riding, "Duarte's Strategy May Work Better in U.S. Than in El Salvador," *New York Times*, 27 September 1981, Sec. IV, 5.

32   Lindsey Gruson, "Peace is Still a Long Shot in El Salvador," *New York Times*, 27 September 1987.

33   Editorial, "Light in El Salvador," *New York Times*, 10 April 1990. The alternative and plausible view that Cristiani, or any other leader, would have to engage in at least a *nominal* effort to investigate charges against the army, when not doing so would seriously jeopardize the flow of U.S. funds, is not suggested by the *Times*. When it was finally disclosed that Cristiani had personally approved army surveillance of the Jesuit victims three days before their murder, the *Times* gave the report very muted treatment. It treated in very low key, also, the evidence that the investigation and case were falling apart.

34   Editorial, "The Lie That Wasn't Shot Down," *New York Times*, 18 January 1988.

35   An article by Edwin Diamond, A. Biddle Duke, and Isabelle Anacker, "Can We Expect TV News To Correct Its Mistakes?," in *TV Guide* (December 5, 1987), that stressed the unwillingness of TV networks to correct errors, notes that newspapers have developed standard practices for doing this through correction boxes, letters to the editor, etc. The authors cite a Gannett Center research report that on average, large newspapers publish "a correction every other day." The authors, however, never discuss the meaning of "error," make no attempt to assess the relationship of number of corrections to the number of actual errors, and fail to note the possibility that the large papers correct a few trivial errors but fail to correct more subtle and important ones. Their undoubtedly just criticism of TV's correction failures is thus juxtaposed with a highly credulous apologetic for the large print media.

36   Duncan Campbell and Patrick Forbes, "Tales of Anti-Reagan Hit Team Was 'Fraud'," *New Statesman*, 16 August 1985.

37   Preston et al., *Hope and Folly*, 246–47, 267–73.

38   Ibid., 273–77; on the later use of this mode of expression, see Edward Herman, "How Paul Lewis Covers UNESCO," *Lies of Our Times* (June 1990), 17–18.

Chapter 6

All the News Fit to Print (Part 1): Structure and Background of the *New York Times*

The masthead logo of the *New York Times*, "All The News That's Fit to Print," dates back to 1896, the first year of Ochs-Sulzberger family control of the paper, and both the family control and arrogant belief in the benevolence and superior judgment of the dominant owners persist to this day. The 1997 proxy statement of The New York Times Company explains the special voting rights that assure family control in terms of the desire for "an independent newspaper, entirely fearless, free of ulterior influence and unselfishly devoted to the public welfare."

The paper's independence, however, and the century long accretion of influence and wealth by the owners, has been contingent on their defining public welfare in a manner acceptable to their elite audience and advertisers. In the 1993 debate over the North American Free Trade Agreement (NAFTA), for example, the *Times* was aggressively supportive of the agreement, and solicited its advertisers to participate in advertorials[1] with a letter that touted the "central importance . . . of this important cause" and the need to educate the public on NAFTA's merits, which polls showed that most citizens failed to appreciate. As the paper regularly takes positions on domestic and foreign policy issues within parameters acceptable to business and political elites, it is evident that the owners have failed to escape class, if not selfish, interests in defining public welfare and what's fit to print.

In debates within the range of elite opinion, moreover, the *Times* has not been "fearless," even in the face of gross outrages against law, morality, and the general interest. During the McCarthy era, for example, the management buckled under to the Eastland Committee by firing former

Communist employees, who spoke freely to the paper's management but would not inform on others, and more generally it failed to oppose the witch-hunt with vigor and on the basis of principle.[2] In fact, an editorial of August 6, 1948, that attacked the use of the Fifth Amendment before the House Committee on Un-American Activities was written by publisher Arthur Hays Sulzberger himself.[3]

Among other cases of accommodation to retrograde policies, the paper did not oppose the Vietnam War till late in the game, and then on the grounds that the war could not be won and would cost us too much (see chapter 8); it failed to oppose either the U.S. sponsorship of a system of National Security States in Latin America or the Central America wars, and protected these murderous enterprises by eye aversion and biased reporting.[4] Even Reagan's "supply side economics" was treated gently by the editors ("No one else has yet offered an option half so grand for dealing with stagflation."),[5] and the paper's top reporter, James Reston, stated (falsely) that Reaganomics involved "a serious attempt . . . to spread the sacrifices equally among all segments of society."[6] The *Times* played a supportive propaganda role in the Cold War and the huge Carter-Reagan era military buildup to contest the inflated Soviet Threat (see chapter 7). Its highly favorable review of *The Bell Curve*, and more recent extensive publicity given the Thernstroms, have been notable contributions to the ongoing assault on affirmative action.

Business Interests

The dominant owners of The New York Times Company—a holding company—control a large and complex business organization, which had revenues of $2.9 billion and earnings of $262 million in 1997. Among its 50 or more subsidiaries, the Times Company owns 21 newspapers in addition to the *New York Times* and the *Boston Globe*, eight TV and two radio stations; various electronic and other news and distribution services; a magazine group that specializes in golf; forest products companies; and 50 percent ownership of the *International Herald Tribune* (the *Washington Post* owns the balance).[7]

The holding company's Class A stock is listed on the New York Stock Exchange, and traded at about $65 per share in February 1998. The Sulzberger family owns 17.5 million shares of the 97.6 million Class A shares outstanding, or 18 percent; but it owns at least 87 percent of the 425,000 Class B shares, which are entitled to elect a majority (nine) of the 14 directors. The value of the Sulzberger family holdings in February 1998 amounted to $1.2 billion. In 1997, family members Arthur Ochs

Sulzberger and Arthur Ochs Sulzberger Jr. also drew compensation from the company in salaries, bonuses, and options that totaled $1.5 million and $1 million respectively.

These owners regularly associate with other rich and powerful people who are anxious to cultivate the acquaintance of those who control the country's most influential newspaper. Such contacts occur on the board of the holding company, which includes business leaders drawn from IBM, First Boston (a major investment bank), the Mercantile Bank of Kansas City, Bristol-Myers Squibb (drugs), Phelps Dodge (copper), Metropolitan Life, and other corporations. The company also has a $200 million line of credit with a group of commercial banks, and periodically uses investment banks to underwrite its bonds and notes and help it buy and sell properties. These financiers and business executives press for a focus on the bottom line, and they would not be pleased if the *Times* took positions hostile to the interests of the corporate community (which, contrary to right-wing mythology, the paper does not do).

Increasing Hegemony of Advertisers

Back in the 1970s, the *Times* was stumbling economically, profits virtually disappeared, and its stock price fell from $53 in 1968 to $15 in 1976. In a 1976 article *Business Week* assailed the management for lethargy, and because it "has also slid precipitously to the left and has become stridently antibusiness in tone, ignoring the fact that the *Times* itself is a business—and one with very serious problems."[8] When this article appeared, measures had already been taken to rectify the paper's business shortcomings and its supposedly "left" tendency as well. A.M. Rosenthal, a close friend of William Buckley Jr. (who referred to Rosenthal as "a terrific anticommunist"), and a self-described "bleeding-heart conservative"[9] (the search for that heart remains a challenge to independent investigators after 25 years), was installed as executive editor. Editor John Oakes was ousted, the editorial board was restructured, with the more conservative Roger Starr and Walter Goodman replacing Herbert Mitgang and Fred Hechinger, and control over all aspects of the paper was more centralized.[10] *Times* policy shifted to the right, the paper was reoriented toward softer and more advertiser friendly news, and the common "policy" root of news reporting, editorials, and book reviews became more conspicuous.

Rosenthal established a Product Committee, and openly emulated Clay Felker's *New York* magazine's pioneering of a news product that featured gossip about the shows, restaurants, discos, attire, decor, and other cultural habits of the upwardly mobile, attractive to fashion trade and other advertisers.[11] More and more articles appeared on the good life of Beautiful People (e.g., "Living Well Is Still The Best Revenge," celebrating the de La Rentas, Dec. 21, 1980), and fashion designers (e.g., "The Business of Being Ralph Lauren," *New York Times Magazine*, Sept. 18, 1983), and entire sections of the paper were allocated to Mens [or Women's] Clothing, House & Home, Food and Dining, and Style. On February 26, 1998, the *Times* introduced a new section entitled "Circuits," which will cover "the personal side of digital technology," and hopefully will attract some of the advertising dollars going to *Wired* and *Electronic Media*.

With the advertising recession of 1991, the pace of integration of advertising and editorial functions was stepped up; regular supplements to the magazine on "Fashions of the Times" and fashion news such as the shortening of women's skirts began to make the front page. On March 23, 1993, the Sunday Magazine featured the big names of fashion—Calvin Klein, Ralph Lauren, Donna Karan, Bill Blass, and Oscar de la Renta—with their photos and sample product lines, in a purported *news* article. Later in 1993, an entire issue of the magazine was devoted to fashion, and in the paper's own Fall 1993 advertising supplement, advertising copy for the A&S department store ad read "All the fashion news that's fit to print" directly above the A&S logo. That is, the *Times* had loaned its own advertising logo that supposedly signified journalistic integrity to an advertising purchaser.[12] The Sunday *Times* now has a regular section on Sunday Style, and the magazine also has a segment devoted to style.

Such attention to advertisers was paralleled by a shift of news interest to the suburbs and other locales in the New York area with affluent householders, and away from the Bronx, Brooklyn, Queens, and Staten Island. It also meant a lightening up of investigative reporting that would threaten local real estate and developer interests, although this was not new. Robert Caro, in *The Power Broker: Robert Moses and the Downfall of New York* (1974), assailed the *Times* for its uncritical support of this political czar, whose ruthless infrastructure development "very nearly destroyed New York's physical fiber."[13] Caro says that the *Times* "fell down on its knees before him, and stayed there year after year." Writing in 1985, John Hess said that "Moses is long gone, . . . yet the *Times* enthusiastically supports billion-dollar projects that will strangle its own neighborhood."[14] The firing of Sidney Schanberg from his metropolitan column beat in 1986 was another clear signal that harsh criticism of local real estate, developer, and associated political interests was no longer acceptable to the paper.

For advertisers, serious consumer reporting is "anti-business," and consumer reporting went into decline in the 1970s and after. Ralph Nader asserted in 1993 that A.M. Rosenthal "did more to damage consumer causes than any other person in the United States," as the *Times*'s lead in downgrading consumer issues was followed by the *Washington Post* and then by the rest of the press.[15] Nader says that more than a dozen *Times* reporters complained to him that they were pushed away from "hot-potato areas into soft consumer advice or other non-consumer assignments." The *Times* was late on many key business stories, like the S&L scandals, the Bank of Credit and Commerce International case, the mid-1980s phony liability crisis contrived by the insurance industry, the misrepresentations of the Bush Task Force on Regulatory Relief, and others. Reporters told Nader that "New York doesn't like these stories," or that they must get company responses to charges against them—and as Nader notes, the companies learned "simply not to return calls, knowing that that tactic would block the story deadline. These companies know about Rosenthal too."[16]

Other Elite (and Government) Connections

Times officials and reporters have other (nonbusiness) ties to the elite that make a class and establishment bias inevitable and natural. In his gentle history of the *Times*, *Without Fear or Favor*, veteran *Times* reporter Harrison Salisbury points out that the paper was dominated in the post World War II era by men "of the same social and geographic circle, [who] had gone, by and large, to the same schools, Groton, again and again, Groton; they had married into each other's families; they were Yale and Harvard and Princeton."[17] They were lawyers, bankers, businessmen, and journalists; and many were notables in the CIA and other parts of the government. These friends had "a common view of the world, the role of the United States, the nature of the communist peril."

Salisbury devotes many pages to the CIA-*Times* connection, questioning but not disproving the claim by Carl Bernstein in *Rolling Stone* in 1977 that Cyrus Sulzberger, long-time chief European correspondent for the *Times*, was a knowing CIA "asset," and that the paper gave cover to some 10 CIA agents from 1950 to 1966. Salisbury supplies an impressive list of CIA people—Allen Dulles, James Angleton, Frank Wisner, Kim Roosevelt, Richard Helms, and others, who were good friends of, and wined, dined, and vacationed with, a large array of *Times* officials and reporters. He acknowledges that in the early years there had been a "relationship of cooperation between *The Times* and the Agency, a relationship of trust betwen the CIA and *Times* correspondents" (quoting CIA official Cord Meyer), and that friendly connections persisted thereafter.[18] When the *Times* published a series on the CIA in 1966, it gave a draft to former CIA chief John McCone for prior review, an action that Salisbury felt was entirely without significance because McCone's reactions could be accepted or ignored by the paper.[19] But Salisbury missed the possibility that the willingness to bring McCone into the editorial process might reflect the limited framework and nonthreatening character of the *Times*'s effort.

The *Times*-CIA relationship, and its complexity, was displayed in 1954, when CIA head Allen Dulles persuaded Arthur Hays Sulzberger to keep reporter Sidney Gruson out of Guatemala, as the U.S. was organizing the overthrow of the Arbenz government. Gruson, although he was a Cold Warrior and strongly supportive of U.S. policy, was not a straight propagandist, so Dulles claimed to possess derogatory information about him, and he was kept away. But Sulzberger kept pressing Dulles for evidence to support his charges against Gruson, and was extremely annoyed when it was never provided. He realized that he had been used by the CIA to fine-tune a propaganda effort.[20] (The *Times* was outrageously biased in its coverage of Guatemala in 1953 and 1954—and later—but not quite biased enough to suit the CIA).[21]

The *Times* today remains very protective of the CIA, as was manifested in its negative reactions to and spectacularly biased news reporting of Gary Webb's story about the CIA link to the contras and contra drug trading,[22] and its equally bad handling of Kathy Kadane's disclosures about the CIA-U.S. connection to the 1965–66 Indonesian massacres.[23] These reactions are almost surely a result of its broader support of U.S. foreign policy rather than any specific links to the CIA, which it will, on occasion, slap on the wrist for demonstrated misbehavior.[24]

Inside Information, Revolving Doors, and Co-optation

Whatever the precise nature of the *Times* link with the CIA and other government agencies, the friendships and common understandings among these Cold Warriors and members of an economic, social, and political elite have made for a built-in lack of scepticism and critical and investigative zeal on the part of the editors and leading reporters. These press recipients of sometimes privileged information from friends have not been inclined to treat the suppliers without favor. Max Frankel, longtime editor, and executive editor after Rosenthal, became extraordinarily close to Henry Kissinger in the Nixon years, and Robert Anson notes that Kissinger "put that intimacy to good use, employing Frankel's trust to delay stories; boost his boss; and, on more than a few occasions—the administration's supposed unconcern about Marxist Salvadore Allende being a prime example—spread flatout falsehoods."[25]

James Reston, the *Times*'s most famous reporter, was on close terms with a string of presidents and secretaries of state, but in the strange mores of U.S. journalism, the resultant compromised character of his reporting did not diminish his professional standing. Bruce Cumings, writing about secretary of state Dean Acheson in 1950, states that "Acheson vented his ideas through our newspaper of record, James Reston's lips moving but Dean Acheson speaking."[26] And Reston himself spoke of his reliance on the "compulsory plagiarism" of "well-informed officials," and he even once titled one of his articles "By Henry Kissinger—With James Reston."[27]

As the Reston story suggests, the most common pattern of serving the political establishment is not by directly telling lies, but rather by omission, and by letting officials tell lies that remain uncorrected. Salisbury describes the internal debate over how far the paper should go in accommodating propaganda, the upshot of which was that the *Times* would "leave things out of the paper," or would publish statements known to be false if U.S. officials "were willing to take responsibility for their statements." What the *Times* would not do is publish unattributed lies.[28] This is the high principle underlying news fit to print!

The *Times*'s close relationship with business and government has also been reflected in a revolving door of personnel. Most notable were Leslie Gelb's moves, from director of policy planning at the Pentagon (1965–68) to the *Times*, then to policy planning at the U.S. State Department (1977–79), and then back to the *Times* as diplomatic correspondent, op ed column editor, and foreign affairs correspondent (1981–93), and then on to head the Council on Foreign Relations, the most important U.S. private organization of foreign policy elites that has ties to business, the CIA, and the State Department. Another notable trip was that of Richard Burt, the *Times*'s Pentagon correspondent during key Cold War years (1974–83), who moved into the Reagan State Department in 1983, where he quickly displayed openly the ultra-Cold War bias that was ill-concealed in his work as a *Times* reporter. Roger Starr's move from the construction business to New York City Housing Commissioner to the editorial board was an important reflection of the *Times*'s new look in the 1970s.

The *Times* has attracted many quality reporters over the years. But power at the paper still flows down from the top, affecting hiring, firing, promotion, assignments, and what reporters can do on particular assignments. As I noted regarding consumer reporting, if "New York" (the editors, who reflect *Times* policy) doesn't like tough stories, reporters will learn to avoid them, or leave the paper, and many good and principled ones have left. If writers are too hard hitting in criticizing theatrical fiascos that represent heavy investments, as Richard Eder was in the 1980s, or about local developer abuses, as Schanberg was, they are eased out. When they write about topics on which the *Times* has an ideological position and "policy," such as the Israeli-Palestinian conflict, Russia and its "reform" process, or health care reform and the Social Security "crisis," the reporters all toe a party line, which either comes naturally to them or to which they adapt. Just as Richard Burt was hired in the 1970s to provide the proper accelerated Cold War thrust in Pentagon reporting, so too during the Central American wars of the 1980s did the *Times* deliberately hire and fire to achieve a policy line that accommodated the Reagan-Bush support of contra terrorism and the violent regimes of El Salvador and Guatemala. The firing of Raymond Bonner and installation of Shirley Christian, James LeMoyne, Mark Uhlig, Bernard Trainor, Lydia Chavez, and Warren Hoge assured this apologetic service.

In short, reporters are underlings, and in an establishment paper like the *Times* they will report within an establishment framework or leave. And the *Times* is without question an establishment newspaper; as Salisbury says of Max Frankel, "The last thing that would have entered his mind would be to hassle the American Establishment of which he was so proud to be a part."[29] What this means, however, is that the paper is not "without fear or favor"—rather, it favors the establishment, and fears those who threaten it.

Notes

1   An advertorial is an advertisement with a great deal of editorial substance rather than material touting a product sold by the advertiser.

2   See especially, James Aronson, *The Press and the Cold War* (New York: Monthly Review Press, 1970), chap. 9; also, Harrison Salisbury, *Without Fear Or Favor* (New York: Times Books, 1980), 473–76.

3   The fact that Sulzberger wrote this editorial was discovered in the *Times* files by Daniel Chomsky in the course of work on his doctoral dissertation, *Constructing the Cold War: The New York Times and the Truman Doctrine* (Ph.D. dissertaion in Political Science, Northwestern University, 1998). I am indebted to him for sharing this and other documentary information from the *Times* files with me.

4   See Edward Herman and Noam Chomsky, *Manufacturing Consent* (New York: Pantheon, 1988), Preface and chap. 3; Noam Chomsky, *Necessary Illusions* (Boston: South End Press, 1989), Appendix IV; Jack Spence, "The U.S. Media Covering (Over) Nicaragua," in Thomas Walker, ed., *Reagan Versus the Sandinistas* (Boulder: Westview Press, 1987).

5   Editorial, "Nit-Picking the Reagan Program," *New York Times*, 17 March 1981.

6   James Reston, "Ends and Means," *New York Times*, February 22, 1981.

7   These data, and those of the next paragraph, are from the holding company's 1997 Proxy Statement and Form 10-K.

8   "Behind The Profit Squeeze At The New York Times," *Business Week*, 30 August, 1976.

9   Salisbury, *Without Fear or Favor*, 531.

10   James Aronson, "The Times is a-changing," *In These Times*, 2–5 March 1977.

11   John Hess, "The Culture Gulch of the Times," *Grand Street* (Winter 1985), 125–28.

12   This is pointed out by Robin Andersen in *Consumer Culture and TV Programming* (Boulder, CO: Westview, 1995), 49.

13   John Hess, "The Culture Gulch," 142.

14   Ibid., 143.

15   Peter Nye, "Interview With Ralph Nader," *Public Citizen* (January/February 1993); for a summary and analysis, see "Nader Decks Rosenthal," *Lies of Our Times* (September 1993), 10–12.

16   Peter Nye, "Interview With Ralph Nader."

17   Salisbury, *Without Fear or Favor*, 565–66.

18   Ibid., 566.

19   Ibid., 523.

20   Ibid., 478–82.

21   For accounts of the biased news coverage of the early years, as well as descriptions of the CIA-Sulzberger-Gruson flap, see Susan Jonas and David Tobias, *Guatemala* (North American Congress of Latin America, 1974) and Stephen Schlesinger and Stephen Kinzer, *Bitter Fruit* (New York: Doubleday, 1982). For a description of later *Times* bias in discussing Guatemala, see Edward Herman, "Gruson on Guatemala: An Update," *Lies of Our Times* (August 1990), 15–16, and Herman and Chomsky, *Manufacturing Consent*, chaps. 2 and 3.

22   On the paper's treatment of Webb, see Alexander Cockburn and Jeffrey St. Clair, *Whiteout: The CIA, Drugs, and the Press* (London: Verso, 1998); "New York Times in Epic Climb-Down, CIA: We Knew All Along," *CounterPunch* (October 1–15, 1998).

23   Months after Kadane's report had circulated in the media, without mention in the *Times*, the paper came forth with a article that had minimal information on Kadane's data, but whose sole objective was to discredit her findings; Michael Wines, "CIA Tie Asserted in Indonesian Purge," *New York Times*, 12 July 1990. For a critique of this effort, see Ellen Ray and William Schaap, "Damage Control At the Times," *Lies of Our Times* (August 1990).

24   See its editorial, "The CIA's Men in Iraq," *New York Times*, 13 May 1997.

25   Robert Sam Anson, "The Best Of Times, The Worst Of Times," *Esquire* (March 1993), 109.

26   Bruce Cumings, *Origins of the Korean War, Vol. II: The Roaring of the Cataract, 1947–1950* (Princeton: Princeton University Press, 1991), 436.

27   "By Henry Kissinger—With James Reston," *New York Times*, 14 March 1979.

28   Salisbury, *Without Fear or Favor*, 486–87.

29   Ibid., 91.

Chapter 7

All the News Fit to Print (Part 2): Biases and Propaganda Service in Covering Foreign Affairs

The *Times* is a strongly ideological paper whose biases and frequent propaganda service give its logo phrase "fit to print" an ironic twist. James Reston acknowledged that "we left [out] a great deal of what we knew about U.S. intervention in Guatemala and in a variety of other cases" at government request or for political reasons satisfactory to the editors. The government lied, but the *Times* published their claims even though the "Times knew the statements were not true." [1] Strategic silences, the conduiting of false or misleading information, the failure to provide relevant context, the acceptance and dissemination of myths, the application of double standards as virtual standard operating procedure, and participation in ideological bandwagons and campaigns have been extremely important components of *Times* coverage of foreign affairs.

Obviously the *Times* is not merely a biased instrument of propaganda service. It does many things well and its reporters often produce high quality journalism. This is especially true when the paper's editorial slant on issues—its "policy"—and ideological biases are not at stake and when major advertisers are not threatened. In the sensitive areas, some of which are described below, critical and probing articles are hardly more common than dogs walking on their hind legs. Furthermore, the paper's reporters are frequently "generalists" who move from field to field and country to country, who must make up for being out of their depth by glibness, a reliance on familiar (and English-speaking) sources, and an ideological conformity that will meet "New York" standards. This helps explain James LeMoyne's reporting in Central America in the 1980s,[2] and Roger Cohen's in France, Serge Schmemann's in Israel, and David Sanger's in Asia today.

In *Without Fear Or Favor*, Harrison Salisbury refers to the *Times* editors pride during the 1960s at the paper's tradition of the "total separation of news and editorial functions," which he implied was still operative in 1980.[3] There is no doubt that there is an organizational separation between these departments, even with the greater centralization of the Rosenthal era and after, and undoubtedly neither department can order the other around. But there is a common line of authority from the top that affects the hiring, firing, and advancement of personnel, and the evidence is overwhelming that on issue after issue a common policy affects editorials, news reporting, and book reviews as well. Alan Wolfe's recent *One Nation, After All*, which fits well the ideological stance of *Times* leaders, was reviewed favorably in both the daily paper and Sunday *Book Review*, and Wolfe immediately got op-ed column space to expound his congenial message. In Central America during the 1980s there was an observable deployment of reporters to adapt news to the editorial line. *Times* news reporters do not often depart from the assumptions and frames of reference that we can read in the paper's editorials.

Anticommunism and the Cold War

The commitment of the *Times* to anticommunist ideology and its acceptance of the Cold War as a death struggle between the forces of good and evil ran deep, and severely limited its objectivity as a source of information. Rosenthal evoked the admiration of William Buckley for his anticommunist fervor. Publisher Arthur Hays Sulzberger was equally passionate, regularly admonishing his editors to focus on the Soviets as "colonialists," to use the phrase "iron curtain," and generally exhibiting the Manichaean world view of anticommunist ideologues.[4]

This corrupting influence dates back at least to the Russian Revolution itself. In a famous, and devastating, critique of *Times* reporting on the revolution, entitled "A Test of the News," published in the *New Republic* on August 4, 1920, Walter Lippmann and Charles Merz found that the paper had reported the imminent or actual fall of the revolutionary government 91 times, and had Lenin and Trotsky in flight, imprisoned, or killed on numerous occasions. *Times* news about Russia was "a case of seeing, not what was there, but what men wanted to see."[5]

The Truman Doctrine and Greece
When the Cold War began in earnest in 1947, the Truman administration found it difficult to get congressional and public support for massive

aid to the far-right collaborationist government that the British had installed in Greece. Truman and Secretary of State Dean Acheson therefore resorted to scare tactics, claiming that Greece represented a case of Soviet expansionism and that we were in a death struggle with the forces of evil. This was disinformation. Stalin honored the postwar settlement with the West. He left it free to dominate Greece and sought to restrain the Greek guerillas.[6] But the lie was taken up by the media with enthusiasm, and on February 28 and March 1, 1947, James Reston had front-page articles in the *Times* that were like State Department press releases: the "issues" allegedly were containment of an expanding Soviet Union and our willingness to aid a government "violently opposed by the Soviet Union" (a lie). Acheson's formulations—Soviet aggression, and "our safety and world peace" at stake in Greece—along with a virtual suppression of the facts on Greece and the quality of our Greek client government—became standard fare in *Times* news coverage and editorials.[7]

An important episode in the history of media coverage of the U.S. effort to "save" Greece by imposing a minority government of the right was the murder of CBS correspondent George Polk in May 1948. Polk had been a harsh critic of the Greek government and his murder presented a public relations problem for that government and its U.S. patron. The Greek government, with complete cooperation from the U.S. government and mainstream U.S. media, pinned the killing on communists, got several to "confess"—after weeks of incarceration—that it had been done to "discredit" the Greek government. Although the case was extremely implausible, and the use of torture to extract suitable confessions was obvious at the time (and conclusively proved in later years), the U.S. media, with great gullibility, accepted as legitimate a staged trial that was a Western equivalent of the trials staged in Moscow by the Stalin regime in the 1930s (and furiously denounced in the West). Walter Lippman even organized a "monitoring" group, which included James Reston, that put its seal of approval on this show trial.[8]

The *Times* reporter in Greece at this time, A.C. Sedgwick, had married into the Greek royal family, and had been accurately described by George Polk himself as a pawn of the right. Even within the *Times* there was a steady stream of criticism of Sedgwick as biased and incompetent. But Cyrus and Arthur Sulzberger supported him—Cyrus had married Sedgwick's niece and was therefore himself linked to the royal family—and Sedgwick remained as a *Times* reporter for 33 years.[9] His coverage of the Polk trial, discussed in detail in Elias Vlanton and Zak Mettger's *Who Killed George Polk?*, was continuously biased, incompetent, and factually unreliable. But his line was compatible with the *Times* support of the Cold War and uncritical acceptance of the party line on the Polk trial, which the editors found to be "honestly and fairly conducted."[10]

Interestingly, the *Times* and its reporter James LeMoyne displayed a very similar patriotic gullibility in treating the murder of Herbert Anaya in El Salvador in 1984. Here also a U.S.-supported right-wing government killed one of its enemies, but produced a tortured student who confessed to having killed Anaya in order to "make the government look bad." LeMoyne and the *Times* took this confession and explanation seriously once again, failed to look at analagous cases of Salvadoran torture (or the Polk case), and failed to follow the case up after the tortured student later recanted.[11]

The Soviet Threat and Arms Race

The *Times* accepted the official view of the Soviet Threat throughout the Cold War, and a huge news and editorial bias flowed from this that served well the propaganda needs of the state. This was notable between 1975 and 1986, when U.S. peddlers of crisis reescalating Cold War frenzy and elite interest in renewing the arms race.

Significant events in this escalation process were the CIA's claims in 1975 and 1976 that the Soviet Union had doubled its rate of military spending, supposedly to 4 or 5 percent a year, and the CIA's Team B report of December 1976, which claimed that the Soviet's were achieving military superiority and getting ready to fight a nuclear war. There had been a Team A report by CIA professionals, which found the Soviets aiming only toward nuclear parity, but CIA boss George Bush found this unsatisfactory and appointed a group of 10 noted hard-liners (including Richard Pipes and Paul Nitze), who came up with the desired frightening conclusions. This hugely politicized report displaced the report of Team A and became official doctrine.

A front-page article in the *Times* of December 26, 1976, by David Binder, took the Team B report at face value, failed to analyze its political bias and purpose, and made no attempt by independent investigation or tapping experts with different views to get at the truth. The paper simply conduited this hardline propaganda. With Richard Burt and Drew Middleton as their regular correspondents on military affairs, *Times* news and commentary featured a steady tattoo painting the Soviets as on the rise and the U.S. in military decline. There was no investigative reporting examining the CIA's estimates, which the CIA itself admitted in 1983 to have been inflated. *Times* editorials complemented this reporting, supporting "prudent" defense expansion, which involved the funding of the Trident submarine, the cruise missile, the MX mobile land missile, and the creation of a rapid deployment force as an "investment in diplomacy."[12]

During the Reagan years, the *Times* contributed to the enormous increase in the military budget by refusing to investigate and contest exaggerations and lies by the administration. Tom Gervasi, who exploded many of these lies in his 1986 book *The Myth of Soviet Military Supremacy*, noted that in one important case where there was a conflict between the claims of Reagan officials and available Pentagon data, the *Times* stated that precise figures were "difficult to pin down," but its reporters made no effort to pin them down even though billions of dollars of excess military spending were at stake. They could have interviewed those giving the figures, "But the *Times* did not do this. It dismissed the issue in six column inches and did not bring it up again."[13] Gervasi put up a four-page compilation of *Times* estimates of U.S. and Soviet warheads for the period 1979 to 1982, compared them with Pentagon data, and showed that the *Times*'s figures were inconsistent, distorted, incompetently assembled, and persistently biased toward overstating Soviet capabilities.[14]

Gervasi was given op ed space in the *Times* in December 1981, after which he was closed out and his book was never reviewed in the paper, although it was of high quality and on a very important subject to which the *Times* devoted much space for official claims. By contrast, passionate supporters of the Reagan military buildup, Edward Luttwak and Richard Perle, were given op ed space nine and six times, respectively, during the Reagan years.

Reagan-Era Propaganda Campaigns

The various propaganda campaigns developed during the 1980s were extremely important in maintaining the vision of an acute Soviet Threat and the need for a huge arms buildup. Such propaganda was used to demonstrate that the Soviet Union was an "evil empire." The *Times* participated in each of these campaigns with a high degree of gullibility.

International Terrorism. One campaign was the attempt to portray the Soviets as the sponsor of "international terrorism." A landmark was the publication and dissemination of Claire Sterling's *The Terror Network* in 1980. This right-wing fairy tale relied heavily on disinformation sources, such as the intelligence agencies of Argentina, Chile, and South Africa, and Soviet-bloc defectors such as Jan Sejna, all of which Sterling took at face value. Sterling also got much of her data from Robert Moss, co-author with Arnaud de Borchgrave of the Soviet-subversion-of-the-West novel *The Spike*, and author of a warm apologia for Pinochet, 10,000 copies of which were purchased by the Pinochet government.[15] Sterling's fanaticism can be inferred from her statement (in *Human Events*, April 21, 1984), at the height of the Reagan era anti-Soviet frenzy, that the Reagan administration was "covering up" Soviet guilt in the assassination attempt against the Pope in 1981 because of the Reaganite devotion to detente!

The *Times* reviewed Sterling's book favorably (compliments of Daniel Schorr), but more importantly, gave her magazine space in which to expound her views ("Terrorism: Tracing the International Network," May 1, 1981). Previously, and just before the 1980 election, the paper also gave space to disinformation specialist Robert Moss, who was peddling the same line ("Terrorism: A Soviet Export," November 2, 1980). These highly misleading flights of propaganda served well the plans of the Reagan administration, featuring and misrepresenting the Soviet connection and diverted attention away from the terrorist holocausts underway in the "constructively engaged" states like South Africa and Argentina. *Times* "news" performed the same service, continuously identifying "terrorism" with retail and left-wing violence, and with the violence of states declared outlaws by the State Department. Little attention was given to the U.S.-sponsored retail (non-state) terrorists of the Cuban refugee network or the wholesale (state) terrorists of Argentina and Guatemala.

The Plot to Murder the Pope. A second propaganda salvo followed the assassination attempt against the Pope in May 1981. As the criminal had stayed in Bulgaria for a period, the Western propaganda machine, with Claire Sterling in the lead, soon pinned the shooting on the Bulgarians and the KGB, and a case was brought in Italy against several Bulgarians (which was eventualy lost). This case rested on what was almost surely an induced and/or coerced confession, and as in the trial for the murder of George Polk in Greece, the *Times* (and most of the mainstream media) performed with shameful gullibility. The will to believe overpowered any critical sense, and investigative responsibility was suspended; official handouts and the speculation of ideologues like former CIA propaganda specialist Paul Henze and Sterling dominated the coverage. The *Times* actually used Sterling as a news reporter in 1984 and 1985; her work during that period included a front-page article on June 10, 1984 ("Bulgarians Hired Agca To Kill Pope"), that was not only biased but also suppressed critically important information.[16]

From beginning to end, the *Times* never departed from the Sterling-Henze party line. This was not altered by the loss of the case in Rome in

1986. When CIA officer Melvin Goodman testified during the hearings to confirm Thomas Gates as head of the CIA in 1990 that CIA professionals knew the Bulgarian Connection was a fraud because they had penetrated the Bulgarian secret services, the *Time* failed to reprint this part of Goodman's testimony. When Allen Weinstein was given permission to examine Bulgarian files on the case in 1991, the *Times* repeatedly found this newsworthy, but when he returned apparently without "success," the *Times* failed to seek him out and report his results. Following Claire Sterling's death, the obituary notice by Eric Pace (June 18, 1995) stated that while her theory of a Bulgarian Connection was "disputed," she asserted in 1988 that Italian courts had "expressed their moral certainty that Bulgarian's secret services was behind the papal shooting." Sterling's unverified hearsay was given the last word.

In sum, having participated in a fraudulent propaganda campaign, the *Times* not only has never cleared matters up for its readers, but it continues to supply disinformation and refuses to publish facts that would correct the record.[17]

Shooting Down 007. The *Times* also got on the propaganda bandwagon when the Soviets shot down Korean Airliner 007 on September 1, 1983. The paper ran 147 articles about the shootdown in September alone, and for ten days it devoted a special section of the paper to the case. As usual, the paper took at face value administration claims, in this case that the Soviets knew that they were shooting down a civilian plane. (Five years later the editors acknowledged this to have been "The Lie That Wasn't Shot Down," June 18, 1988). The columnists and editors were frenzied with indignation, using words like "savage," "brutal," and "uncivilized," and the editors stated that "There is no conceivable excuse for any nation shooting down a harmless airliner" (September 2, 1983). But when the USS *Vincennes* shot down an Iranian airliner in 1988, killing 290, no invidious language was employed, and here the patriotic editors found that there *was* a good excuse for the act—a "tragic error" and irresponsible behavior by the victims.

Subsequently, when David Carlson, commander of a nearby ship, wrote in the September 1989 issue of the U.S. Naval Institute's *Proceedings* that the actions of the commander of the *Vincennes* had been consistently aggressive, and that Iranian behavior had been entirely proper and unthreatening, the *Times* failed to report this information, which contradicted its editorial apologetics. The *Times* also failed to report that in 1990 President Bush had awarded the commander of the *Vincennes* a Legion of Merit award for "exceptionally meritorious conduct" in recognition of his deadly efforts. On the other hand, on December 9, 1996, the

Times did find newsworthy an interview with the Soviet pilot who shot down KAL 007, showing his picture on the front page, with a brief lead entitled "Pilot Describes Downing of KAL 007," the text including the statement that "he recognized [007] as a civilian plane." But the fuller text on page 12 quotes him saying "It is easy to turn a civilian plane into one for military use." The *Times* distorted his message on page 1, in an almost reflexive continuing effort to portray the Soviet Union as barbaric, as it continued to suppress evidence that put the shooting down of the Iranian airliner in a bad light.

Fresh and Stale History. In fact, the *Times* regularly selects and ignores history in order to make its favored political points. For example, Soviet forces killed perhaps 10,000 Polish police and military personnel in the Katyn Forest in 1940. In the period between January 1, 1988 and June 1, 1990, the *Times* had 20 news stories and two editorial page entries on this massacre, including five front-page feature articles. Many of these articles were repetitive and referred to disclosures that were anticipated but had not yet occurred. This was an old story, but it was not stale because political points could be scored. On the other hand, the *Times* treated differently the story that broke in Italy in 1990 about Operation Gladio, the code name for a secret army in Europe sponsored by the CIA, that was closely tied to the far right, and that used weapons secreted through this program for terrorist activities. The three back-page *Times* stories on the case all featured its old age, although the use of Gladio-related weapons in terrorist activities during the 1980s gave it a currency absent in the Katyn Forest massacre story. But its political implications made the Gladio story stale.

Notes

1   Harrison Salisbury, *Without Fear Or Favor* (New York: Times Books, 1980), 486.

2   For a brilliant and devastating critique, see Noam Chomsky, *Necessary Illusions* (Boston: South End Press, 1989), Appendix IV.

3   Salisbury, *Without Fear or Favor*, 43.

4   This statement is based on numerous internal memos and letters in the *Times* files, cited in Daniel Chomsky, *Constructing the Cold War: The New York Times and the Truman Doctrine* (Ph.D. dissertation in Political Science, Northwestern University, 1998).

5   Walter Lippmann and Charles Merz, "A Test of the News," *New Republic* (August 4, 1920), Part II (Supplement), 3.

6   For a good account, see Lawrence Wittner, *American Intervention in Greece, 1943–1949* (New York: Columbia University Press, 1982).

7   Editorials, *New York Times*, 3, 11, and 12 March 1947.

8   See Elias Vlanton and Zak Mettger, *Who Killed George Polk: The Press Covers Up a Death in the Family* (Philadelphia: Temple University Press, 1996).

9   C.L. Sulzberger, *A Long Row of Candles* (Toronto: Macmillan, 1969), 69–71.

10   Editorial, *New York Times*, 22 April 1947.

11   Edward S. Herman, "Disinformation as News Fit to Print: Lemoyne and the Times on the Murder of Herbert Anaya," *CovertAction* (Winter 1989).

12   Editorial, *New York Times*, 24 February 1978; Editorial, *New York Times*, 1 February 1980.

13   Tom Gervasi, *The Myth of Soviet Military Supremacy* (New York: Harper and Row, 1986), 119.

14   Ibid., 122–25.

15   For critiques of Sterling's methodology, see Diana Johnstone, "The 'fright story' of Claire Sterling's tales of terrorism," *In These Times* (20–26 May 1981); Edward Herman, *The Real Terror Network* (Boston: South End Press, 1982).

16   See Edward Herman and Frank Brodhead, *The Rise and Fall of the Bulgarian Connection* (New York: Sheridan Square Press, 1986), 190–94.

17   For a summary account, see Herman and Chomsky, *Manufacturing Consent*, chap. 4; for further developments, see Herman and Friel, "'Stacking the Deck' on the Bulgarian Connection," *Lies of Our Times* (November 1991), 14–15.

Chapter 8

All the News Fit to Print (Part 3): The Vietnam War

It is part of conservative mythology that the mainstream media, and notoriously the *New York Times*, opposed U.S. involvement in Vietnam, and effectively "lost the war." Liberals, on the other hand, who often agree that the press opposed the war, regard this opposition as a display of the media at its best, pursuing its proper critical role. But they are both wrong: the conservatives, because they identify any reporting of unhelpful facts as "adversarial" and want the media to serve as crude propaganda agencies of the state; the liberals, because they fail to see how massively the mainstream media serve the state by accepting the assumptions and frameworks of state policy, transmitting vast amounts of state propaganda, and confining criticism to matters of tactics while excluding criticism of premises and intentions.

Before examining the applicability of these myths to the *New York Times*, let us look briefly at the factual background and context of the war.

Vietnam War Context

The United States became involved in Vietnam after World War II, first in support of the French from 1945 to 1954 as they tried to reestablish control over their former colony following the Japanese occupation. After the Vietnamese defeated the French, the United States refused to accept the 1954 Geneva settlement, which provided for a temporary North-South division that would be ended by a unifying election in 1956. Instead, it imported its own leader, Ngo Dinh Diem, from the United States, imposed him on the south, and supported his refusal to participate in the 1956 election. Eisenhower acknowledged that Ho Chi Minh would have swept a free election, and from 1954 to 1965 a stream of U.S. experts conceded that our side had no indigenous base, whereas the Vietnamese enemy had the only "truly mass-based political party in South Vietnam."[1] Pacification officer John Vann stated in 1965 that "A popular political base for the Government of South Vietnam does not now exist," that our puppet regime is "a continuation of the French colonial system . . . with upper-class Vietnamese replacing the French," and that rural dissatisfaction "is expressed largely through alliance with the NLF [National Liberation Front]."[2]

When our puppet could no longer maintain control by the early 1960s, even with massive U.S. aid, the U.S. engaged increasingly in direct military action from 1962, including the chemical destruction of crops and mass relocations of the population. In 1963 the United States collaborated in the assassination of Diem, replacing him with a series of military men who would do our bidding, which meant, first and foremost, refusing a negotiated settlement and fighting to the bitter end. As U.S. official William Bundy put it, "Our requirements were really very simple—we wanted any government that would continue to fight."[3] The United States was determined to maintain a controlled entity in the south, and a negotiated settlement with the dominant political force there—which opposed our rule—was consequently dismissed. The strategy was to escalate the violence until the dominant indigenous opposition surrendered and agreed to allow our choice to prevail. We assured that only force would determine the outcome by manipulating the governments of "South Vietnam" so that only hard-line military men who met our demands would be in charge. General Maxwell Taylor was frank about the need for "establishing some reasonably satisfactory government," replacing it if it proved recalcitrant, possibly with a "military dictatorship."[4]

Having imposed a puppet, refused to allow the unifying election, evaded a local settlement that would give the majority representation, and resorted to extreme violence to compel the Vietnamese to accept our preferred rulers, a reasonable use of words tells us that the United States was engaging in aggression in Vietnam.

The official U.S. position, however, was that the North Vietnamese were the aggressors because they supported the southern resistance, and, in April 1965, actually sent organized North Vietnamese troops across the border. In one remarkable version, the southerners who were members of the only mass-based political party in the south, but who opposed our choice of ruler, were engaged in "internal aggression"! We were allegedly "invited in" by the government to defend "South Vietnam." Members of the mainstream U.S. media never accepted the view that the Soviets were justifiably in Afghanistan because they were "invited in"—they questioned the legitimacy of the government doing the inviting. If the Soviet-sponsored government was a minority government, the media were prepared to label the Soviet intrusion aggression. Their willingness to apply the same principles to the Vietnam war was a test of their integrity, and they—and the *New York Times*—failed that test decisively.

The Times As Apologist for U.S. Policies

In *Without Fear Or Favor*, Harrison Salisbury acknowledged that in 1962 the *Times* was "deeply and consistently" supportive of the war policy. He also admitted that the paper was taken in by the Johnson administration's lies about the 1964 Tonkin Bay incident that impelled Congress to give Johnson a blank check to make war.[5] Salisbury claims, however, that in 1965 the *Times* began to question the war and move into the increasingly oppositional stance that culminated in the publication of the Pentagon Papers in 1971.

Although there is some truth in Salisbury's portrayal, it is misleading in important respects. For one thing, from 1954 to the present, the *Times* never abandoned the framework and language of apologetics, according to which the United States was resisting somebody else's aggression and protecting "South Vietnam." The paper never used the word "aggression" to describe the U.S. invasion of Vietnam, but applied it freely to North Vietnamese actions. And its supposedly liberal and "adversarial" reporters like David Halberstam and Homer Bigart referred to NLF actions as "subversion" and the forced relocation of peasants as "humane" and "better protection against the Communists." The liberal columnist Tom Wicker referred to President Johnson's decision to "step up resistance to Vietcong infiltration in South Vietnam." The Vietcong "infiltrated" in their own country; the United States "resisted." Wicker also accepted without question that we were "invited in" by a presumably legitimate government,[6] and in the very period when the United States was refusing all negotiation in favor of military escalation to compel enemy surrender, James Reston declared that we were in Vietnam in accord with "the guiding principle of American foreign policy . . . that no state shall use military force or the threat of military force to achieve its political objectives."[7] In short, for all these *Times* men the patriotic double standard was internalized, and any oppositional tendency was fatally compromised by their acceptance of the legitimacy of U.S. intervention, which limited their questioning to matters of tactics and costs.

Furthermore, although from 1965 onward the *Times* was willing to publish more information that put the war in a less favorable light, it never broke from its heavy dependence on official sources or its reluctance to check out official lies or explore the damage being wrought by the U.S. war machine. In contrast with its eager pursuit of refugees from the Khmer Rouge after April 1975, the paper rarely sought out testimony from the millions of Vietnamese refugees who fled U.S. bombing and chemical warfare. In its opinion columns as well, the new openness was toward those commentators who accepted the premises of the war and would limit their criticisms to its tactical problems and costs to us. From beginning to end, those who criticized the war as aggression and immoral at its root were excluded from the debate.

Times Propaganda Service

The *Times* also remained to the end a gullible transmitter of each propaganda campaign mobilized to keep the war going, as the following examples illustrate:

Demonstration Elections

The Johnson administration sponsored "demonstration elections" in Vietnam in 1966 and 1967 to show that we were respecting the will of the Vietnamese people. Although that country was occupied by a foreign (U.S.) army and was otherwise thoroughly militarized, free speech and freedom of the press were nonexistent, and the only "mass-based political party" (NLF) as well as all "neutralists" were barred from participation, the *New York Times* took these elections seriously. Their news reports stressed the heavy turnouts, and the editorials noted the "popular support" shown by the peasants' willingness "to risk participation in the election held by the Saigon regime."[8] In both news reports and editorials the paper suggested that the elections might lead to peace, because by legitimizing the generals it "provides a viable basis for a peace settlement."[9] As the whole point of the exercise was to keep in place leaders who would fight, this was promotional deception of the worst sort.[10]

Phony Peace Moves

Every six months or so, the Johnson administration would make a "peace move," with a brief bombing halt, which was described by the analysts of the Pentagon Papers as "efforts to quiet critics and obtain public support for the air war by striking a position of compromise," that "masked publicly unstated conditions . . . that from the communists' point of view was tantamount to a demand for their surrender."[11] Although from early 1965 onward the *Times* editorially favored some kind of negotiated settlement, it was institutionally incapable of piercing the veil of deception in the peace move ploy, of presenting evidence of the fraudulence and public relations design of such ploys, and calling president Johnson and his associates liars. Reston greeted each of them at face value, asserting that Johnson "has now tried to meet every honorable proposal for a negotiated accommodation," and that "the enduring mystery of the war in Vietnam is why the Communists have not accepted the American offers of unconditional peace negotiations."[12]

The *Times* gave back-page coverage to disclosures late in 1966 that the United States had sabotaged a string of negotiating efforts in 1964, and the peace talks in late 1966 that involved Poland, which ended with a series of bombings of Hanoi, were given minimal publicity.[13] Altogether, from beginning to end, the editorials and news articles of the *Times* failed to portray the true role of the "peace moves," even while allowing some modest criticism of their flaws.[14]

Paris Peace Agreement

In October 1972 an agreement was reached between the Nixon administration and Hanoi that would have ended the war on terms similar to those the United States had rejected in 1964, with the NLF and Saigon government both recognized in the south and an electoral contest to follow. The United States, however, following the heaviest bombing attacks in history on Hanoi in December 1972, proceeded to reinterpret the agreement as one that left the south to the exclusive control of its client, in contradiction to the clear language of the document.[15] The *Times*, along with the rest of the mainstream media, accepted the Nixon administration's reinterpretion without question, and continued thereafter to repeat this false version and to cite the incident as "a case study of how an agreement with ambiguous provisions could be exploited and even ignored by a Communist government."[16]

The POW/MIA Gambit

Nixon used the U.S. prisoners of war and men missing in action "mainly as an indispensable device for continuing the war," allowing him to prevent or sabotage peace talks.[17] The *New York Times* editors jumped quickly onto this bandwagon, denounced the Communists as "inhuman," accepted the disinformation that 750 U.S. POWs were still alive, and claimed that the POW question "is a humanitarian, not a political issue."[18] Reston argued that Americans "care more about the human problems than the political problems . . . The guess here is that they will be more likely to get out of the war if the prisoners are released . . . than if Hanoi holds them as hostages and demands that Mr. Nixon knuckle under to them."[19] The ready transformation of the POWs into hostages, and the failure to see the cynicism and managed quality of this concern over POWs, shows the *Times* at its most gullible as it joined once more a deceptive propaganda exercise that contributed to further large-scale violence and deaths.

Postwar Continuation of Imperial Apologetics

After the Vietnam War ended, and during the ensuing 18 years of U.S. economic warfare against the newly independent Vietnam, the adherence of the *Times* to the traditional and official viewpoints never wavered. That the United States was guilty of aggression has never been hinted at; the United States fought to protect "South Vietnam." In 1985 the editors chided the public for ignorance of history, evidenced by the fact that only 60 percent of its readers knew that this country had "sided with South Vietnam"[20]—a creation of the United States with no legal basis or indigenous support. Even so, South Vietnam was legitimized for the *Times* because this was official doctrine, just as *Pravda* might have found that the Soviet Union "sided with Afghanistan" in its fight against foreign-aided rebels.

In reconstructing imperial ideology it was also important that the enormous damage inflicted on the land and people of Vietnam by this country be downplayed and that the Vietnamese who took command be put in an unfavorable light. The *Times* accommodated the demands of the state by giving the damage minimal attention and by consistently attributing the difficulties of the smashed (and then boycotted) country to communist mismanagement.[21] While featuring selected refugees who presented the most gruesome stories and blamed the communists, the *Times* repeatedly sneered at the "bitter and inescapable ironies . . . for those who opposed the war" and who had "looked to the communists as saviors of the unhappy land."[22] This, of course, implicitly denied U.S. responsibility for the unhappiness. The statement also misrepresented the position of most antiwar activists, who did not look on the communists as saviors, but did object to the murderous aggression designed to thwart their rule, an aggression that the *Times* supported.

For the *Times*, our only debt was to those fleeing "communism." On the other hand, with the POW/MIA gambit institutionalized in the United States, throughout the boycott years the *Times* adhered to the view that the Vietnamese were never sufficiently forthcoming about U.S. servicemen missing in action (the vast numbers of missing Vietnamese have never been a concern of the U.S. establishment or of the *Times*). In 1992 the editors even retrospectively criticized Nixon for having failed to pursue the issue sufficiently aggressively with Hanoi![23] Their gullibility quotient in this area also continued at a high level, so that when, with normalization of relations threatening in 1993, the rightwing anti-Vietnam activist Stephen Morris allegedly found a document in Soviet archives showing that Hanoi had deceived on POWs, the *Times* featured this on the front page, without the slightest critical scrutiny.[24] This was in the tradition of convenient gullibility that was displayed earlier in the paper's evaluation of the Polk trial and the KGB plot to kill the Pope.

When Vietnam invaded Cambodia in 1979, despite the serious provocations that led it to do so and the frenzied Western outcries over Pol Pot's murderous behavior, Vietnam immediately became the "Prussia of Southeast Asia" for the *Times*, who gave the country no credit for ousting the Khmer Rouge (nor did it criticize the ensuing U.S. support of the Khmer Rouge). And Vietnam's failure to withdraw over the next decade was given as a reason that justified its ostracization.[25] The contrast with the *Times* treatment of the regular Israeli assaults on Lebanon and Israel's refusal to withdraw from occupied neighboring territories is striking. In one of the most revealing displays of the arrogance and double standard of the *Times*, in 1993 Leslie Gelb classed Vietnam as one of the "outlaw" states, for its behavior in Cambodia, its foot-dragging on the MIAs that counted, and because "these guys harmed Americans."[26] As in the case of Nicaragua in the 1980s, the *Times* line is that nobody has a right of self-defense against any U.S. exercise of force, which is by definition just and right.

Concluding Note

In sum, the *Times* was not only not "adversarial" during the Vietnam war, it was also for a long time a war promoter. As antiwar feeling grew and encompassed an increasing proportion of the elite, the *Times* provided more information and allowed more criticism within prescribed limits (the war could be presented as a tragic error, despite the best of intentions, because of unwinnability and excessive costs—to us). But even then it

continued to provide support for the war by accepting the official ideological framework, by frequently and uncritically transmitting official propaganda, by providing very limited and often misleading information about
government intentions and the damage being inflicted on Vietnam, and
by excluding fundamental criticism. It is one of the major fallacies about
the war that antiwar critics were given media access—those who opposed
the war on principle were excluded from the *Times*, and the antiwar
movement and the "sixties" have always been treated with hostility by the
paper.

Notes

1   Douglas Pike, *Viet Cong* (Cambridge: MIT Press, 1965), 110.

2   Vann gave his untitled and unpublished document to Professor Alex Carey in 1965, who circulated it widely.

3   Quoted by George Kahin in *Intervention* (New York: Alfred Knopf, 1986), 183.

4   For a short account of this history, see Noam Chomsky and Edward Herman, *The Washington Connection and Third World Fascism* (Boston: South End Press, 1979), chap. 5. For fuller studies, George Kahin, *Intervention: How America Became Involved in Vietnam* (New York: Knopf, 1986); Gabriel Kolko, *Anatomy of a War* (New York: Pantheon, 1985); Marilyn Young, *The Vietnam Wars, 1945–1990* (New York: HarperCollins, 1990).

5   Harrison Salisbury, *Without Fear or Favor*, 45–46.

6   For cites to these reporters, and others as well, see Edward Herman and Noam Chomsky, *Manufacturing Consent* (New York: Pantheon, 1988), 191–206.

7   James Reston, "The Guiding Principle in Vietnam," *New York Times*, 26 February, 1965.

8   Editorial, "Voting in Vietnam," *New York Times*, 4 September 1967.

9   Ibid.

10 For further details, see Edward Herman and Frank Brodhead, *Demonstration Elections: U.S.-Staged Elections in the Dominican Republic, Vietnam, and El Salvador* (Boston: South End Press, 1994), chap. 3.

11 The Senator Gravel Edition, *The Pentagon Papers*, vol. 3 (Boston: Beacon Press, 1972), 291.

12 James Reston, "The Danger of Miscalculation in Vietnam," *New York Times*, 19 May 1965; "The Historic Skepticism of Hanoi," 31 December 1965.

13 "Pessimism in Warsaw," *New York Times*, 15 December 1966, 4.

14 Two books that described Johnson's peace moves as public relations efforts, published at the time, were Richard DuBoff and Edward Herman, *The Strategy of Deception* (Washington, D.C.: Public Affairs Press, 1966), and Franz Schurmann et al., *The Politics of Escalation in Vietnam* (New York: Fawcett, 1966).

15 For a discussion, see *Manufacturing Consent*, chap. 5.

16 Neil Lewis, *New York Times*, 18 August 1987.

17 H. Bruce Franklin, *M.I.A. or Mythmaking in America* (New York: Lawrence Hill, 1992), 48.

18   Editorial, "Inhuman Stance on Prisoners," *New York Times*, 29 May 1969.

19   James Reston, "Tragedy of Ignorance," *New York Times*, 21 April 1972.

20   Adam Clymer, "What Americans Think Now," *New York Times*, 31 March 1985.

21   For details, see Noam Chomsky and Edward Herman, *After the Cataclysm: Postwar Indochina and the Reconstruction of Imperial Ideology* (Boston: South End Press, 1979), chap. 3.

22   Editorial, "'Liberation' Comes to Vietnam," *New York Times*, 21 March 1977.

23   Editorial, "What's Still Missing on M.I.A's," *New York Times*, 18 August 1992.

24   Celestine Bohlen, "Files Said to Show Hanoi Lied in '72 On Prisoner Totals," *New York Times*, 12 April 1993. For a good analysis of this forgery, see Bruce Franklin, "M.I.A.sma," The *Nation* (May 10, 1993).

25   Editorial, "Coming Soon: The Vietnam Peace," *New York Times*, 28 October 1992.

26   Leslie Gelb, "When to Forgive and Forget," *New York Times*, 15 April 1993.

Chapter 9

The *Wall Street Journal* as Propaganda Agency: Yellow Rain and the El Mozote Massacre

The Two Wall Street Journals

The *Wall Street Journal* is in a sense two different newspapers: a high-quality news operation, and an editorial page that pushes right-wing causes and themes relentlessly, often with a blatant disregard of evidence. Occasionally the two arms of the paper come into conflict, as in *Journal* reporter Jonathan Kwitny's August 1985 series detailing the shady qualities of the Italian secret services and political culture and its U.S. connections.[1] The articles shed unflattering light on frequent *Journal* editorial page contributor, neoconservative activist and propagandist Michael Ledeen, and his erstwhile ally, Italian spy and fixer Francesco Pazienza, who was then residing in a U.S. jail.

Kwitny's two-part report was the first time the *Journal* had focused on some of the doubtful features of the alleged Bulgarian-KGB involvement in the assassination attempt on Pope John Paul II in May 1981. Previously, the editorial page had run numerous articles that supported the alleged connection, with Claire Sterling as favored contributor and Gordon (the "Crowbar") Crovitz, the inside hatchet person. The editorials had also pushed the line that Italian politics and police operations were clean as a whistle. "Mind you," wrote Suzanne Garment in an editorial-page article about the Italian government's decision to prosecute the Bulgarians, "this is the Italians—no American hawk paranoids but instead people who live with a new government every thirty days. You simply cannot doubt their word."[2] The P-2 scandal was ignored in editorial page commentaries to preserve the vision of a wholesome Italy. Kwitny's critical facts about Pazienza and other unpleasant types, which he linked to editorial favorite Ledeen, were painful, and Ledeen and Sterling were given generous letter space to rebut Kwitny. The editors took some cracks at him as well.

Purging the Editorial Page

For some years the editorial page ran semiregular columns by Alexander Cockburn, Hodding Carter III, Arthur Schlesinger Jr., and Walter Heller, giving readers at least occasional relief from the otherwise incessant barrage of right-wing opinion and propaganda. But the ending of the Cold War brought this system to an end, and the editorial page has since become much freer of the taint of any alternative points of view.[3]

In a way, however, the news and editorial pages do complement one another rather well. The function of the news pages is to provide reliable information about matters relevant to the *Journal*'s readership. Ideological corruption would undermine the performance of this function, and it is mainly on issues like "terrorism" that the news department allows ideology to submerge the world of reality.[4] The news reporters are exceptionally free to examine the seamy sides of the corporate and political system, and have exposed many important cases of corporate and political malpractice, conflicts of interest, and abuses of regulation arising out of business influence. The paper is powerful enough to be able to ignore the complaints of those corporations and government officials that are being criticized that would render lesser papers more careful or altogether silent. It is surely helped in this by the fact that it can point to a solidly reactionary editorial page, which supports an unfettered capitalism and each and every imperialist venture.

The editorial page serves other functions as well. It offers an open forum and testing ground for right-wing opinion and provides readers with rationales for supply-side economics, monetarism, capital gains tax reductions, deregulation, the death penalty, generosity to police and prisons, Salvadoran and Guatemalan death squads, Pinochet, Fujimori, Savimbi, etc. It supports state and right-wing agendas through the aggressive espousal and dissemination of propaganda themes. Thus it pursued with ideological fervor each major Reaganite policy thrust and claim of the 1980s, including supply-side tax cuts, the trashing of the poor, the Soviet threat and arms build-up, the menace of Marxism-Leninism in Central America, Salvadoran guerrilla and Sandinista terrorism, the Bulgarian-KGB attempt to assassinate the Pope, and the alleged communist use of "yellow rain" chemical warfare in Laos and Cambodia.

Finally, the editors have helped to discipline and contain critics of the approved views. The editorial page has been a flak machine, like Accuracy in Media, except that it operates from within the mainstream media itself. This function is performed in part by the sheer aggressiveness and self-assurance of the editorial proclamations of higher truths. But the editors also launched attacks in the Reagan years, in parallel with those of the government, on human rights groups such as Americas Watch and Amnesty International, that were too critical of the Guatemalan government in 1981–1982, or against reporters like Raymond Bonner and Alma Guillermoprieto, whose claims that the Salvadoran army engaged in mass killings in El Mozote in 1982 were denied by the administration, as described below.

Yellow Rain

The *Wall Street Journal*'s service as a propaganda arm of the state reached its zenith in its handling of the Reagan administration's propaganda campaign from 1981 to 1986, which claimed that the Soviet Union and its allies in Laos and Cambodia were using chemical poisons against local insurgents that took the form of yellow rain. In an unusual admission, the principal *Journal* editorial writer on yellow rain, William Kucewicz, acknowledged that the *Journal* had responded to an appeal by the administration to support this "cause": " . . . some people in government—in the administration—contacted us [after the initial yellow rain announcements had been put on the back burner by the press] and said, 'Gee, can't you guys keep this going, because it is a vital issue.' After we saw how extensive this was and what it meant for the future of arms control and how inhumane these types of weapons were, we decided to take this on as a cause."[5] The *Journal*'s pursuit of the yellow rain campaign was confined almost entirely to its editorial page, whose coverage of the issue was intensive, hysterical, uncompromisingly biased, and unbending in the face of the complete collapse of the evidence. The editors were still operating as if these confuted claims were true in the 1990s.

Background

Charges of chemical warfare and the use of poison gas in Laos originated in the mid-1970s, based largely on claims of certain Hmong tribespeople who were refugees in Thailand. The charges escalated in 1978 and 1979, as the State Department and the Pentagon dispatched teams to interview refugees, and the press and the right-wing latched on to the claims to push their own agendas. The official position, however, until Reagan came into office, was that the evidence was circumstantial but justified intensive inquiry.[6]

Under Reagan, the circumstantial evidence became definitive truth. Secretary of State Alexander Haig stated in a speech in Berlin on September 13, 1981, "we now have physical evidence from Southeast Asia which has been analyzed and found to contain abnormally high levels of three potent mycotoxins—poisonous substances not indigenous to the region and which are highly toxic to man and animals."[7] Richard Burt and other officials claimed that the symptoms suffered by the victims were precisely what such poisons would produce—"the fit was perfect," said Burt. The physical evidence at that time consisted of a single leaf and stem that purportedly came from Cambodia, which was furnished by a Thai military officer to the U.S. Embassy. No control sample of leaves was obtained, nor were the original tests verified by an independent check. The claim that such mycotoxins—also referred to as trichothecenes—were not indigenous to the area was not checked out, and turned out to be false. The same was true of the allegation that the symptoms of the victims were a "perfect fit."

It should be recalled that this was the same administration that in 1981 alleged there was a Libyan "hit squad" allegedly after Reagan, which turned out to be a fabrication; that in 1981 and 1982 charged that the Soviet Union was the organizing force of world terrorism (a charge alleged by Claire Sterling, but rejected by the CIA's own professionals);[8] that between 1982 and 1986 supported the Sterling-Henze claims of the Bulgarian-KGB involvement in the shooting of the Pope in 1981; and that in 1983 charged that the Soviet Union knowingly shot down the civilian airliner KAL 007, when in fact the administration *knew* that this was not the case. In other words, this was a government for which deliberate lying as an instrument of political ends was not "second nature," it was a primary modus operandi.

From 1981 on it was U.S. policy to vilify the Soviet Union by any means, fair or foul. The yellow rain charge had the additional merit that the chemical warfare lobby had suffered a setback in the post-Vietnam War environment and was aggressively seeking to enlarge its domain in the late 1970s.[9] In the Reagan years, the lobby obtained the support of the executive branch, which saw the yellow rain story as an effective tool to restore chemical weapons development "to counter the perceived Soviet threat."[10] The administration engaged in intensive lobbying to get congressional authorization and funding for the full-scale production of new binary nerve-gas munitions."[11] It pressed its European allies to condemn the Soviets and to agree to repair Western chemical weapons deficiencies, claiming that a Soviet surprise attack could breach NATO defenses and allow a Soviet victory.[12] There were the usual claims that Western governments were aware of or had evidence of Soviet guilt in the use of yellow rain, but were "politically constrained" from exposing them. (Actually, the constraints worked the other way: as discussed below, the British government sat for years on evidence that cast doubt on the yellow rain evidence.)

The Case Disintegrates

Refugee Testimony. The Hmong tribespeople from Laos fought the Laotian government for years and were attacked periodically by ground and air fire. Back in 1964, Cambodia had accused the United States and South Vietnam in the UN Security Council of dropping yellow powder on villages, killing residents. And in the early 1970s the United States sprayed Hmong poppy fields with herbicides, which the Hmong reported resulted in human deaths. So in both Cambodia and Laos there was "a collective history of aerial spraying and, perhaps, a basis for present day rumors."[13] It is not impossible that the Hmong were attacked after the U.S. withdrawal from Indochina by planes that dropped tear gas and defoliants, which the Vietnamese had inherited from the departed U.S. forces, but this has not been proven and of course any tie-in of Vietnamese or Laotian yellow rain attacks with prior U.S. policy in Indochina is avoided by the Western propaganda system.

Given Hmong experience and fears they would be inclined to blame their ills on enemy attacks, and certainly with a bit of urging that derogatory testimony against the enemy was desired, would tend to provide it. Biochemist Matthew Meselson uncovered a 1977 Chinese scientific article which gave an account of what peasants in Jiangsu province called yellow rain, which aroused fear of poisoning from the air, and led to an investigation that found that the "rain" was bee feces. The Hmong would have more reason than the Chinese to fear poison from the air and attribute their sicknesses to yellow rain dropped by enemy forces.

There is also evidence that many of the early Hmong witnesses were asked leading questions and were not interrogated very rigorously. They were also given a line to follow by their military leaders. When independent investigators and U.S. Army and State Department follow-up teams questioned the refugees more rigorously, the stories turned out to be almost entirely hearsay, full of contradictions, and inconsistent over time.[14]

It is also important to note that no material evidence supporting yellow rain attacks—artillery shells, bombs or bomb fragments, or containers—was ever provided.[15] Furthermore, "At no time, then or later, was any case documented in which diagnostic examination or autopsy provided clear evidence of exposure to chemical warfare agents."[16] The medical investigators of the Defense-State Department chemical and biological warfare team visited a dozen suspected chemical warfare attack sites reported to them, "but none yielded confirmatory evidence."[17] The Haig-Burt team's claim of a "perfect fit" between symptoms reported and the known toxic effects of the trichothecenes did not hold up either, as the Army-State Department medical interviews found that "only 2 of the 60 alleged witnesses interviewed reported that particular constellation of symptoms. Over time this ratio did not increase. In a total of 217 interviews accumulated by 1984, only 5 matched the constellation of medical symptoms described in the Haig report."[18]

The Collapse of the Scientific Case. The scientific quality of the Reagan administration's case was negligible from its inception. The single leaf-stem sample first used as evidence was provided by a Thai military officer. That sample and three others showed only minute traces of trichothecenes. Eventually it was demonstrated that over 99 percent of the leaf contaminants was pollen in feces dropped by honeybees. This raised the question of how the Soviets and their clients had managed to get toxins linked to bee droppings. This point was usually evaded, but at one point the administration claimed that the pollen had been commercially prepared by the Soviets "to help ensure the retention of toxins in the human body."[19] There was no evidence offered to support this claim, and the absurdity of the Soviets manufacturing and collecting bee feces in order to cover up a toxin, which was itself hard to make and an inefficient weapon, was obvious.

The scientific case also broke down as more rigorous testing procedures were applied to leaf samples from southeast Asia. The early confirmations of trichothecenes in the original leaf samples were done by rudimentary methods at Fort Detrick, Md., and a laboratory in Minnesota. After the Army's acquisition of more advanced testing facilities at its Chemical Systems Laboratory, the army ran tests on 80 samples from alleged attacks in Southeast Asia, including one reported to contain trichothecenes by the Minnesota laboratory. The Chemical Systems Laboratory found no trichothecenes in any of the 80 samples.[20] Another large testing operation on samples of both vegetation and the blood and urine of victims of alleged chemical attacks was carried out at the British government laboratory at Porton Downs in 1982. The findings were kept under cover till May 1986, when the government finally reported that no trace of trichothecenes was found in any of the samples.[21] Very low levels of trichothecenes were occasionally found in bee feces samples from Thailand and elsewhere. A Canadian government report, however, indicated that the tiny quantities of trichothecenes found in such samples were "comparable to the levels found worldwide for natural occurrences of trichothecenes on stored cereals."[22] These levels also showed up in Thai blood test samples of people who had not experienced any chemical attacks. In short, they were levels that could be explained by natural processes.

The final scientific blow was the finding that trichothecenes were produced naturally in southeast Asia. In August 1985, Canadian government investigators "reported that a leaf sample collected at the site of the Ban Sa Tong episode was found to have a trichothecene-producing mold on it."[23] In 1987, British government scientists at Porton Downs reported the natural occurrence of trichothecenes in samples of food crops from Thailand. The U.S. claim that these toxins were not indigenous to southeast Asia was proven false. The case was dead, but not for the editors of the *Wall Street Journal*.

The Role of the *Wall Street Journal*

The *Wall Street Journal*'s editorial page served as a virtual propaganda arm of the Reagan administration during the yellow rain controversy. As noted earlier, the chief editorial writer on the subject acknowledged as much, stating that the editors took the issue on as a "cause" after an appeal by the administration to keep this vital issue alive. The editorials that ensued all served the propaganda function in two important respects: they accepted the claims of the state at face value as a higher truth, and they pressed hard the larger themes that the state wanted to get over: that the Soviet Union was an insidious, cruel enemy not to be trusted; that arms control agreements with them were suspect; and that our CB warfare operations needed drastic enlargement.[24]

Hypocrisy (1): Editorial Concern for the "Helpless People." The editors of the *Journal* waxed eloquent and furious over the use of such a cruel weapon as yellow rain against a "helpless people," an "unsophisticated and defenseless people." They frequently expressed their horror at the "ghastliness" of such weaponry, and at the image of "children choking on their own blood."[25] This was the same editorial board that had accepted with great equanimity the U.S. use of napalm, phosphorus bombs, CS-2 gas, and the massive chemical defoliation of peasant crops and forests in South Vietnam. That was far and away the largest application of chemical warfare since World War I, and the victims were peasants without medical resources or means of defense against technological warfare by a great industrial power. We will see below, also, that the only thing about the mass killing of men, women, and children in Central America that bothered the editors was that U.S. reporters gave credence to the claims of such unworthy victims.

In the numerous *Journal* editorial-page discussions of yellow rain in the years 1981 to 1986, the background of U.S. chemical warfare in Indochina was unmentioned. In a September 9, 1992 article by *Journal* publisher Peter Kann, entitled "Clinton Ignores History's Lessons In Vietnam," Kann demonstrated our superior moral position in the Vietnam War and clarified "who were the good guys and who were the bad guys" by citing "the poisoned fields of Laos." The vastly larger U.S. chemical war in Vietnam is blacked out, but the "poison" in Laos, his euphemism for yellow rain, is still front and center in this account. The discredited myth proves enemy evil; the well established large-scale chemical war by the United States is written out of history, allowing the United States to be as always the benevolent Uncle. Could Stalinist historiography surpass this?

Hypocrisy (2): The Bias of Anyone Who Contests the Propaganda Line. In an even more remarkable display of hypocrisy, the editors of the *Journal* expressed great indignation over the alleged personal and political biases of the investigators and scientists who were undermining the yellow rain case in the years 1982 through 1986. Scientists who merely failed to confirm the yellow rain claims were largely ignored. But Grant Evans, an Australian anthropologist who cast severe doubts on the reliability of Hmong refugee accounts, was red-baited (February 15, 1984), and the *Journal* editors castigated Matthew Meselson, who wrote extensively on the subject, for having a "personal and intellectual stake in the issue." They also suggested political bias on the part of one of 64 sources cited in an outstanding and critical review article by Lois Ember in the *Chemical & Engineering News*.[26]

In short, those who agreed with the editors were good guys. Only the motives of the bad guys needed to be examined. This was sometimes funny. One of the editors' favorite scientists was Professor Aubin Heyndrickx, a toxologist at the University of Ghent in Belgium, who explained that he was not political and had no political axe to grind in his support of the yellow rain hypothesis; his only care "is protecting freedom and human rights from the totalitarians." Furthermore, the accusations against his research "are the usual aggressive tactics of the Soviet bloc."[27] Clearly this is an objective scientist.

The Preferential Method. Throughout the 1980s the *Journal*'s editors dealt with the evidence on yellow rain by the "preferential method" of research: i.e., select the findings that fit and are preferred; ignore, distort, or sneer at conflicting evidence. On the question of refugee testimony and its reliability, the editors never once analyzed the problems involved that eventually led the Pentagon-State Department chemical warfare team to raise real doubts about this evidence. The "Yellow Rain" articles by Thomas Whiteside, Julian Robinson, Jeanne Guillemin, and Matthew Meselson (see notes 5 and 14) gave detailed accounts of the inconsistencies and other problems with the reports that the official team raised. The preferential method led the editors of the *Journal* to fail to mention this material, even though it came from an official source. When the official teams tried to follow up on alleged yellow rain attacks in 1983 and 1984, they were regularly unable to confirm the presence of trichothecene or appropriate symptoms in the alleged victims. This might suggest to the independent observer that the earlier claims were invalid. For the editors, since the earlier claims were true according to the preferential method, the failure to find evidence in the later period showed that U.S. protests and *Wall Street Journal* publicity were stopping the enemy from using yellow rain![28]

Similarly, as regards the bee feces theory, the editors of the *Journal* simply evaded or lied about its content and significance. It was the refugees who identified the yellow spots with the poisonous rain. If these spots consisted invariably and largely (over 99 percent of the material) of honeybee feces, how do we explain this composition if the yellow rain was deposited by the Soviets and their clients engaged in chemical warfare? The editors never addressed the point. The quantity of tricothecenes found in the few samples where it showed up were also extremely tiny and could not plausibly account for serious illness. Why it was found so rarely and how the tiny quantities could have an effect were not preferred questions. When the British reported in 1986, after a four-year silence, that they were unable to confirm the presence of trichothecenes in any samples they had examined, the editors did not report this. The fact that the Army itself, with more sophisticated technology, failed both to confirm one of the Minnesota lab's positive finding of trichothecenes or to find the toxin in 79 other samples, was mentioned only in passing, as if the facts did not devastate the *Journal*'s position.

Editorial writer William Kucewicz published an article on September 6, 1985, entitled "The 'Bee Feces' Theory Undone." In Kucewicz's view the theory was undone because Meselson's samples of bee feces from Thailand "admittedly" contained no trichothecenes. But this was not inconsistent in any way with Meselson's "theory" and most samples from areas allegedly subject to attacks also showed no such toxins in local samples of bee feces. At this point Kucewicz was relying heavily on the continuing claim that trichothecenes did not occur naturally in the area. The Canadian findings of 1985 and 1986, however, disclosed that a leaf sample collected at Ban Sa Tong had a trichothecene-producing mold on it. In two articles in which he focused on the Canadian reports,[29] Kucewicz never mentioned this finding, which undercut a key element in his argument. (He also failed ever to mention the British finding of trichothecenes in Thai food crops.) And although he cited another Canadian report on the Ban Sa Tong findings, he reported only the description of the attack, the symptoms of the victims, and the finding of trichothecenes in the area—he failed to mention that the document found the quantities of the toxin very small and comparable to the levels found world-wide on stored cereal. This is the preferential method with a vengeance.

El Mozote and Unworthy Victims

The *Wall Street Journal*'s editorial handling of the yellow rain controversy was in stark contrast with its treatment of massacres in Central America, which were carried out under U.S. sponsorship. Perhaps the greatest massacre of unarmed civilians during the Salvadoran struggle of the 1980s occurred at El Mozote and nearby towns in December 1981. The U.S.-trained Atlacantl Battalion swept through the villages unopposed, and proceeded to destroy homes, rape and slaughter women, and kill everyone else in sight. The number of dead, according to lists compiled by surviving peasants, totalled 733, of whom 280 were children. At the time, the U.S. Embassy and State Department furiously denied an army massacre. But investigations of the Mozote gravesites in connection with the new peace accord have now fully corroborated claims of a major massacre. Forensic scientists "were surprised only by the size of the skeletons. 'We never thought we would find so many kids, . . . and so young.'"[30]

Although the El Mozote massacre was possibly the largest, there was a steady stream of lesser but sizable massacres of civilians as the Salvadoran army conducted a series of sweeps through the countryside in the early 1980s. An article by Raymond Bonner of the *New York Times* on July 12, 1981, was entitled "Mass Killings Rack Salvador," and in this and other articles similar slaughters were described at Rio Lempa, Cabanes, the Guazapa Volcano, Cerro Pando, La Joya, La Capilla, San Pedro, Barrios, and elsewhere. Bonner pointed out, for example, that after the Atlacantl Battalion swept through the Guazapa Volcano in the spring of 1983, "'the signs of slaughter were everywhere,' [according to] free-lance journalist Don North [who] reported for *Newsweek*. North, who spent forty-two days with the guerrillas in their Guazapa stronghold, wrote about the 'charred and scattered bits of clothing, shoes and schoolbooks.' A villager from Tenango showed him shallow graves in which he said the soldiers had buried dozens of men, women, and children, after executing them with guns and machetes."[31] Murdering children was a specialty of the Salvadoran army: twelve of those massacred at Barrios were less than 5 years old.[32]

The Atlacantl Battalion, trained by U.S. advisers just prior to the El Mozote massacres, was headed by Lt. Commander Domingo Monterrosa, who "became a convert to American-style tactics and the greatest army hero of the war."[33] Another leader of the army troops that killed civilians was Lt. Col. Sigifredo Ochoa Perez. Colonel John D. Waghelstein, a senior U.S. adviser to the Salvadoran army, was enthusiastic about Ochoa and his methods,[34] so we may surely conclude that the civilian massacres were consistent with de facto U.S. advice and policy.

For the Reagan administration, the ongoing massacres were merely a public relations problem, and honest reporting was a threat to policy. The El Mozote massacre, for example, occurred inopportunely just before a required administration certification that the Salvadoran government was making a concerted effort to improve human rights. Thomas Enders, the U.S. Ambassador to El Salvador, not only denied an army massacre, claiming that "there were probably no more than 300" persons living in Mozote at the time anyway, he launched a furious attack on Bonner and Alma Guillermoprieto (of the *Washington Post*) for providing evidence of the killings. Enders was even lying about the embassy's own knowledge, as two investigators sent to the scene concluded that "there had been a massacre."[35] The Enders statement that there were only 300 people in Mozote was doubly false: the reporters had claimed the killings applied to Mozote *and* nearby villages, and a representative of the International Red Cross with close experience in the area said that at least a thousand people lived in Mozote at the time.[36]

The Journal's War on the Media

On February 10, 1982, the editors of the *Wall Street Journal* published a long editorial entitled "The Media's War," which criticized Bonner in particular for his reporting on El Mozote and the press in general for alleged credulity and failure to serve the higher purposes of U.S. foreign policy. In contrast with their reactions to the purported victims of yellow rain, the editors expressed not the slightest interest in, let alone indignation over, the slaughter of "helpless" children butchered by the Atlacantl Battalion. As victims of U.S.-organized forces, they were "unworthy" and Bonner was by definition "overly credulous" to have believed the claims of a dozen survivors and his eyewitness experiences in the face of official denials.

This was, in essence, an editorial war on the media under the guise of concern over media improprieties. The editors quoted Thomas Enders' denials, and his assertion that only 300 people lived in Mozote as serious evidence. No question was raised about government credibility, nor did the editors mention the already large record of similar army massacres. Because the reporters got evidence in rebel-held territory, they were alleged to be naive victims of a "propaganda exercise." It was not mentioned that they saw large numbers of bodies and got the testimony of at least 13 different survivors.

But the editors moved quickly to a more global attack, alleging that reporters in general tend to romanticize revolution, etc., giving selected illustrations (Herbert Matthews on Cuba, David Halberstam on Vietnam). No mention was made of possible patriotic bias or pressures on reporters from editors and officials to toe the government line, or the murder of journalists in El Salvador and Guatemala that might make reporters overly cautious.[37] At a still higher level, the editors asserted as fact that Cuba controlled the Salvadoran rebels and that a rebel victory would mean Cuban-style repression. The "big story" for the editors was that when U.S. enemies win, it is bad business; therefore, reporters should "bring some perspective to the story." Translated, this means that reporters should "get on the team" and reserve their credulity for government claims, not those unhelpful to the higher truth. This "conservative" formula for reporting would have caused the now acknowledged truth about El Mozote to be completely suppressed, and the fabricated yellow rain damage to the "helpless people" to be given massive publicity. The truth is purely instrumental for a propaganda agency.

Bonner himself was fired by the *Times* not long after the government-*Journal* assaults in what was widely regarded as an object lesson in the costs of reportorial integrity. The editors of the *Wall Street Journal* surely deserve credit for this reportorial "cleansing" operation. Bonner stated in his book that "It is widely believed that the *Journal's* editorial had a significant impact on the reporting from El Salvador, in favor of the administration. The editorial 'turned the press around,' General Nutting told a reporter some months later. The foreign editor of one major newspaper sent copies of the editorial to his correspondents in Central America. 'Let's not let this happen to us' was the message, according to one of the paper's reporters."[38] This is an example of the editorial page serving in its role of enforcer of state propaganda.

Conclusion

The *Wall Street Journal*, by virtue of the focused attention of its editorial page, was in the vanguard in pushing virtually every big lie of the Reagan era, and it did its best for many other right-wing causes. This involved remarkable hypocrisy and exceptional levels of intellectual dishonesty, both of which were consequences of the editors' internalized belief that they were instruments of higher ends. This made inaccuracies on details of little importance (and even useful to the various "causes").[39]

In helping clear the ground for the arms build-up, counterrevolutionary intervention abroad, and the Reagan policies of deregulation and upward redistribution of income, the *Journal* editors served the short-term ends of the business class well. But whether their wedding of uncompromisingly reactionary economics and politics with a brazenly instrumental conception of truth will serve the long-term interests of their business constituency is more doubtful.

Notes

1   Jonathan Kwitny, "Tales of Intrigue: How an Italian Ex-Spy, Who Also Helped U.S. Landed in Prison Here," *Wall Street Journal*, 7 August 1985; "Why Italian Ex-Spy Francesco Pazienza Got Closely Involved in the Billygate Affair," 8 August 1985.

2   Suzanne Garment, "Soviet Connection: How Much Proof Do We Need?," *Wall Street Journal*, 15 June 1984. The logic by which rapid government turnover makes for wisdom is not obvious. Garment doesn't mention that virtually all of those governments were run by the Christian Democrats. Nor does she mention that the Italian state had been heavily penetrated and manipulated by the U.S. secret services and military, as the 1991 Gladio exposures further revealed. For the corrupt political background of the case against the Bulgarians in Italy, see Edward Herman and Frank Brodhead, *The Rise and Fall of the Bulgarian Connection* (New York: Sheridan Square, 1986), chap. 4.

3   Following the new homogenization, I sent a tongue-in-cheek letter to the editor proposing, in the name of freedom of choice, that the paper decouple the news and editorial pages, allowing those who want only news *or* rightwing propaganda to buy it without the previously tied-in offering. It pointed out, also, that with a spun-off editorial page there would be so much more room for coverage of the opinions of Oliver North, Jonas Savimbi, Hector Gramjo, Augusto Pinochet, Alfredo Cristiani, Richard Perle, Dinesh D'Souza, Jude Wanniski, and the other true-blue doers and thinkers of the world. The editors didn't think well of my plan for enlarging free choice.

4   The *Journal* is no different from other mainstream papers in this respect: on terrorism, the "privileged definitions" of the state conquer all. See Edward Herman and Gerry O'Sullivan, *The "Terrorism" Industry* (New York: Pantheon, 1990), chap. 7.

5   Quoted from a 1986 article in the *Technology Review* by Thomas Whiteside, "Annals of the Cold War: The Yellow Rain Complex-II," *The New Yorker* (February 18, 1990), 48. Hereafter Whiteside—II.

6   See Thomas Whiteside, "Annals of the Cold War: The Yellow Rain Complex-I," *The New Yorker* (February 11, 1990), 44ff. Hereafter Whiteside—I.

7   Quoted in Whiteside—I, 51.

8   When presented with the Sterling thesis by Ray Cline at the 1980 meeting of the Association of Former Intelligence Officers, the recently retired CIA Moscow station chief, Howard Bane, said: "We've got to get Cline off this Moscow control of terrorists. It's divisive. It's not true. There's not a single word of truth in it." Retired CIA officer Harry Rositzke said: "It's that far right stuff, that's all. It's horseshit." [Quoted in Jeff Stein, "Old Spies and Cold Peas," *Inquiry* (December 29, 1980).] These CIA men weren't aware that this "horseshit" was about to become official doctrine.

9   See Whiteside—I, 42–46.

10 Ibid., 65.

11 Ibid.

12 Ibid., 66.

13 Lois Ember, "Yellow Rain," *Chemical and Engineering News* (January 9, 1984), 24–25.

14 "Documents recently reclassified show that when the Defense-State CBW team began to address these matters, it discovered serious problems with the reliability of the previous interviews." Julian Robinson, Jeanne Guillemin, and Matthew Meselson, "Yellow Rain: The Story Collapses," *Foreign Policy* (Fall 1987), 113. Among independent investigators, see especially Grant Evans, *The Yellow Rainmakers* (London: Verso, 1983), and Jacqui Chagnon and Roger Rumpf, "Search for 'Yellow Rain`," *Southeast Asia Chronicle* (June 1983).

15 One possible exception is a piece of plastic bag allegedly found at Ban Sa Tong, that tested positive for trichotecenes, but which Canadian investigators treated with great caution as of uncertain authenticity, given that it was supplied to them by others. The *Journal*'s William Kucewicz treated this—like anything else supporting his case—as authentic and conclusive evidence. The possible doctoring of evidence never occurred to him for any claim supporting the preferred conclusion. "Yellow Rain Confirmed," *Wall Street Journal*, 25 August 1986.

16 Robinson, et al., "Yellow Rain," 114–15.

17 Ibid., 115.

18 Ibid.

19 This was stated by Kenneth Adelman, in Whiteside—I, 105.

20 Robinson et al., "Yellow Rain," 109.

21 Ibid., 110.

22 Ibid., 111.

23 Ibid.

24 This was spelled out most clearly in the editorial "Yellow Rain & Arms Control," *Wall Street Journal*, 21 September 1981.

25 See ibid.; also, "Anyone Serious?," *Wall Street Journal*, 13 November 1981.

26 The *Journal* editorials attacking Ember were "Science and Windmills," 15 February 1984; and "Who Speaks for Science?," 4 November 1985.

27 Gordon Crovitz, "Belgian Keeps Faith With 'Yellow Rain' Victims," *Wall Street Journal*, 15 February 1984.

28 "The yellow rain attacks have apparently stopped, for example, an accomplishment for which the Reagan administration and The Wall Street Journal can claim

some credit." "Who Speaks for Science?," *Wall Street Journal*, 4 November 1985. The editors fail to note that *reports* of yellow rain did not stop, but rather the reports could not be verified using methods other than taking them at face value.

29   William Kucewicz, "Yellow Rain Confirmed," *Wall Street Journal*, 31 March 1986; "Canada's Other 'Yellow Rain' Findings," 25 August 1986.

30   Tim Golden, "Salvador Skeletons Confirm Reports of Massacre in 1981," *New York Times*, 22 October 1992.

31   Raymond Bonner, *Weakness and Deceit* (New York: Times Books, 1984), 335.

32   Ibid., 320.

33   Golden, "Salvador Skeletons."

34   Bonner, *Weakness and Deceit*, 335.

35   Quoted in ibid., 341. The embassy investigators had never gotten to El Mozote and had never interviewed survivors, which the two reporters had done.

36   Ibid., 342.

37   See Julia Preston, "Killing off the News in Guatemala," *Columbia Journalism Review* (January/February 1982); Michael Massing, "Central America: A Tale of Three Countries," *Columbia Journalism Review* (July/August 1982).

38   Bonner, *Weakness and Deceit*, 341.

39   Referring back from the growing evidence of fraud in the yellow rain case to the proven lies in the 1981 White Paper on El Salvador, the editors wrote: "Doubtless there will be an effort, as with the El Salvador White Paper, to discredit the charges. Just as minor inaccuracies couldn't hide the basic truth of the subversion effort in El Salvador," etc., etc. "Yellow Rain & Arms Control," *Wall Street Journal*, 21 September 1981. Any inaccuracies are minor for the editors when it comes to a "basic truth" as asserted by the state.

Chapter 10

The Inky and Me: A Study in Market Driven Journalism

The *Philadelphia Inquirer* (the Inky) is widely regarded as a very good newspaper. This reputation derives in part from its great superiority over its predecessor, Walter Annenberg's *Inquirer*, notorious as a partisan Republican rag and instrument of Annenberg's personal vendettas (most famously, his refusal to allow mention of the name of the liberal Democratic Governor of Pennsylvania, Milton Shapp). After the Knight system acquired the Inky (and the Annenberg-owned *Philadelphia Daily News*) in 1970—Knight merged with the Ridder chain in 1974 to form Knight-Ridder—it brought in professional managers, sharply upgraded the news operation, and terminated the paper's service as a personal political vehicle of the owner.

The paper's favorable reputation also rests on positive accomplishments. Knight-Ridder (KR) has had such first rate journalists as Frank Greve and Juan Tamayo, whose reports occasionally appear in the Inky (these reporters have been attached directly to the KR-owned *Miami Herald*). The Inky itself has had a fair number of in-house news articles and investigative studies of issues such as the wetlands, police abuses, local political corruption, and others that are very good journalism. Donald Barlett and James Steele's periodic multipart investigative reports on the tax burden and income distribution, despite limitations (noted below) have been worthy efforts.[1] The paper is not closed, and publishes news articles and occasional opinion pieces that conflict with the party line the paper supports editorially.

Despite these positive elements, however, the Inky has always been an establishment institution that keeps news and opinion very much within the bounds of establishment parameters. It is a market-driven paper, increasingly so over the past decade, and as a result has done a very poor job of maintaining a "public sphere" within which issues important to the entire citizenry are freely discussed and debated. Its news arm has the deficiency of all mainstream commercial papers—it depends too heavily on official sources, so that it is regularly led by the nose in the direction officials desire; and when officials want silence and afford few leads, the paper fails to follow a story and allows silence to prevail. (Often, however, the editors of the Inky already want to go in the same direction as officials want the paper to go.) One result is that the Inky has frequently served as a propaganda arm of the state, as in the case of its news/editorial treatment of the NAFTA debate and the Mexican bailout, where the news coverage was thin and uncritical and the editorial page was extremely biased and demagogic (see chapter 14).

Market-Driven Journalism

The Inky's parent, KR, is a publicly-owned company that is traded on the New York Stock Exchange, and as a consequence is under steady pressure to attend to the bottom line. This pressure sharpened over the past decade, during which newspaper profits suffered from recession, high newsprint prices, and competition for advertising from cable and other rivals. John Knight, a liberal Republican with an old-fashioned respect for investigative journalism, died in 1981; the Ridder half of the combine was always more business oriented, and Tony Ridder, now the CEO, is noted for his marketing focus. Under Ridder, and his predecessor as president, James Batten, KR has pursued a number of strategies: it has tried to diversify into new media (unsuccessfully), it has engaged in union busting in Detroit, and it has tried to cut costs in all its papers by reducing personnel. This led to the departure of the Inky's top executive, Eugene Roberts, in 1990, and then to the resignation of executive editor James Naughton in 1995. In leaving the *Philadelphia Daily News* in 1995, editorial page editor Richard Aregood remarked that KR "was becoming a company on the standard model of corporations rather than on the Knight model."[2] David Von Drehle, who once worked for the *Miami Herald*, stated that the recent deterioration of standards at KR led him to conclude "that it's time to pronounce the experiment of publicly traded newspapers a failure."[3]

The other line of attack by Knight-Ridder has been a more aggressive (or sycophantic) catering to readers and advertisers. James Batten, president of KR from 1988 until his death in 1995, pioneered this new phase of market-driven journalism, and was featured in the recent books *When MBAs Rule Newsrooms* (Doug Underwood) and *Market-Driven Jour-*

nalism (John McManus). From 1988, Batten campaigned within KR for what he called "customer obsession," the word customer encompassing both readers and advertisers. The marketing underpinning of this "obsession" was clear: it was closely tied in with an intensified focus on profit margin targets, and the *Wall Street Journal* noted back in 1990 that KR seemed to be "borrowing heavily on the innovations of Gannett Co.'s USA Today...[with] graphics and bright colors [that] highlight stories on baby-boomer 'hot buttons,' such as divorce, personal finance, housing trends and the workplace."[4] According to *Miami Herald* Executive Editor Doug Clifton, the paper should be answering the main question asked by readers: "What does this mean to ME?"[5] Accordingly, his paper proceeded to downgrade nonlocal news and as a matter of policy began to confine news coverage to nine areas that focus groups indicated were of primary interest to readers (the list excluded national politics and world affairs!). David Remick wrote in the *New Yorker* that the *Miami Herald* was now "thin and anemic, a booster sheet."[6]

Boosterism and Phony Empowerment

The Inky was slower than the *Miami Herald* to succumb to the "obsession" that KR pressed on its subsidiaries, but it took heavy cost-cutting hits and gradually adopted important features of the new order. Its boosterism was evident in its editorial support of a locally produced helicopter boondoggle ("Save the Osprey: Here's a strange-looking plane we really need," July 9, 1990), and more dramatically in November 1998 as Philadelphia's victory in the competition to host the year 2000 Republican convention caused the paper to give rapturous front-page coverage to this great achievement for the better part of a week.

The increased pandering tendency of the Inky was dramatically illustrated at the time of death of Philadelphia-based Cardinal John Krol on March 3, 1996. For an entire week the Inky ran huge front page spreads with pictures of the Cardinal, his bier, and his funeral, accompanied by adulatory language—"a towering presence," "Philadelphia's Servant for 27 Years," etc.—the inside pages full of detail and drivel. Krol, an admirer of Richard Nixon, ally of the regressive Pope John II, and a mediocrity in every respect, could be given a wholly uncritical hero's celebration only by a newspaper that was pandering to an important power center and bloc of readers.[7]

The 1990 *Wall Street Journal* account of the new "reader friendly" KR noted that KR papers' editorial pages now featured "'empowerment boxes' giving names and phone numbers, so readers can take action." The Inky was one of those papers. Many KR papers also installed Citizens Voice programs that encourage readers to get together to exchange opinions and to have them expressed in a special part of the paper. The Inky has adopted this with energy and has devoted many pages to brief expressions of "citizens voices." This new "civic journalism," sometimes called "commercial populism," is a cop-out and fraud. It is a cop-out in that the paper abandons its own responsibility to address issues and treat them in depth; it is fraudulent in its pretended interest in ordinary people's views and in the notion that allowing controlled expressions of opinion by these citizens in any sense "empowers" them (when in fact the brevity and range of voices assures that they will have no coherence or consequences).

The Inky also has a reader-friendly ombudsman, who displayed his and the Inky's true colors in an incident involving the publication of a front-page article on Rush Limbaugh, "The king of talk, leading the charge," with an accompanying picture that showed Limbaugh grimacing.[8] The article was a superficial puff piece that quoted Rush at length. Only on the continuation page did the author mention that Limbaugh's "no less strident" critics assert that he plays fast and loose with facts and has a mean streak. No quotes or citations were given and no mention was made of the well-publicized Fairness and Accuracy in Reporting (FAIR) book *The Way Things Aren't: Rush Limbaugh's Reign of Error*. Enter the ombudsman, to apologize not for the omissions and puffery but for the photo that showed Limbaugh grimacing! And while the Inky also gave Limbaugh an op ed column, a submission by Jeff Cohen (co-author of the FAIR volume) detailing Limbaugh's errors was rejected.

This pandering to the right has characterized the Inky's handling of the letters and op ed page for many years. These features are not designed to illuminate issues or encourage in-depth debate, which might upset important constituencies. The Inky sees its market as mainly the affluent suburbanites of Philadelphia; the affiliated *Daily News* is for the lunch pail citizenry of the city. A recent Inky solicitation of advertisers asserted that the paper is read by 83 percent of Philadelphians with incomes of $100,000 or more. The Inky management has long perceived that this market segment wants a generous treatment of conservative and right-wing pundits and the Inky has provided such treatment for decades.

A problem for the management has always been that there are many liberals and leftists who read the paper and didn't like Nixon, the Vietnam War, Reaganomics, the Central American wars, and don't like racism, the attack on the welfare state, and much else that leaders, advertisers, and suburban conservatives support. The Inky has never been friendly to this large set of readers; fending them off has been a major and ongoing task.

During the 1980s, opponents of the Central American wars steadily protested the Inky's op ed page overgenerosity to the war party. In response, the editor Edwin Guthman wrote two columns that acknowledged that the antiwar letters were outnumbering those supporting Reagan, but then literally appealed to right-wing readers to write in to correct the imbalance and presumably justify the pro-war columns.[9] We may be sure that no Inky editor has ever appealed to liberals and leftists to write in to support a liberal-left position or program. In an editorial commenting on the reception to a populist Barlett-Steele series in 1996, the Inky editor noted that letters supporting Barlett and Steele greatly outnumbered those in opposition. This once again suggests that the conservative bias of the op ed page and close rationing of liberal-left commentary is not justified by the voices that reach the paper, but results from the desire to provide a page that satisfies *important* readers and advertisers.

In an August 1990 letter to Central American protestors explaining the paper's letters policy, the letters editor wrote that the letters column is "primarily for plain old ordinary readers first, not for groups and organizations seeking a platform to expound their beliefs." Citizens Voices for the Inky are not people in Central American protest groups, but "ordinary" citizens. This is a formula for using the letters columns as a lightning rod, to give the impression of being democratic while keeping it pretty free of letters that might enlighten. This is the working basis of Inky letters policy today.

Pandering to the Pro-Israel Lobby

The Inky makes exceptions to the policy of avoiding letters by organized groups when the groups are powerful and effectively threatening. A conspicuous case involved the pro-Israel lobby and the Specter-Yeakel senatorial election campaign of 1992. The paper is under steady pressure from this lobby, and one form of cave-in has been very generous allotment of letter and op ed column space to its members. Notable has been its treatment of Morton Klein, the very aggressive, Philadelphia-based president of the Zionist Organization of America, who had seven letters and four op ed columns published in 1991 and 1992 (and many thereafter). Klein strongly favored Arlen Specter in 1992, and one Inky insider informed me that Klein faxed the Inky a message of criticism of its coverage of the election and Israel-related issues every day. The pro-Israel lobby also besieged the Inky with visits; one of its members noted in a local paper that his group visited the editors, who "listened very carefully and, to their credit, took steps to redress the imbalance in subsequent editions."[10]

One consequence of this lobbying effort was that Inky coverage of the Specter-Yeakel campaign was assigned mainly to reporter Nathan Gorenstein, whose pro-Specter bias was blatant. He, and other reporters as well, repeatedly referred to Yeakel's wealth and the fact that some of her own money went into her campaign, but he never mentioned the much greater sums poured into the Specter campaign by the pro-Israel lobby, and real issues and Specter's record were not covered. One of the sinister features of Specter's campaign was the claim that Yeakel's Bryn Mawr Presbyterian Church was anti-Semitic, because they had included some pro-Palestinian speakers on the Middle East among a large set that included Specter himself (this last point was never mentioned by Gorenstein). Gorenstein's stories treated the charge of anti-Semitism as a genuine issue, not a smear tactic, and from beginning to end the Inky never explored the use of this dirty trick by Specter and his supportive lobby.

I sent a letter to the Inky that criticized Gorenstein's coverage, but instead of publishing it executive editor Naughton answered me in a six-page single-spaced letter. The Inky also supported the lobby and Specter by publishing successive letters by Klein and two of his associates, Gary Wolf and Rabbi Michael Goldblatt, attacking the Bryn Mawr Presbyterian Church. Goldblatt's letter was featured by the Inky, although it was full of errors that any competent editor should recognize, such as "No Jewish leader has attempted to equate criticism of Israel with anti-Semitism," and it made ad hominem and false charges about Church leaders Rev. Eugene Bay and Paul Hopkins.[11] The Inky refused to publish Hopkins's low-keyed reply to Goldblatt.

My Decade on the Blacklist

I had a painful experience of my own with the pro-Israel lobby's muscle with the Inky. After having three successive op ed columns taken by the Inky in 1981 and 1982, a fourth column was published on state terrorism, which identified Israel (among others) as a terrorist state. This elicited flak, including some from important pro-Israel power brokers in Philadelphia. For the next decade (until 1991) I couldn't get an op ed column into the paper, and while I have no hard evidence of cause I am pretty confident that the Inky was responding to a power center to which it often grovels, and that I was de facto blacklisted.

During this period I published a number of books on matters of extreme topicality, but op eds on these topics by a "local author" were not salable. One proposed op ed, on the alleged Bulgarian-KGB plot to kill the Pope in 1991, an important propaganda ploy of the Cold War, was based on the book, *The Rise and Fall of the Bulgarian Connection* (written with Frank Brodhead). The Inky published only one op ed column on this subject, by rightwinger Michael Ledeen, who took the "plot" as already proven. The Inky not only rejected my offering, they also turned down an opinion piece on the subject by Diana Johnstone, the well-informed *In These Times* correspondent from Paris, which I submitted on her behalf. In its news columns, also, the Inky's reporters never once departed from the party line; its "specialist" was completely uninterested in pursuing counter evidence that I pointed out to him. When the case against the Bulgarians collapsed in an Italian court in 1986, the Inky offered no reassessment; nor did it review the issue in 1991 when former CIA official Melvin Goodman told Congress during the Gates confirmation hearings that CIA professionals knew that the case against the Bulgarians was fraudulent because they had penetrated the Bulgarian secret services. In short, in this major propaganda exercise the Inky was a gullible instrument of disinformation.

The Central American Wars

Several of my rejected columns during the blacklist years were about the Central American wars. One was based on the book *Demonstration Elections*, written with Frank Brodhead, that tried to show that the 1982 Salvadoran election met none of the conditions of a genuine free election, but was a public relations gambit designed to prove to the U.S. public that our intervention was justified, thereby allowing the war to continue. (At the same time, both here and in El Salvador it was claimed that the election was a means of terminating the fighting.) The only op ed column in the Inky during the 1984 Salvadoran election period was by James Kilpatrick, who of course found it a wonderfully democratic exercise. The Inky was editorially "against the war," but interestingly this did not cause its editorials to challenge the demonstration elections as fraudulent, nor in the case of Nicaragua did it expose the Reagan peace plans as cynical and call the contra war state-sponsored terrorism. Instead, it regularly lauded the good intentions of the terrorist sponsors, agreed that Nicaragua had a "dictatorship" and that their hot pursuit of contras into Honduras was reprehensible, etc. So, in the case of the Salvadoran elections of 1982 and 1984, with the news department as ever following the official lead, and the editorials weakly critical, the Inky on balance supported the war policy.

The same conclusion was arrived at later by the Media Committee of the Philadelphia Pledge of Resistance in two detailed studies of the Inky's coverage of Central America for 1989 and 1990, which showed that the Inky was "twice as likely to use [derogatory] labels" for "enemies" than U.S. allies; that it depended excessively on U.S. official sources and "rarely quoted or interviewed" civilians or victims; that its photo selection policy supported State Department policy (no photos of civilian victims in El Salvador or Panama); and that it rarely covered Salvadoran military killings and almost never mentioned the army's responsibility for the vast majority of civilian deaths. As U.S. officials ignored Guatemala, so did the Inky, and it gave "very limited coverage to the unprecedented upsurge in U.S. national and local demonstrations/civil disobedience against U.S. policy and intervention." The paper's bias as regards each country in the region was substantial and supportive of U.S. intervention.

Columnists: From Center to Far Right

Back in the 1970s when the Inky had as columnists George Will and William Rusher of the *National Review* and far-rightists John Lofton and Smith Hempstone (feebly balanced by Mike Royko and David Broder), I visited the editorial offices to try to sell them on Howard Zinn, who then had a syndicated column. I failed in this, and the Inky has never had a regular columnist as far "left" as Mary McGrory. They have had lightweight, issue-evading centrists like Broder, who is easily overpowered by aggressive rightwingers like Will and Charles Krauthammer, who all through the 1980s pressed the Reaganite propaganda lines on Central America, the Soviet menace, and the Welfare Mother Threat, with only weak opposition. The Inky defends the columnist imbalance on the ground that their own editorials are liberal, as is their cartoonist Tony Auth, so the "left" is well covered. But this argument does not hold water: even when they tend toward opposition to official policy Inky editorials are badly compromised, and on many policies they are distinctly illiberal. The Inky editorially supported the Panama, Persian Gulf, and Yugoslav wars; Clinton's bombing and starving of Iraq; NAFTA; the anti-PC crusade; privatization;

the urgent need to balance the budget; the desperate state of Social Security and need for its "reform"; and Boris Yeltsin as savior of the highly desirably Russian "reforms." With liberalism like this who needs conservatives?

Each new right-winger who comes on board in this country goes straight into the Inky op ed columns—Greg Easterbrook and Michael Silverstein on the threat of the environmentalists, Mickey Kaus on the end of equality, Richard Rector of the Heritage Foundation on the welfare threat, Christina Sommers and Camille Paglia on the menace of feminism. Sommers and Paglia are no longer needed as the op ed page has latched on to Cathy Young, who has had over 50 columns since 1993, a large fraction of which have aggressively attacked feminists. It is true that the Inky often carries Ellen Goodman and Sally Steenland, but these women are general interest columnists who rarely address and defend feminist concerns. They in no way offset the steady antifeminist aggression of Young, supplemented by columnist and former editor David Boldt, local rightwing contributing editor Mark Randall, and local fanatic Ronald James ("Where are the feminists when a sister needs help? Free Leona!," July 8, 1992).

The Inky has also been very kind to Dinesh D'Souza. His book *Illiberal Education* was given a featured double review (one favorable, one critical). His followup new racist tome *The End of Racism* led to his being given generous op ed space (and identified as a conservative "scholar"), a featured book review, plus an accolade by David Boldt. When D'Souza spoke at St. Joseph College following publication of *Illiberal Education*, his speech got a generous Inky write-up complete with a flattering picture of the speaker. At almost the same moment Noam Chomsky was in Philadelphia, giving a fund-raising speech at a downtown church. Not only was Chomsky's speech never mentioned in the Inky, the paper refused to report that it was to take place, despite repeated requests. Chomsky has never had an op ed column in the Inky; he supplied one, by invitation, several years ago, but it was never published, and no explanation was ever given for the failure to do so.

The most frequently published economist on the op ed page—22 columns between 1994 and 1996—is Walter Williams, the black reactionary who was first syndicated by the Heritage Foundation and is now the holder of an Olin Foundation chair. He specializes in attacking entitlements (of poor people), welfare, and affirmative action. The local progressive economist, Richard DuBoff, gets published much less frequently—two columns between 1994 and 1996—and his submissions put the op ed editor under stress. For example, DuBoff submitted an op ed on July 16, 1996, that defended Social Security. The op ed editor, when pushed, told DuBoff that he couldn't find a "peg" for the piece, although Social Security is a hot issue and he was publishing "unpegged" feel-good tripe and Walter Williams columns without a problem. The piece was never published. DuBoff submitted another one in January 1997 on the immensely topical issue of investing Social Security money in the stock market. The editor was trapped, so he solicited an "answer" from Michael Tanner of the rightwing Cato Institute to set alongside DuBoff's piece (which he also cut and softened) to provide "balance." In short, the occasional and carefully rationed "left" entries get "balance," the feel-gooders and rightists don't need either balance or "pegs."

The two most frequently published Inky insiders are Claude Lewis and Trudy Rubin. Lewis, who is black, is perfect for the Inky as he gives ethnic balance while staying nicely within bounds that are acceptable to the white establishment. He strongly supported Clarence Thomas (although to his credit he recently expressed regret and admitted having made a mistake), supported Arlen Specter for the Senate in 1992, and found that "So far Bush is a pleasant surprise" (September 13, 1989). He argued along Reagan lines that the homeless made a free choice and asked for it ("Homeless, by deciding not to work," December 27, 1989), and in a marvel on the crack-cocaine CIA connection, noted that "Even if the CIA flooded inner cities with crack, blacks didn't say 'no`'" (September 25, 1996). Lewis shows his black solidarity by bravely denouncing Texaco officials for racist talk and talk show hosts for racist innuendo.[12]

Trudy Rubin, the Inky's editorial page foreign policy specialist, was once a pretty good reporter, but her long stint on the Inky editorial board has taken a heavy toll and it has been years since she has said anything that departs one iota from the establishment foreign policy consensus. She also makes grossly inaccurate statements, like "[the Europeans] opposed U.S. moves to quarantine Saddam Hussein before 1990" (August 7, 1996—the U.S. was appeasing Saddam up to August 2, 1990; this factual error was uncorrectible in the letters column). Her apologetics for Yeltsin, the attack on the Russian Parliament and the Constitution in 1993, the 1996 election, the Chechnya War, and the devastating effects of Russian reform have been grounded in a simple avoidance of inconvenient facts. They have made the editorial and op ed page a travesty in this important area. Bombing Iraq, Serbia, Afghanistan and Sudan has met with her enthusiastic approval, just as she has offered no criticism of the supportive U.S. policy toward Turkey and Indonesia.

The Sobran Case

In September 1995, Inky editor Jane Eisner announced changes in the syndicated columnists that replaced a few tired centrists with others and substituted Joseph Sobran for George Will. Sobran is on the far right among the regulars of the right-wing *National Review*. Eisner explained Sobran's selection on the ground that "we've heard often from readers who complain that this kind of unvarnished conservatism is not represented on our pages."[13]

Eisner had not done her homework. Sobran's outbursts and warm affiliation with the pro-Nazi, anti-Semitic, and racist *Instauration* in the mid-1980s had caused Midge Decter to label him "a crude and naked anti-semite" and had even led William Buckley to distance himself from Sobran, briefly. In 1994 Sobran criticized the film *Schindler's List* as "holocaust harping" that has "gotten out of control," and in another column assailed Roosevelt for having gotten us into war in 1941 because of his unreasonable antipathy to Nazi Germany.

Eisner took quite a bit of flak for bringing in Sobran, but she defended herself in print by a selective reading of his work and his personal assurances that he regretted some of his past remarks. She also stated with great pomposity that "I understand that some readers wish to open these pages and find a set of opinions that conform pleasantly to their own views. I am afraid that I can't accommodate them."[14] Eisner apparently forgot her previous statement admitting her accommodation to right-wing readers desirous of an "unvarnished conservative." A letter signed by 55 individuals pointing out her inconsistency, and asking why the left has to be satisfied with beltway centrists who never challenge the status quo, was refused publication. The letters editor did, however, publish a letter extolling Eisner's "clear reasoning."

During the next year Sobran was quietly dropped and another rightwinger, Linda Chavez, was substituted for him. But this was done without any public announcement. Eisner and company had had enough of openly discussing their biased structuring of the opinion page. So much for Citizens Voices.

The Barlett-Steele Anomaly

Donald Barlett and James Steele's populism doesn't fit too comfortably into today's Inky, and in fact, shortly after the publication of their Inky series and book on *America: Who Stole the Dream*, the authors left the paper. The paper has moved steadily to the right and become increasingly reluctant to give a voice to critical fact and opinion. Barlett and Steele had built a strong reputation for investigative research, and their productions bolstered Inky circulation and enhanced its reputation, even if they "went too far" and appeared only very episodically. The Inky could support NAFTA and year after year largely evade the income distribution issues that Barlett and Steele focused on, with only rare discomfort from the house populists.

Barlett/Steele populism also has its limits. They don't urge a vigorous full employment policy or strengthened unions as means of improving income distribution; nor do they propose cutbacks in the military budget or decentralization of the corporate system and media. They support campaign financing reform, which everybody agrees to but which is hard to enact or enforce with existing inequalities intact. They also take dubious positions on trade and immigration—they support more aggressive efforts to open foreign markets, and, although they urge higher taxes on transnational corporation incomes, they offer no useful proposals for controlling U.S. foreign investment or international money market speculation. They fail to recognize that a great deal of immigration pressure comes from U.S. and International Monetary Fund and World Bank policies abroad that produce political and economic refugees.

One Historical Success

Back in the mid-1970s, when the Committee for a Sane Nuclear Policy (SANE) was a vigorous membership organization in Philadelphia, we organized a membership protest against the very conservative editor of the Inky, Creed Black, with many scores of letters and numerous phone calls to John Knight and others in the top management. Black was replaced by Ed Guthman shortly thereafter, and the Inky did become a somewhat better paper.

But we failed to maintain that organization and level of activism, and the liberals and left of Philadelphia have largely sat on the sidelines as citizens without representation, as far as the Inky goes. And the Inky remains a "part of the problem," speaking consistently for the establishment, giving the right ample voice, and marginalizing citizens voices from the left. We need new media for a real voice, but we also have to fight harder to get fair representation and a modest public sphere operating in the existing media, which will accommodate to some extent those who press hard and with tenacity.

Notes

1 As discussed below, Barlett and Steele left the Inky later in 1997.

2 Quoted in Susan Paterno, "Whither Knight-Ridder?," *American Journalism Review* (January/February 1996), 26.

3 Ibid.

4 Patrick Reilly, "Friendly Format: Knight-Ridder Makes A Costly New Effort To Engage Its Readers," *Wall Street Journal*, 6 December 1990.

5 William Glaberson, "Media," *New York Times*, 23 October 1995.

6 Quoted in Paterno, "Whither Knight-Ridder?."

7 In an interesting followup, in 1998, Richard Cipriano, who had been the Inky's religious editor for several years in the 1990s, got into a publicly aired struggle with the paper, in which he sued the editor for libel and was fired. Cipriano had been removed from his religious beat on the paper following complaints by Krol's successor, Cardinal John Bevilaqua and his supporters that Cipriano had been unfair to the Cardinal. Cipriano went outside the Inky to publish a severe attack on Bevilaqua and his operation in the *National Catholic Reporter*, under the title "Lavish spending in archdiocese skips inner city" (May 29, 1998). Cipriano sued the Inky editor when the latter published a letter in the *Washington Post* suggesting that Cipriano was careless with the facts, and failed to check all relevant sources. But the Inky is very selective in its concern for a balanced use of sources in covering stories—or in expressions of opinion.

8 Joe Logan, "The king of talk, leading the charge," *Philadelphia Inquirer*, 2 June 1995.

9 Edwin Guthman, "Reagan doesn't poll well in letters to this editor," *Philadelphia Inquirer*, 6 April 1986.

10 Herbert Linsenberg, Letter to the editor, *City Paper* (Philadelphia), 27 November 1992.

11 Michael Goldblatt, "Criticism of Israel or Anti-Semitism?," *Philadelphia Inquirer*, 27 November 1992.

12 Lewis retired later in the year 1997, but continued to contribute columns quite frequently.

13 Jane Eisner, "We're Changing the Lineup of Our Syndicated Columnists," *Philadelphia Inquirer*, 10 September 1995.

14 Jane Eisner, "Sobran Has Drawn Fire—But His Views Are Important," *Philadelphia Inquirer*, 1 October 1995.

Chapter 11

David Broder and the Limits of Mainstream Liberalism

Several years ago, a Philadelphia opponent of U.S. policy in Central America asked the editor of the *Philadelphia Inquirer* where on his opinion page there was a leftist to offset his regular offerings of George Will and Charles Krauthammer? The editor named David Broder. Broder himself would quite properly deny the designation of leftist, but it is significant that he would be so categorized, and it is a fact that in the spectrum of opinion of leading syndicated columnists he *is* on the left. Eric Alterman points out that "Broder is the only non-right-wing pundit who begins to challenge the circulation numbers of the likes of Will, Kilpatrick, and Buchanan," and that in the print media "the 'responsible' political dialogue on the Great Issues of the Day is thus often perceived to fall between Will on the one hand and Broder on the other."[1] We may recall, also, the neoconservative opinion that the elite media has been captured by the left. It may be of interest, therefore, to examine Broder's positions on major issues,[2] to see just how far left opinion reaches in the mainstream press today.

General Characteristics

Since 1966 Broder has been a reporter and (from 1975) syndicated columnist based at the *Washington Post*. He won the Pulitzer prize in 1972 and has received many other awards within the fraternity of journalists. Although alleged by some to be a card-carrying liberal, he is rarely attacked by right-wing media enforcers and politicians, as Anthony Lewis sometimes is and as Drew Pearson used to be. This is understandable because Broder takes conservative positions on many issues, and in those instances in which he is inclined toward liberal and dissident views his voice is faint and he leans over backwards to cause no conservative distress.

No Agenda and No Pugnacity

Broder has no discernible agenda as a columnist, with the possible exceptions of the threat of budgetary deficits and the need to fend off attacks that suggest fatal flaws in the two-party system or other basic U.S. institutions. Furthermore, in contrast with right-wingers like Krauthammer, Safire, and Will, he does not press issues. He shifts from topic to topic like a butterfly, touching lightly on a point of current interest and moving quickly on. But he avoids many of the tough issues that the conservatives repeatedly address. For example, on Nicaragua, during the 1980s Broder several times noted in passing that he opposed the contra war, but his only full column on the subject lauded Reagan for finally "turning to diplomacy" and working on "a sounder premise than the maintenance of a mercenary army of 'contras'."[3] In fact, Reagan was trying to undercut the efforts of several Central American governments to stop the war, so that in this one and only column Broder misrepresented the facts and issues and served as an instrument of official propaganda.[4]

On numerous other important but controversial issues, Broder has been silent or evasive. He has written only passing phrases on the Israeli-Palestinian conflict. Racism, environmental issues, gender and sexual preference questions, and developments in and policies toward problematic states such as Pinochet's Chile and Guatemala he rarely if ever discusses. His two articles on feminism over the past dozen years dealt with infighting among feminists: one was about the possibility of feminists working within the Republican Party, the other about who deserves feminist political support.[5] His several columns on abortion evaded taking a position (and the issues) by writing in a "horse race" mode—on the balance of factional power in the political arena and on who is winning and losing in the court battles.[6] A column about Clinton's early compromise on the issue of gays in the military did stress the historic significance of Clinton's rally with gay activists in May 1992 and the "important step [of the compromise itself] toward eliminating one of society's last prejudices," but Broder framed it all in terms of Clinton's weakness and inability to carry through on commitments.[7] In another article that touched on gay and lesbian issues, Broder described his attendance at Tony Kushner's "Angels in America-Perestroika," but again, although the column was sympathetic in tone, it failed to address real issues.[8] Broder has been entirely silent on Guatemala, Chile, El Mozote, Oscar Romero, the U.S. with drawal from UNESCO, Otto Reich and the Office of Public Diplomacy, the Boland amendment, the Cuban Democracy Act, and the intensified boycott of Cuba.

Kindness Toward Conservatives

Broder not only doesn't fight on the tough issues, he is exceedingly kind to conservatives. Thus, Lee Atwater, the organizer of the Willie Horton campaign of 1988 was "tough and effective"; campaign manager James Baker was merely "manipulating paranoia" in using Willie Horton; and George Bush, ultimately responsible for the Horton ploy, used that racist strategy despite a "life-long history of tolerance and decency in racial matters."[9] Broder was apparently unaware of Bush's opposition to the crucial Civil Rights Act of 1964 (on the ground that it "violates the constitutional rights of all people").[10] Broder wrote this accolade while commenting on Bush's new "quota bill" campaign against civil rights. Bush was also described as a "man of moderate temperment and pragmatic instinct" and his foreign policy was one of "practical idealism."[11] Dick Cheney had "an emotional balance and a mental discipline remarkable" in government.[12] Reagan himself was repeatedly lauded for his "presidential" qualities and "national leadership of a high order" in handling Grenada and in pushing through his economic program; any shortcomings as president were "overshadowed by the grace with which he functions as chief of state in moments of national tragedy and triumph."[13]

Broder's generosity to the Reaganites went far beyond any he extended to Democrats, except New Democrats. Those who attacked the Bork appointment Broder spoke of as "quick-lip liberals" who "pop off in opposition."[14] Those who signed a petition opposing the invasion of Panama he dismissed as "left-wing politicians and activists" (they included former Senator J. W. Fulbright).[15] Jerry Brown, campaigning in 1992, Broder paired with Buchanan, and dismissed harshly as a "loud-voiced protester" offering "leftwing populism" and "phony salvation."[16]

Lazy Insider

One of Broder's favorite themes is the danger of reporters getting too close to their sources, and he congratulates the press for "its determination to keep its distance from government, not only to avoid censorship, but to avoid co-optation."[17] He clearly puts himself in the class of outsiders who are "inquisitive, impudent, incorrigibly independent," who "hold their [government officials] feet to the fire and devil them with questions and make them, if they can, explain and justify what they do."[18]

But surely Broder is describing somebody like the late I.F. Stone, or Robert Parry, formerly with A.P and *Newsweek*, not himself. Broder's columns never display a serious investigative effort. His citations to scholarly articles and books are infrequent; he rarely if ever refers to government hearings and out-of-the-way government documents. In his numerous articles on economics, he never cites Ralph Nader, Jeff Faux or the Economic Policy Institute, Robert McIntyre or Citizens for Tax Justice, or representatives of the Center for Budget Priorities or the Center for Defense Information. Rather, he quotes spokespersons of the right-wing Cato Institute, the New Democrat's Progressive Policy Institute, the Georgetown Center for International and Strategic Studies, the Hoover Institution, and other conservative think tanks. The farthest left Broder goes in tapping policy institute sources is the Brookings Institution, now run by former Republican officials and safely back in the conservative fold.

Broder's reliance on government officials is heavy. He reports on interviews with Bush, Cheney, Moynihan, William Gray, Lee Hamilton, Les Aspin, Colin Powell, and William Bennett, and he cites many other officials. He treats them with a light touch, rarely comparing their claims with evidence from independent sources. He never questions their motives, and with rare exception takes what they say at face value. On Reagan's bombing of Libya in 1986, Broder assured his readers that "Reagan has been insistent that every possible step be taken to spare the innocent,"[19] an unverifiable official claim of no value except as official propaganda. As noted, Broder praised Reagan for having taken the diplomatic track in Nicaragua in 1987, lazily accepting official claims at face value and failing to consider other possible reasons for the new line, as would a pundit who holds officials' "feet to the fire and devils them with questions."

In his speech before the National Press Club in which he spoke on the threat of co-optation, Broder flattered the press and public, saying that the U.S. system of journalism "somehow works." The voters "sniff out the phony from the real, the poseur from the politician who merits trust."[20] This was said in December 1988, after the Iran-Contra affair disclosures and toward the end of actor-president Reagan's second term in office.

Elitism and Limited Vision of Democracy

Broder's touching faith in the voters ability to find their way to essential truth is hyperbole in the service of the status quo. When the voters don't agree with an elite agenda, his respect for their grasp of the truth vanishes. This was dramatically evident in the struggle over NAFTA. Despite the overwhelming press bias in favor of NAFTA, the general public consistently opposed it. In July 1991, a CBS/New York Times poll found 55 per cent opposed and 27 percent in favor of NAFTA; in March 1993, a Gallup/CNN poll found 63 percent opposed and 31 percent in favor; and in July 1993, Gallup/CNN found 65 percent opposed and 28 percent in favor. Elected Democrats didn't like it either. But the Business Roundtable and corporate elite were enthusiastic—so Broder sneered at those Democrats who opposed NAFTA, who were once again siding with "the losers" instead of "the winners." He made it clear that the winners were the affluent, upwardly mobile suburbanites who the Democrats had foolishly neglected, whereas the losers were "the older, poorer and black Democrats."[21]

Broder ignored the polls, which suggested that the "losers" were a majority of the population and constituted the great majority of those who had voted for Clinton. He did not mention the back-room construction of NAFTA, its capacity to override domestic law, and the fact that Clinton had to engage in egregious bribery to win enough pro-NAFTA votes. Apparently, democracy for Broder means that elected representatives should pay no heed to their voting constituencies when the "winners" have spoken.

Similarly, in discussing the health care debates of 1993–94, polls have indicated that the public strongly prefers a single payer system and universal coverage. Broder's articles on the subject never mentioned the polls or discussed the Canadian system, and only once addressed the single payer plan—one of three Broder interviewees favored single payer, but Broder did not ask this individual to state the reasons for his preference.[22] Because the elite had declared single payer impracticable, Broder didn't allow voter and democratic preference to influence *his* assessment of health care politics.

Political and Civil Rights Issues

Politics Lite

Broder attacked Jerry Brown in 1992 on the ground that "politics is more than protest. For people's anger to be salved, policies must be put in place that address their needs and right the wrongs of which they properly complain. The problem with populism . . . is that it is long on indignation but notably short on solutions."[23] But what solutions did Broder or his favored New Democrats have for the big problems? In a 1992 apologia for New Democrat Paul Tsongas, Broder stressed Tsongas's alleged integrity, religious faith, and fighting qualities; he mentioned only in passing his "belief in capital-gains [tax] cuts and industrial policy" and Broder didn't discuss how Tsongas's policies would address the needs and wrongs of ordinary people.[24] Apparently only "populists" have to produce viable policies; New Democrats are acceptable on the basis of faith and personal qualities.

Broder sometimes writes about the unaffordability of political office and the rise of rich people to Senate preeminence,[25] but he never discusses who owns newspapers and TV stations, who funds elections, who can move capital in and out of the country according to the investment climate, and how these factors together might constrain policies that serve ordinary citizens and affect publicity and votes on an issue such as NAFTA. He offers only "politics lite"—politics as a horse race, personal qualities of establishment politicians, programmatic failings of populists, inexplicable public anger and frustration at policy failure in a system that is a "triumph" and with a media that is "working well" to serve the public interest.

Court Appointments

Broder was extremely kind to the Reagan-Bush court appointees of the past decade, and raised no objection to the resultant ideologically based restructuring of the courts. Broder's article that discussed Scalia's nomination was entitled "Finally the Reagan Stamp";[26] that is, Broder treated the topic "objectively," using as a peg the fact that Reagan was merely conforming to expectations, which allowed Broder to avoid addressing substantive issues. He even complimented Scalia and Rehnquist for their "commanding intellect and considerable personal charm," and offered no critique of these strongly ideological jurists; presumably intellect and "charm" are enough. Souter was "a superb choice—both substantively and politically" for Broder—despite "grumbles from the political extremes."[27] Broder failed to provide one fact or argument in support of the alleged "substantive" merits of Souter; most of this article was about the political adeptness of the appointment.

On Clarence Thomas, Broder was once again "objective," devoting most of his attention to the politics of the selection, very little to qualifications, and none to the ideological stacking of the court.[28] And Broder took no position on the merits of the appointment. He did mention Thomas's somewhat esoteric notion of "natural rights," and civil rights leaders' objections to Thomas's having worked for the Office of Economic Opportunity under Reagan (where he helped gut poor people's claims). But Broder never mentioned Thomas's close association with two black lobbyists for the South African apartheid government (Jay Parker and William Keyes), or the terrible irony and racist insult that this anti-affirmative action ideologue should be named to replace Thurgood Marshall (who was himself outraged). The Anita Hill sequel was never taken up by Broder.

Guinier and Civil Rights

Broder's virtual enthusiasm for Scalia and Souter, and acceptance of Thomas and the final Republican contruction of an extremist court, contrasted sharply with his critique of Lani Guinier and approval of Clinton's decision to drop her nomination.[29] No mention was made of Guinier's "intellect and personal charm"; in this case an analysis of the alleged theoretical position of the appointee on voting rights in scholarly law reviews (which Broder gave no internal evidence of having read) was the basis for a conclusion on fitness for office. The right-wing court nominations that Broder approved were lifetime appointments, unlike Guinier's, yet Broder felt no obligation to examine closely the thinking of those nominees and to try to see where they might take the country in the future.

His response to Guinier (and Thomas et al.) did not speak well for Broder's commitment to civil rights or civil liberties. He never mentioned the political and symbolic importance of Guinier—that she represented a potentially reinvigorated enforcement of the civil rights laws that had been gutted in the Reagan-Bush years. It is significant that that gutting had never energized Broder—he had no column on civil rights or William Bradford Reynolds, who had been in charge of *non*-enforcement during the Reagan tenure. *After* Reagan's departure, Broder wrote one good article, based on a Brookings Institution briefing on Kirschenman and Neckerman's book, *The Urban Underclass*, in which Broder summarized their grim empirical evidence of serious racist discrimination among employers; and in another article he quoted Eddie Williams of the Joint Center for Political Studies, asking whether Reagan "did not allow the genie of racism to escape the bottle."[30] But these came too late; and it was only the proposed appointment of Guinier that aroused and upset him, as it did the Republicans and New Democrats.

Iran-Contra

Broder's dozen articles on the Iran-Contra affair and its followup were an unmitigated journalistic disaster. He came to the subject late, never deviated from the lines put forward by the Reagan team and leading Democrats, and failed to follow up on the Banco Lavoro case or the Walsh report. He never cited independent investigators such as reporters Robert Parry or Brian Barger, or analyst Peter Kornbluh. His main source was Democratic congressman Lee Hamilton, who was one of the engineers of the Democratic political collapse over Iran-Contra (protecting a dubious "national interest" in unity that the Republicans never honor in connection with a Democratic president). His leading secondary sources were George Bush and "an influential Republican." He never criticized the extremely limited scope of the congressional investigation, its granting of immunity to Oliver North, and the incompetence and cowardice of the Democrats, who let North take over the proceedings. Most important, Broder saw the whole affair as mainly a policy "fiasco" based on executive mismanagment—he underplayed or ignored the very serious law violations.[31] For Broder, the main problem was the failure of Reagan to control his subordinates and inform the congressional intelligence committees what they were up to.[32] He implied that this was all that was needed. He therefore agreed with Hamilton that no legislative change was necessary, and expressed satisfaction that Reagan had taken steps to put his house in management order.[33]

Broder's downgrading of the legal and constitutional issues in the Iran-Contra affair was shown further in a column in which he equated the Democrats' attempts to legislate limits on contra aid with the Iran-Contra actions of the Reaganites.[34] The former, which were entirely within the bounds of law, he characterized as "legislative usurpation"; the Iran-contra actions, which involved hidden, direct violations of law and an overriding of constitutional provisions on the separation of powers, Broder characterized as "executive usurpation."[35]

Broder wrote several columns arguing against both the trial and then the imprisonment of Oliver North. He argued that North did violate the law, but had already suffered by being fired from the White House and retired from the Marines; and a trial and imprisonment would be "a copout for our failure to ban—or shun—a prominent ne'er do well."[36] The "critical question" is "whether we as a society are prepared to treat him as someone who has betrayed his trust," etc. That, he wrote, "is up to us," not a jury.

The notion that the law should be enforced as a matter of principle, and that the *jury* is "our" representative in treating matters of trust that are also law violations, escaped Broder; as did the fact that his own opinions fed in to how the public viewed North and his legal position (and helped exonerate him). Broder's evasions can be explained as follows:

large numbers felt North should not be tried or imprisoned (believing him to be either justified or a secondary character and fall guy), and Broder didn't want to offend this substantial constituency. So he worked both sides of the issue—he castigated North, but also constructed a pathetic argument that rationalized the non-application of the law in North's particular case.

Political Forecasts
David Broder doesn't often offer prognostications of the future, but when he does the results are not impressive. Although his forte is politics, in 1987 he predicted that poor George Bush was not likely to be a candidate given his vulnerable record and political innocence. If Bush did venture into today's "shark tank" political environment, we were likely to witness "the slaughter of the innocent."[37] It turned out, of course, that the sharks were on Bush's payroll, organizing tactics like the Willie Horton ploy, or were pundits who feed only on Democrats. Broder's forecast that the candidate would be somebody with the "spontaneity for common truth," an outsider not loaded down "with political-government connections,"[38] was a bit off the mark.

On international affairs, his Panglossian tendency was dramatically evident in his view that in the New World Order ethnic conflict would surely be on the downgrade; the column in which he spoke of "the waning force of the clashing nationalisms" was unfortunately timed to usher in its global resurgence.[39]

Economic and Social Issues

Reaganomics, the Deficit, and Social Security
Broder's finest moments were his attacks on Reagan's economic program in the years 1981 to 1984, in which he assailed Reagan (and the supportive Democrats) for a damaging policy mix that promised dire consequences. He stressed the implausibility of supply side reasoning, the deficits that would ensue, and the favoritism to the rich in the tax cuts that were supposed to (but wouldn't) serve the general interest.[40] Reaganomics was grounded in "greater inequality and greater poverty for millions of our fellow citizens."[41]

Over succeeding years, however, Broder's focus was increasingly on the deficit and its threat alone. And in urging policy changes in the years 1987 to 1994 he did not call for rectifying the regressive income distribution changes of the early Reagan (and late Carter) years. Instead he stressed the menace of "runaway entitlement spending" and the threat to the "integrity of the social security trust fund."[42] In other columns, however, Broder cited Patrick Moynihan's critique of deficit accounting, which stressed that the accounts for the "runaway entitlements" were in surplus and masked the real deficit.[43] This contradiction was based on muddled thinking, but the focus on entitlements—non-corporate—is in accord with elite priorities.

More recently, with the establishment claiming that Social Security is in crisis, threatened with bankruptcy in several decades, Broder says the same, but as usual offers not a phrase of coherent analysis, and fails to tap even one of the large number of economists who say that this crisis is mythical (e.g., Robert Eisner, Dean Baker, Richard DuBoff, Mark Weisbrot).[44]

For years Broder has been keen to scale down the size of government and privatize, both also in accord with corporate, Republican, and New Democrat ideology. Broder discusses these issues with great superficiality, using as his sources a Cato Institute study that urges massive cuts in non-military outlays, the example of privatization by Mayor Daley of Chicago, and recommendations of David Osborne and the New Democrats Progressive Policy Institute.[45]

Military Budget

Broder was somewhat ambivalent about Reagan's military buildup and occasionally suggested that its rate was perhaps excessive; but in the end he accepted the level of military outlays and never regarded military expenditures—like entitlements—as a source of potentially large budget savings. He never spoke of a "runaway" military budget. In 1987 he wrote an admiring column on a Hollings budget proposal that incorporated a further 2 percent annual real growth in military spending.[46] He has had no column over the last 15 years devoted to the military budget and its possible excesses (although he had one full column critical of Star Wars).[47]

Broder even lauded Reagan in retrospect for his military buildup, that made us ready for the Gulf War, and he expressed worry lest we shortchange our military establishment. The Gulf crisis proved to Broder that we can't "safely solve every budget problem by 'whacking the Pentagon'."[48] Broder never ever hinted at the possibility that the Gulf (or any other) war could be even partially *explained* by the power of the security establishment and its need to justify its command over resources.

The Republicans, said Broder, in a final accolade, "did not let America's armed might wither away."[49] He did not mention that they let other things wither away instead, such as human and social capital. There was no hint by this chronic worrier about entitlement excesses that the Republicans might have spent too much on America's armed might.

NAFTA and Free Trade
As noted earlier, Broder strongly favored NAFTA, on the grounds that it represented the "winners" and would enlarge U.S. markets. Furthermore, voting down the treaty would have stopped the "liberalizing trend" of Salinas and the PRI; Broder never mentioned the impact of these changes on ordinary Mexicans—he just assumed that their interests were being served by something called "reform." He did speak with Harley Shaiken, an "anti-NAFTA guru," but Broder only reported Shaiken's admission that the defeat of the treaty would shock Mexico—he did not report a word on Shaiken's analysis of the substantive issues.[50] Instead, he relied heavily on journalist William Orme's book *Continental Shift*, published by The Washington Post Company, which said what Broder wanted to hear about the wonders of NAFTA.[51]

Broder argued in a number of columns for the unqualified benefits of free trade, and repeatedly claimed that the Great Depression of the 1930s resulted from the imposition of the Smoot-Hawley tariff (a position that would not be supported by most economic historians; the index to economic historian Peter Temin's well regarded book on the causes of the Great Depression has no listing for "tariff" or the "Smoot-Hawley Act").[52] He congratulated Reagan for his support of free trade, apparently unaware of the great Reagan era expansion of Voluntary Export Agreements and what has been described as a policy of "aggressive unilateralism" (the title of a book by Jagdish Bhagwati and Hugh Patrick).[53] The possible damaging effects of NAFTA on the environment and income distribution he ignored or treated as transitory; and as with his discussion of the health care issue, Broder never mentioned the Canadian experience with a 1988 free trade agreement. The essence of Broder's approach was a simple-minded and demagogic support of a policy favored by the national business elite, and a failure to discuss alternative views and analyses.

Crime
On crime and crime legislation Broder deserves commendation for several pieces in which he argued that imprisonment as a main solution to the crime problem is both enormously expensive and ineffective as well. He didn't delve very deeply into what would be effective, but he mentioned policies addressed toward jobs, education, gun control, and identification and treatment of drug and alcohol abuse.[54]

Welfare and Family Values

On welfare and family values, however, Broder joined the Republican-New Democratic throng in their focus on family stability and family values while downgrading economic conditions and racism. Broder cited as main sources William Bennett; the "estimable" David Gergen; Clinton's in-house Moynihan clone, William Galston; and of course Deborah Dafoe Whitehead's *Atlantic Monthly* article, "Dan Quayle Was Right." Broder quoted Gergen's assertion at an Aspen Seminar that the participants agreed that "the best anti-poverty program for children is a stable, intact family,"[55] a remarkable statement that makes family instability the *cause* of poverty but doesn't even suggest that family instability might be a *result* of poverty. Broder said that "liberals now acknowledge the centrality of values like family stability, personal responsibility and work." This is a misleading partial truth; many liberals contend that family values, while important, are fundamentally derivative and are not central in a causal sense. Broder featured Whitehead's claim that Dan Quayle was right that two-parent families are best for children, implying that family instability is primarily a matter of personal morality, not of economic and social conditions. That Whitehead's views are contestable, and that "Dan Quayle's attack on Murphy Brown was an attempt to play the Willie Horton card in whiteface,"[56] was beyond Broder's vision, as he followed the elite in making welfare a moral issue, with conservative (and money-saving) policy conclusions that follow.

Education

Broder wrote two columns on the Reagan educational aid cutbacks of the early 1980s. Although the columns were superficial, they did offer a serious critique on the grounds of damage to the less affluent and to the educational system (and national interest) in general.[57] In an article on school choice, however, Broder framed the story around the failure of organized conservatism to support a school voucher plan referendum in California.[58] He made it a story of betrayal, and in the process failed to discuss the merits and demerits of school choice and voucher plans.

Environment

Although the environment is an exceedingly important issue, over a 15 year period Broder provided no coverage of the problem in general, Reagan policies in particular, national forest policy, or Bush and the Rio Summit. Surprisingly, in the one article during the Reagan era in which he devoted a few paragraphs to environmental policy, he sided with the Reaganites and castigated Carter as an environmental extremist. Speaking of Beaver Island, Michigan, his vacation site, he wrote: "Deregulation—and particularly the change in the Environmental Protection Agency since Anne Gorsuch took over—has helped the island. For a time, under what Interior Secretary James Watt would rightly call the environmental extremism of the Carter administration, the Beaver Island dump was threatened with closure. There were rumbles we would have to take our tax money and build an incinerator. Let me tell you, an incinerator would be as out of place on Beaver Island as an All-Star on the Chicago Cubs. But, thanks to Reagan, the dump is still in business."[59] This is all Broder had to say about Gorsuch, Reagan's gutting of the EPA (which went too far even for the chemical industry), and environmental issues, in the 1980s.

In 1990, in connection with Earth Week celebrations, Broder addressed environmental issues once again.[60] One main point of his article was that everybody now agreed that the environment was important and "the 'conservation ethic' has become one of the fixed guiding stars of American politics." This vacuous statement confused the nominal and real; the *words* were now being used, but that said nothing about real beliefs, and obscured the likelihood that powerful interests would find public concern over the environment an obstacle to overcome. His second prominent theme was the threat of environmentalist alarmism and too-frequent pushing of the panic button, which might discredit environmentalism. There was no suggestion that the strength of the business interests that opposed genuine environmental protection might be a major problem. The experience of the EPA under Reagan was not mentioned.

Foreign Affairs

Imperialist Apologetics

Except for the low-intensity Nicaraguan and Salvadoran conflicts, Broder got onto the war bandwagons of the Reagan-Bush era with enthusiasm. The Grenada invasion he found entirely justifiable based on our natural imperial rights: "We are old-fashioned enough to think that, even in a nuclear age, there are such things as spheres of influence and geographical areas of vital national interest. The Caribbean is such an area for us. The use of American power against a regime of thugs backed by forces that want to weaken American influence in the area does not strike us as unconscionable."[61] In connection with the Panama invasion of 1989, for which Broder was equally keen, he did note that in an open letter to the president "69 left-wing politicians and activists" called attention to his violations of the UN Charter and OAS agreement. Broder's reply was: "What nonsense. This static on the left should not obscure the fact that Panama represents the best evidence yet that 15 years after the Vietnam War ended, Americans really have come together in recognition of the circumstances in which military intervention makes sense."[62] The evasion of the question of international law is laughable, and the "analysis" is sheer demagoguery. The public always rallies around the flag after an enemy has been demonized and "our boys" are in action. Making this into a careful calculus by the public that justifies intervention is worthy of Charles Krauthammer.

In commenting on the Iran-Contra affair, Broder wrote that the Reagan administration's "defiance of law by its own staff members [caused it to be] terribly weakened when confronting a dictator who chooses to ignore . . . laws that inconvenience him."[63] The hypocrisy of this position, in light of Broder's comprehensive apologia for Bush's ignoring laws that inconvenienced him in invading Panama, is striking.

On Panama, Broder quoted Bush on our need "to send a clear signal when democracy is imperiled," as otherwise "the enemies of constitutional government will become more dangerous."[64] Broder did mention in passing that the Reagan administration had earlier supported the "tin-pot dictator" and drug trader Manuel Noriega, but he never mentioned George Shultz's presence and sanctioning of the fraudulent Panamanian election of 1984, which left Noriega in charge. He did not discuss Oliver North's negotiations with Noriega that sought help in destabilizing Nicaragua, and he did not explain why the tin-pot dictator suddenly became objectionable in 1986. And in his usual superficial way, Broder failed to enumerate the vast array of tin-pot dictators supported by U.S. power, nor did he mention George Bush's 1981 toast to the tin-pot dictator Ferdinand Marcos: "We love you, sir . . . we love your adherence to democratic rights and processes."[65]

During and after the Gulf War, Broder exceeded himself in patriotic ardor, several times even castigating the Democrats for "dithering" in failing to give Bush immediate powers to fight ("the best hope of salvaging the peace"), and then hypocritically citing the congressional debates on the war as evidence of democracy at work.[66] There was no patriotic lie and obfuscation that Broder did not swallow. In an early article, Broder quoted a Republican politician's prescient observation: "My concern is that before election day, the question will be not how well Bush reacted but whether we did all we could have done to prevent the crisis from arising."[67] But Broder made no effort to examine the background of appeasement, which virtually invited an invasion of Kuwait; he simply parrotted the official propaganda line that it was all Saddam's fault ("the miscalculations were all on Saddam's side").[68] He also accepted without question that we were helping the people of Kuwait "keep their freedom"![69] And he failed to question the central propaganda lie that the Bush administration had made a serious effort at a diplomatic solution; he stated that Saddam had applied the "diplomatic stiff-arm . . . to all proposals for a peaceful solution,"[70] when in fact it was Bush and Baker who had fended off every diplomatic move (for a good review, see Chomsky's chapter in Mowlana, Gerbner, and Schiller, *Triumph of the Image*). Broder reported Baker's failed conference with Iraqi Foreign Minister Aziz in January 1991 as simply one more sad instance of Iraqi intransigence.[71] This was pundit service to the war party that once again Charles Krauthammer could not surpass.

South Africa and Savimbi

Broder ignored South Africa in the Reagan-Bush years. He never discussed the apartheid system, the South African assault on the frontline states, "constructive engagement," or Jonas Savimbi, South Africa's proxy within Angola. He had one sentence on the subject: "An American negotiated agreement promises to bring peace to Namibia, a land fought over by South Africa and Angola, with the involvement of thousands of Cuban troops."[72] In fact, Namibia had been illegally occupied by South Africa for decades, and was used by South Africa as a jumping off place to invade Angola; Cuban troops were never in Namibia and only entered the conflict in response to South African aggression against Angola. Describing Namibia as having been "fought over" by Angola and South Africa is a gross distortion of the record, and Broder's focus on Cuban aid and failure to note U.S. support of South Africa (and Savimbi) under the cloak of "constructive engagement" is seriously biased reporting.

Broder made a more general statement that would seem to laud the Reagan achievement in Angola: "But from Afghanistan to El Salvador, the United States under the leadership of these Republicans effectively supported people whose values and aspirations came closest to our own—and helped them prevail."[73] This incredible sentence is on a par with Reagan's identification of the contras with our founding fathers. Under this construction the Afghan Islamic fundamentalist terrorist leader and drug dealer Gulbuddin Hekmatyar, Salvadoran death squad leader Roberto D'Aubuisson's ARENA party, and presumably the Argentinian and Guatemalan generals as well as Savimbi "share our values." I suspect Broder was carried away with sentimental yearnings for the Reagan-Bush era in which he thrived as a columnist "on the left," and would possibly not agree with his own statement if he were to be confronted with the details—Broder is not a very careful writer.

It is obvious that in this important area (South Africa), in which the conservative pundits pushed a reactionary agenda that cost black South Africans dearly, David Broder offered not the slightest opposition.

Libya and Terrorism

When Reagan bombed Libya in 1986, purportedly in response to a Libyan terrorist attack at a German discotheque, Broder, far from distancing himself from government, once again took the official version as true and asked no questions. The strike was "a necessary and proper step," and Americans could "take justifiable pride" in the President's response to "deliberate provocation."[74] Could Reagan be lying about Libyan involvement? Could there be a hidden agenda in the stoking up of anti-Libyan fervor? Wasn't the attack an attempt to kill Khadaffi, and therefore contrary to U.S. law, which prohibits foreign assassinations? No such questions were asked by the gullible Broder. He lists as the other major "terror states" Syria and Iran—not South Africa, or Guatemala, or the United States in Nicaragua—in accord with the official line.

Haiti and El Salvador

Broder's only redeeming columns on foreign policy were one that criticized Clinton for following Bush's policy of repatriating fleeing Haitians, contrary to his campaign promises,[75] and a 1983 column that reported on the slaughter of doctors in El Salvador.[76] The trouble is that these are, or were, major issues and demanded sustained attention; a journalist with an aim to enlighten on issues of great public importance would have held Reagan's and Clinton's "feet to the fire" on these matters and made them "explain and justify what they do," in Broder's own description of the function of a journalist.

Broder on the Press

Broder is a Pollyana about the press, which "has always been tough on itself" and is notable for successful maintenance of a "distance" and "apartness" from government, despite the attraction of closeness to insiders and the existence of a revolving door between media and government, which Broder acknowledges.[77] Broder never gets beyond these superficial assertions. He does not discuss the economics of the media that make for dependency on powerful sources, nor does he examine the economic interests, power, and policy of media owners and advertisers. That Katherine Graham and Ben Bradlee were part of the dominant power structure and close friends of many government leaders he doesn't consider to be a salient consideration.

Although the 1980s witnessed a major merger movement in the media, Broder never addressed the issue. The Reagan administration's attacks on the media and its major propaganda and disinformation effort, paid for by the taxpayer and based in the Office of Public Diplomacy, were never discussed by Broder, although he did have a celebratory (but fact-free) column on our wonderful Bill of Rights.[78]

Broder did criticize the Republican administration's censorship of the media during the Grenada invasion and the Gulf war, but in neither instance did he discuss government disinformation (which he failed to recognize as such) or the media's de facto collaboration in propaganda. During the Gulf War, he didn't even object to the pool system of censorship; he objected only to the delays in release of information and the government's lack of trust in the press.[79]

On "the deterioration in the tone and quality of public discourse in this country," Broder is encouraged by the recent "sensible dialogue between press and government" which is "a start on improving public understanding and reducing cynicism."[80] He has no further recommendations on the subject.

Concluding Note

David Broder has prospered as a syndicated columnist because, although a decent person, he never threatens the *larger* special interests—the "winners" who he advises the Democrats to heed in contests like that over NAFTA. When his better instincts would lead to opposition, as in the case of the contra war against Nicaragua, the Israeli-Palestinian conflict, or gay and lesbian issues, he remains exceedingly quiet and his tiny forays have no weight. On most foreign and economic policy issues—NAFTA; the Grenada, Panama, and Iraq wars; attacks on Libya; fear of runaway entitlements; the need for a lavish military budget; welfare as a personal morality question; the tendency toward environmentalist excesses—Broder lines up with the conservatives. He relies heavily on official and conservative institutional sources, engages in minimal independent research, and rarely asks hard questions. He even helps keep debates within proper bounds by castigating those who challenge establishment premises as extremists (Jerry Brown, J.W. Fulbright), or by simply ignoring them (Ralph Nader, Jeff Faux, Robert Eisner, Harley Shaiken, Robert Parry, Peter Kornbluh, Noam Chomsky). In sum, David Broder is an ideal "leftist" for a media and political establishment that can't even abide a serious liberal challenge.

Notes

1   Eric Alterman, *Sound and Fury* (New York: Harper Perennial, 1992), 156.

2   This study is based on a reading and analysis of 136 Broder opinion columns in the *Washington Post* (WP) or *Philadelphia Inquirer* (PI) dating from 1980 through July 1994. The items from the *Post* were obtained by a Lexis-Nexis search by topic area and key words covering some 45 major topics (example: EPA, S&L, Grenada, Angola, Iran-Contra, Guinier, civil rights, and William Bradford Reynolds). They supplement items from the author's personal collection of Broder op ed columns that appeared in the *Inquirer*. The author was assisted in this project by Adam Horowitz.

3   David Broder, "Bailing Out on Nicaragua," *Washington Post*, 19 August 1987.

4   For a good account of the Reagan ploy, see Noam Chomsky, *Necessary Illusions* (Boston: South End Press, 1989), 223–61.

5   David Broder, "Can a Feminist Be a Republican?," *Washington Post*, 26 August 1987; "Feminist Dilemma," *Washington Post*, 18 July 1983.

6   David Broder, "Why the Abortion Issue Won't Go Away," *Washington Post*, 29 May 1991.

7   David Broder, "Big Talk, Weak Hand," *Washington Post*, 25 July 1993.

8   David Broder, "Stonewall America: Another group of Americans claims its place in the culture," *Philadelphia Inquirer*, 29 June 1994.

9   David Broder, "As Republican chief, Bennett will raise the national political consciousness," *Philadelphia Inquirer*, 26 November 1990; "The High Cost of Coalition Government," *Washington Post*, 9 April 1989; "Bush has mastered the psychological art of blaming other side for his tactics," *Philadelphia Inquirer*, 10 June 1991.

10 Quoted in Susan Page, "Once a Foe of Civil Rights Bill, Bush Lauds It on Anniversary," *Newsday*, 1 July 1989.

11 David Broder, "Leashing the Dogs of War," *Washington Post*, 21 December 1988.

12 David Broder, "Cheney for the defense: Vietnam legacy of public cynicism has been vanquished," *Philadelphia Inquirer*, 28 February 1991.

13 David Broder, "It's Not Enough to Say Thank You Mr. President," *Washington Post*, 4 November 1984; "The Revolution Continues," *Washington Post*, 22 December 1985.

14 David Broder, "Deficits: Still in the Land of Oz," *Washington Post*, 14 August 1987.

15   David Broder, "Panama: An Intervention That Made Sense," *Washington Post*, 14 January 1990.

16   David Broder, "Buchanan and Brown have nothing to offer, but media give them a free ride," *Philadelphia Inquirer*, 26 February 1992.

17   David Broder, "Beware the Insider Syndrome," *Washington Post*, 4 December 1988.

18   Ibid.

19   David Broder, "Another 'Yellow Ribbon'?," *Washington Post*, 20 April 1986.

20   Broder, "Beware the Insider Syndrome."

21   David Broder, "NAFTAmath: the fight has shown that Clinton does not want the Democrats to be seen as the party of losers," *Washington Post*, 19 November 1993.

22   David Broder, "On the Front Line of Health Care," *Washington Post*, 28 April 1993.

23   Broder, "Buchanan and Brown have nothing to offer."

24   David Broder, "Ignore 'Greek-from Massachusetts' dismissal; Tsongas deserves a full hearing," *Philadelphia Inquirer*, 12 February 1992.

25   David Broder, "The Senate seems to have become increasingly unrepresentative of the United States," *Philadelphia Inquirer*, 4 August 1993.

26   David Broder, "Finally the Reagan Stamp," *Washington Post*, 22 June 1986.

27   David Broder, "The Next Three Court Nominees," *Washington Post*, 27 July 1990.

28   David Broder, "Thomas: Dilemma for Democrats," *Washington Post*, 7 July 1991.

29   David Broder, "Lani Guinier's own words prove why the President made the correct decision," *Philadelphia Inquirer*, 16 June 1993.

30   David Broder, "Blunt Talk About Race," *Washington Post*, 21 April 1991; "Presidents, Race and Politics," *Washington Post*, 4 April 1990.

31   David Broder, "Listen to Lee Hamilton: A Good Congressman's Thoughts on the Iran-Contra Affair," *Washington Post*, 17 June 1987; "The Innocent George Bush," *Washington Post*, 9 August 1987; "The Longer Edwin Meese Stays: The Grimmer Things Look," *Washington Post*, 10 November 1987.

32   David Broder, "North's Trial Notice To Us All," *Washington Post*, 9 July 1987.

33   David Broder, "Listen to Lee Hamilton"; "Deficits: Still in the Land of Oz," *Washington Post*, 14 August 1987.

34   David Broder, "The High Cost of 'Coalition Government'," *Washington Post*, 9 April 1989.

35   Eric Alterman has a good discussion of Broder's apologia for Reagan and the administration's Iran-Contra performance in *Sound and Fury*, 154–55.

36   David Broder, "The North Trial is a Cop-Out," *Washington Post*, 5 April 1989.

37   David Broder, "The Innocent George Bush," *Washington Post*, 9 August 1987.

38   David Broder, "Still Searching for a Hero," *Washington Post*, 14 July 1987.

39   David Broder, "Leashing the Dogs of War," *Washington Post*, 21 December 1988.

40   David Broder, "The Budget: Both Dishonest . . . And Too Honest," *Washington Post*, 10 February 1982; "A Recipe For Disaster," *Washington Post*, 23 May 1982; "A Vote for Economic Realism," *Washington Post*, 6 October 1982.

41   David Broder, "It's Not Enough to Say, 'Thank You Mr. President'," *Washington Post*, 4 November 1984.

42   David Broder, "Curb Those Entitlements," *Philadelphia Inquirer*, 2 January 1994; "The message is getting home: We can't ignore the movement for fiscal discipline," *Philadelphia Inquirer*, 4 October 1992.

43   David Broder, "A Spiraling and Hidden Tax," *Washington Post*, 25 March 1990.

44   David Broder, "Who Will Rescue Social Security," *Washington Post*, 29 November 1998.

45   David Broder, "After the Tax Fight: Enter a New Hero," *Washington Post*, 22 July 1982; "When Mayor Daley starts pushing privatization, it's no flash in the pan," *Philadelphia Inquirer*, 10 July 1991; "To Slim Down the Federal Goliath," *Washington Post*, 13 July 1993.

46   David Broder, "Hollings Warning: His Dissents are Getting Sharper—But Will the Other Democrats Listen?," *Washington Post*, 11 May 1987.

47   David Broder, "Science Protectionism," *Washington Post*, 22 September 1985.

48   David Broder, "America's Wake-Up Call," *Washington Post*, 29 August 1990.

49   David Broder, "12 Pretty Good Years For The GOP," *Washington Post*, 17 January 1993.

50   David Broder, "Can the President Save the Deal?," *Washington Post*, 14 November 1993.

51   David Broder, "A Last-Minute Pitch for NAFTA," *Washington Post*, 3 November 1993.

52   Peter Temin, *Did Monetary Forces Cause the Great Depression?* (Harmondsworth, England: Penguin Books, 1973).

53   Jagdish Bhagwati and Hugh T. Patrick, *Aggressive Unilateralism: America's 301 Trade Policy and the World Trading System* (Ann Arbor, MI: University of Michigan Press, 1990).

54   David Broder, "When Tough Isn't Smart," *Washington Post*, 23 March 1994; "All Locked Up," *Washington Post*, 17 April 1994.

55   David Broder, "Quayle Right on the Family," *Washington Post*, 24 March 1993.

56   Judith Stacey, "The New Family Values Crusaders," *The Nation* (July 25–August 1, 1994).

57   David Broder, "Another Watt," *Washington Post*, 24 February 1985; "Philosophizing While Education Burns," *Washington Post*, 3 April 1985.

58   David Broder, "Shameful Silence on School Vouchers," *Washington Post*, 27 October 1993.

59   David Broder, "Life at the 'Center of the Real World'," *Washington Post*, 25 July 1982.

60   David Broder, "Beyond Folk Songs and Flowers," *Washington Post*, 22 April 1990.

61   David Broder, "Gunboat Gamble," *Washington Post*, 2 November 1983.

62   David Broder, "Panama: An Intervention That Made Sense," *Washington Post*, 14 January 1990.

63   David Broder, "The North-Noriega Lesson," *Washington Post*, 14 May 1989.

64   Broder, "Panama: An Intervention That Made Sense."

65   "In Toast to Marcos, Bush Lauds Manila Democracy," *Washington Post*, 1 July 1981.

66   David Broder, "The Gulf Debate—Less Disunity Than Meets the Eye," *Washington Post* 16 December 1990.

67   David Broder, "Reactive President," *Washington Post*, 18 August 1990.

68   David Broder, "End of a War," *Washington Post*, 10 April 1991.

69   David Broder, "How We'll Know We've Won," *Washington Post*, 18 January 1991.

70   Ibid.

71   David Broder, "A Really Bad Week," *Washington Post*, 11 January 1991.

72   David Broder, "Leashing the Dogs of War," *Washington Post*, 21 December 1988,

73   David Broder, "12 Pretty Good Years for the GOP," *Washington Post*, 17 January 1993.

74   David Broder, "Another 'Yellow Ribbon'?," *Washington Post*, 20 April 1986.

75   David Broder, "Haiti: Headache for Presidents," *Washington Post*, 7 March 1993.

76   David Broder, "When Doctors Disappear," *Washington Post*, 26 June 1993.

77   Broder, "Beware the Insider Syndrome."

78   David Broder, "Individual Freedom," *Philadelphia Inquirer*, 16 December 1991.

79   David Broder, "Of the media's big complaints with Pentagon, one was right, the other wrong," *Philadelphia Inquirer*, 21 March 1991.

80   David Broder, "Dialogue between government and the press is necessary to fight against cynicism," *Philadelphia Inquirer*, 6 July 1994.

Part 3

MEDIA COVERAGE OF FOREIGN AND DOMESTIC POLICY

Chapter 12

The Media's Role in U.S. Foreign Policy: The Persian Gulf War

Spokespersons for the media in the United States regularly portray them as the country's watchdogs, who "root about in our national life, exposing what they deem right for exposure," without fear or favor.[1] Such self-congratulatory statements are traditionally supported by reference to the Watergate exposures, which "helped force a President from office,"[2] and the media's news coverage of the Vietnam War—allegedly so open and critical that it helped firm up popular opposition and forced the war's negotiated settlement.

The media's generous self-appraisal is supported in a curious and indirect way by neoconservative and business attacks, which have frequently charged that the media are dominated by a liberal elite, hostile to business and government.[3] The same Watergate-Nixon evidence and Vietnam War coverage that is cited by defenders of the media as evidence of their constructive role is used by conservative critics to demonstrate media excess. Peter Braestrup's *Big Story*, for example, purported to show that the media's coverage of the 1968 Tet offensive was inaccurate, adversarial, and unpatriotic.[4] Cited often and without criticism, *Big Story* contributed to the now conventional belief not only that the media was hostile to the war, but also that "the outcome of the war was determined not in the battlefield, but on the printed page, and above all, on the television screen."[5] John Corry of the *New York Times* conceded that the media bias argued by Braestrup existed but contended that it was thoughtlessness, not deliberate subversive intent, that brought about this result.[6]

Critical Analyses of the Media

In fact, the media do *not* root about and expose abuses freely and without discrimination. Rather, the media serve mainly as a supportive arm of the state and dominant elites, focus heavily on themes serviceable to them, and expose and allow debates only within accepted frames of reference.

The dominant media are themselves members of the corporate-elite establishment. Furthermore, media scholarship has regularly stressed the tendency of the media to rely excessively on the government as a news source and to defer to its positions. A classic and often-cited study by Leon Sigal showed that nearly three-quarters of the front page stories in the *Washington Post* and *New York Times* depended on official sources.[7] Lance Bennett, Noam Chomsky, Mark Cooper, Lawrence Soley, and Jack Spence have also quantified the media's extraordinary deference to official views during the Central American wars of the 1980s.[8]

Media analysts have long noted that the economics of the media push journalists into the hands of "primary definers," who offer a daily supply of supposedly credible stories.[9] Offbeat news and sources, in contrast, require careful verification for accuracy and, thus, added expenses. State Department and White House handouts are provided daily at the same place and do not require an accuracy check; they are news by virtue of their source. A symbiotic relationship tends to develop between primary definers and their regular beat reporters, who are rewarded for cooperativeness and penalized for unfriendly reporting. These old-boy networks are reinforced by linkages between officials and senior managers and editors in the mainstream media.[10]

Structural aspects of the media also make them sensitive to the demands of the government. Contrary to neoconservative analyses, the controlling media elites are the owners, not the reporters and anchors. The owners are extremely wealthy individuals or large corporations, such as Westinghouse and General Electric Company, with a major stake in the status quo and extensive social and business connections to other business and government leaders. They also depend on the government for television licenses, contracts to provide goods and services, and support for overseas activities.[11] Furthermore, the media must sell their programs to advertisers, who are not likely to look favorably on "adversarial" messages.[12]

Given this kind of media, what is the explanation for business and neoconservative complaints of adversarial and unpatriotic media? Part of the explanation lies in the fact that business leaders and the neoconservatives frequently resent any messages that don't serve their public relations needs or advance policies they favor.[13] And the media are not simple tools of individual companies, nor are they closely controlled by the "capitalist class," although they broadly reflect dominant class interests. Frequent disagreements crop up among these interests, and the media often criticize established institutions, their abuses, and their policies, although virtually never at the level of institutional arrangements themselves. The accusations and debates mentioned earlier are intra-establishment conflicts in which the complaining parties, although not necessarily badly treated, are dissatisfied and have the resources to press for closer conformity to their views.

The business community, angry at the media's treatment of the Nixon-era bribery disclosures and the oil-price increases of the 1970s, made its dissatisfaction known, directly by vociferous complaints and a barrage of publicity, and indirectly by the funding of critical analysts and institutions like The Media Institute and Accuracy in Media to press its case. Similarly, neoconservative critiques of the media on foreign policy issues have essentially objected to deviations from the official party line. The proper role of the mass media in the neoconservative view is conduiting official claims, as is implicit in Michael Ledeen's plaint about the media: "Most journalists these days consider it beneath their dignity to simply report the words of government officials—and let it go at that."[14] Braestrup's *Big Story* had offered a similar complaint about the Vietnam War. The media were too pessimistic during and after the Tet offensive, he contended.[15] Braestrup's documentation, however, showed that the U.S. military leaders were even more pessimistic than the media, but his premise was that a free press should act as a marketing agent for official policy when reporting on any national venture. During the U.S.-led 1991 Persian Gulf War, likewise, Reed Irvine of Accuracy in Media complained that the media were reporting facts that were not helpful to the war effort; like Braestrup and Ledeen he wants the media to serve as public relations agents of the state and adjust the news accordingly.[16]

It is noteworthy that in early 1988 the Soviet press was assailed by Defense Minister Dimitri Yazov for disclosing negative facts about the Soviet war in Afghanistan, which he claimed "played into the hands of the West."[17] Ledeen, Irving, and Braestrup equivalents in the former Soviet Union would surely have supported Yazov's claim that the Soviet press was too liberal and "adversarial," as his criticisms of the Soviet press matched their own for the U.S. media. In fact, the "adversary press" in the Soviet Union followed the party line in all essentials in 1988. Similarly, the mass media in the United States accepted that the United States fought to protect South Vietnam, sought democracy in Nicaragua in the 1980s, and intervened in the war in the Persian Gulf in 1991 to fight for the principle of nonaggression. The Bush administration wanted to censor the media during the Gulf War, not because they were adversaries, but for the reason implicit in Yazov's critique of the Soviet media—to avoid *any* inconvenient or negative reports.

Criteria for Evaluating the Media's Role in Foreign Policy

There is a strong elitist tradition in the United States concerning the proper roles of the government and ordinary citizens in the conduct of foreign policy. In this tradition, the most notable exemplar of which was the journalist Walter Lippmann, the public is seen as stupid, volatile, and best kept in the dark, with policy properly left in the hands of a superior elite who can better judge the national interest.[18] Government officials regularly look upon themselves as the best judges of the national interest and regard the public and media as obstacles to be overcome or managed.[19] This view fits with the contemporary neoconservative opinion that the media are properly an arm of the government. The difference is that the liberal-elite tradition recognizes and allows debate and disputes among the elite. In the neoconservative view, even dissenting elites are a subversive and unpatriotic threat. Both traditions, however, share the view that the public has no legitimate role in determining foreign policy.

These views are blatantly undemocratic. The mainstream media themselves, in principle, espouse the view that they are responsible for informing the public, thereby enabling it to properly assess policy and potentially influence decision-making. As instruments of a democratic order, they should be condemned—and in theory would condemn themselves—if they served as tools of the government, deprived the public of essential information, and, in effect, *sold* government policy.

If the media should serve a democratic polity, then they ought to inform the public about the major issues of the day with sufficient context, depth, and honesty for the public to be able to make thoughtful judgments and influence the course of policymaking. Because all governments lie and manipulate evidence, a democratically oriented media would not take government claims at face value and allow themselves to become another propaganda arm of the government. They would try to establish the substantive reasons for actions and not accept nominal claims as valid. They would be alert to double standards and selective use of criteria and evidence to justify policy. They would carefully evaluate claims of the probable effects of proposed policies. Finally, they would follow up on policy actions to see whether the claimed objectives were met; they would not allow the government to mobilize support for a policy action, carry it out, and then drop the subject.

The Persian Gulf TV War: A Case Study in Media Bias

The invasions of Grenada and Panama during the 1980s and the Persian Gulf War in 1991 were military successes, but disastrous media failures. In part, the failures were a result of military restrictions on access, but the media did not react to these official constraints by more aggressive investigative and reporting efforts in areas that were open to them, nor did they struggle very energetically to get the restraints removed. In the cases of Grenada and Panama, once the great military triumphs over two of the tiniest countries in the world were completed and officials turned their attention elsewhere, the mainstream media dutifully did the same.

The Persian Gulf War was a larger scale effort, with international dimensions, and its preparation and the war itself were of longer duration, even though the imbalance of forces between the West and Iraq was overwhelming. This meant that there was more room for debate and public discussion before the outbreak of hostilities. The main focus in what follows will be on this early period in which the media could have fostered a democratic debate about issues of war and peace.

Phase 1. August 2, 1990, through January 15, 1991

Following the occupation of Kuwait by Iraq on August 2, 1990, the Bush administration very quickly decided to use this invasion for Bush's and the security state's political advantage, by compelling Saddam Hussein to leave Kuwait in total defeat and humiliation ("with his tail between his legs," in Defense Secretary Dick Cheney's memorable phrase). This required the administration to fend off all attempts at a negotiated settlement that would have allowed Saddam a dignified exit, and to ready the public for war.

The media's role was crucial. The Reagan-Bush administration had actively supported Iraq's aggression against Iran during the period 1980 to 1988, and subsequently the Bush administration continued to aid and appease Saddam Hussein through July 31, 1990. On July 25, 1990, a week before the invasion, U.S. ambassador to Iraq, April Glaspie, had assured Saddam that the United States had "no opinion" on his conflict with Kuwait, which was "Arab" business. And on July 31, John Kelly, the highest ranking Bush official directly concerned with Middle Eastern affairs, told a congressional committee that this country had no obligation to defend Kuwait.[20] Numerous CIA alerts that Iraq was massing troops on Kuwait's border and that an invasion was imminent did not cause the Bush administration to issue a word of warning. This was either entrapment or colossal incompetence and blundering. It was important for Bush's freedom of action that his virtual go-ahead to the invasion, and the prior appeasement policy, be buried. The media obliged.[21]

Because Bush was allegedly taking a high moral stance against "naked aggression," it was also important that the background of Reagan-Bush support of Iraq's aggression against Iran be ignored. Furthermore, less than a year before Iraq's invasion, the Bush administration had invaded Panama, in violation of the UN and OAS Charters and in the face of a UN oppositional majority, which was vetoed by the United States. South Africa had been ordered to leave Namibia by UN and World Court orders from 1968, and it regularly invaded Angola from Namibia from 1975 into the 1980s. But Reagan-Bush policy in that case was "quiet diplomacy" and "constructive engagement," with the United States supporting a "linkage" between South Africa's gradual withdrawal from Namibia and the departure of Cuban troops from Angola. Israel, also, was in long-standing violation of Security Council orders to leave the occupied territories, which led to no cutbacks in massive U.S. aid, let alone sanctions or bombing. Attention to these double standards would have called into question the purity of Bush's insistence that aggression could never be allowed to stand or to pay. The media obliged by rarely, if ever, allowing these matters to surface.[22]

Similarly, the United States had long failed to meet its legal obligations to UN financing, had withdrawn from UNESCO, and was far and away the dominant user of the veto against UN attempts to oppose violations of international law. It simply ignored a 1986 World Court decision that its attacks on Nicaragua constituted an "unlawful use of force." In the case of Iraq's invasion of Kuwait, however, because the Soviet veto and military capability were no longer an obstruction, the United States was able to mobilize the UN to attack this particular law violator. The double standard here, and the turnabout in treatment of UN authority, were dramatic, but were essentially ignored in the mainstream media, which reproduced the U.S. official view that the UN was finally resuming its proper role in maintaining the peace, etc.[23]

In addition to the decontextualization of issues just described, the Bush administration depended heavily on mass media cooperation in its various strategies for mobilizing consent, all of which involved the use of traditional propaganda techniques. One technique was the demonization of Saddam Hussein, who, like Muammar Khadaffi and Manuel Noriega in earlier years, was made into the embodiment of evil and "another Hitler." Effective propaganda here required that the mass media repeat the propaganda claims and supply the evidence of the new villain's evil acts, but avoid mention not only of any positive features of his rule, but also of the fact that the villain was for a long time nurtured by the U.S. government as a valuable ally, and treated with similar apologetics by the mainstream media (earlier, Saddam had been characterized in the media as a "pragmatist," the evils featured after August 2, 1990, had been glossed over).[24] Demonization was accompanied by new atrocity stories that were often inflated and sometimes wholly fabricated. A classic example was the alleged Iraqi removal of incubators from several hundred babies in Kuwaiti hospitals following the occupation. This story, created by a Kuwait-financed propaganda operation, was accepted and transmitted without verification by the mainstream media, and was still repeated by CNN and others long after it had been shown to be a complete fabrication.[25]

An important part of the Bush war program was to place a large U.S. contingent in Saudi Arabia and elsewhere in the Middle East, partly in order to get the media focused on military maneuvers and to bond them and the public with warriors facing a ruthless enemy. This was accomplished, first, by claiming that Iraq was planning to invade Saudi Arabia. This claim was a propaganda lie, as Iraq not only consistently asserted that it had no such intention, it also had insufficient troops and supplies for such an operation, and almost certainly recognized that such an action would have been a suicidal declaration of war against the United States. The U.S. mainstream media nevertheless accepted the official version without question and quickly urged vigorous military action against Iraq.[26]

Having gotten a large U.S. force in place, the Bush team enlarged it substantially immediately after the November elections. With our fighting personnel over there, the media cooperatively spent a large fraction of their organizational resources in exploring military deployments, possible scenarios of war, and the conditions and opinions of our troops. This not only diverted attention from real issues, it also readied the public for war.

The most important official lie and the greatest media service to the war policy was on the question of diplomacy. It was crucial to the Bush strategy that a diplomatic solution be averted; Thomas Friedman noted in the *New York Times* of August 22, 1990, that the diplomatic track needed to be blocked lest negotiations "defuse the crisis" while allowing Iraq "a few token gains." The administration therefore carefully subverted an early Arab effort to resolve the crisis.[27] Iraq itself, taken aback by the Bush administration's furious reaction, made at least five diplomatic approaches and proposals, all summarily rejected by the United States.[28] The French and Russians also tried to open diplomatic lines, to no avail.[29] The mainstream media served administration policy by giving these diplomatic efforts, and their immediate summary rejection by the United States, minimal attention; even further, in the end, when the Bush administration kept repeating that the United States had tried and exhausted the diplomatic option, the media accepted this lie as true.[30]

The significance of this Big Lie and its media support is highlighted by a national public opinion poll reported in the *Washington Post* on January 11, 1991, which indicated that two-thirds of the public favored a conference on the Arab-Israeli conflict if it would lead to an Iraqi withdrawal from Kuwait.[31] The poll was biased against a positive response, as it indicated that the Bush administration was opposed to the proposal. As it happens, about one week earlier a diplomatic proposal had been floated by the Iraq government, supported by the Iraqi democratic opposition,[32] which embodied the elements of the resolution supported by at least two-thirds of the U.S. public. The Iraqi proposal was flatly rejected by the Bush administration, and went virtually unreported by the U.S. mass media. That is to say, the media suppressed and failed to allow or encourage a debate on a political solution that was favored by the public; instead it allowed the administration to pull the country into war, based on a media-sustained lie that all the diplomatic routes had been exhausted.

The War—January 16 to February 27, 1991

During the war proper, access to military personnel was closely controlled by a pool and censorship system, which caused exceptional reliance on government handouts. The aim was to get the media to focus on the new weaponry, to convey the image of a clean war, to minimize images of human suffering, and to give the impression of warmakers in excellent control of the situation.

The result was one of the great successes in the history of war propaganda. The media were incorporated into a system of serious censorship with only mild protests,[33] they focused throughout on precisely what the censors wanted them to, and they helped produce a genuine war hysteria. The control of information by government "couldn't have been better," stated Michael Deaver, the number two image-making official in the Reagan administration.[34] Douglas Kellner, in his extensive examination of media coverage, concluded that the mainstream media

> presented incredible PR for the military, inundating the country with images of war and the new high-tech military for months, while the brutality of war was normalized and even glamourized in the uncritical media coverage. Throughout

the Persian Gulf TV war, the culture of militarism became *the* mainstream culture
after a period when war and the military were in disfavor.[35]

During the war, the media passed on innumerable rumors and official
and unofficial fabrications concerning Iraqi atrocities, the size of Iraq's
forces in Kuwait and chemical and other arms capabilities, the alleged
exclusive Iraqi responsibility for oil spills, the number of Iraqi hostages
taken from Kuwait in the final Iraqi exodus, and the legitimacy of U.S.
targeting and "turkey shooting."[36] Although it was clear from official statements during the war that the United States was deliberately destroying
the infrastructure of Iraq beyond military necessity, the media never picked
this story up or discussed its compatibility with the UN mandate or international law and morality. When U.S. officials adamantly claimed that an
infant formula factory destroyed in Baghdad actually made biological weapons, the U.S. media accepted the story as true, despite the fact that the
denials of Peter Arnett and Iraqi officials were confirmed by numerous
independent sources.[37]

When the U.S. military engaged in its final orgy of massacre on the
Highway of Death, destroying many thousands of fleeing Iraqi soldiers
and, almost surely, thousands of Kuwaiti hostages and other refugees, the
U.S. media provided an apologetic cover: they averted their eyes to a
maximum degree; they failed to discuss the use of napalm, fragmentation
bombs, and fuel air bombs; they claimed that the fleeing Iraqis were "loot-
ers" and ignored the large numbers of hostages and refugees slaughtered
along with the Iraqis (although they had given close attention to the earlier claims of Iraqi hostages taken from Kuwait); they repeated the official
explanation that it was important to destroy Iraq's military capability, but
failed to note the limited UN mandate and international law that condemned the slaughter of completely helpless and fleeing soldiers and the
practice of burying large numbers of them in unmarked graves.[38] After
discussing what he called "probably the most appalling episode" in the
war, and quoting an Air Force officer that "it was close to Armageddon,"
Kellner said: "And that's it. Armageddon for the Iraqis but no details, no
follow ups, and certainly no outrage."[39]

The Aftermath—February 28, 1991, to the Present

The euphoria that followed the pulverizing of a completely overmatched
Third World country continued for some months, but eventually faded as
neglected internal problems came to the fore *and* as the results of the war
came under closer scrutiny. Belated attention was given to the earlier

appeasement policy and the Bush administration's role in building up Saddam Hussein's military establishment, although almost nothing was said of the administration's virtual enticement of Iraq to invade Kuwait and its subsequent complete refusal to allow a diplomatic resolution of the conflict. The fact that the "allied" military effort stopped short of removing "another Hitler," but left him with just enough arms to crush dissident and oppressed Kurds, Shiites, and any democratic opposition, was noted, but its full implications were not discussed. There was some slight publicity given to the fact that Bush and the CIA had encouraged the Kurds to fight, but virtually no publicity was given to the administration's refusal to provide arms to those fighting Saddam Hussein.

The fact that the United States was again selling arms to the Middle East on a massive scale was barely noted in the media, and was certainly not contrasted with earlier pious claims about bringing a new era of peace to that area. The media touched lightly on the fact that the fight for principle did not include bringing democracy to Kuwait or Saudi Arabia, and little attention was paid to the retaliatory killings in Kuwait, which may have exceeded the inflated and indignant accounts of executions in Kuwait by Iraq.[40]

Most notable in the aftermath coverage was the continued attention to Iraq's obstructions and refusals to allow inspections, overflights, and destruction of its military resources. This was the basis for the continued limitations on Iraqi trade and oil sales that made more difficult its recovery from the "near apocalyptic conditions" reported by a UN team in June 1991.[41] In perfect accord with the U.S. foreign policy agenda, the media paid almost no attention to Iraqi civilian hunger, sickness and death, but focused unrelentingly on Iraq's alleged footdragging on weapons control.

Concluding Note

In sum, in the three phases of the Persian Gulf War, U.S. mass media coverage was to an extraordinary degree a servant of official policy. In the crucial months before the war, the mainstream media allowed themselves to be managed in the service of war mobilization, and failed to provide the factual and opinion basis for public evaluation. Then and later the mass media served ongoing government policy, not the democratic polity.

Notes

1   See Anthony Lewis, "Freedom of the Press—Anthony Lewis Distinguishes Between Britain and America," *London Review of Books*, 26 November 1987.

2   *Ibid.*

3   For expositions of the neoconservative view, see Michael Ledeen, *Grave New World* (New York: Oxford University Press, 1985); Robert Lichter and Stanley Rothman, "Media and Business Elites," *Public Opinion*, (October/November 1981); Michael Novak, "The New Elite in an Adversary Culture," *Business and the Media*, Conference Report, Yankelovich, Skelly & White (November 19, 1981), 8–11.

4   Peter Braestrup, *Big Story* (Boulder, CO: Westview, 1977).

5   Robert Elegant, as cited in an Accuracy in Media (AIM) rebuttal to the Public Broadcasting System (PBS) series "Vietnam: A Television History," AIM episode entitled "Inside Story Special Edition: Vietnam Op Ed," 1985. For a critical examination of Braestrup's book, see Edward Herman and Noam Chomsky, *Manufacturing Consent* (New York: Pantheon, 1988), chapter 5 and appendix 3.

6   John Corry, "Is TV Unpatriotic or Simply Unmindful," *New York Times*, 12 May 1985.

7   Leon V. Sigal, *Reporters and Officials: The Organization and Politics of Newsmaking* (Lexington, MA: D.C. Heath, 1973), 48.

8   For a discussion, with citations to these and other authors, see Noam Chomsky, *Necessary Illusions* (Boston: South End Press, 1989), 76–79; also, Lawrence Soley, *The News Shapers* (New York: Praeger, 1992).

9   Primary definers are major news sources who by virtue of their importance as sources are able to define what is newsworthy. The term is used and explained in Stuart Hall, Charles Critcher, Tony Jefferson, John Clarke, and Brian Roberts, *Policing the Crisis: Mugging, the State and Law and Order* (London: Macmillan, 1978), 53–76. See also Herman and Chomsky, *Manufacturing Consent*, 18–20, and sources cited there.

10   Herman and Chomsky, *Manufacturing Consent*, 8–16; Soley, *The News Shapers*, chaps. 2, 3, and 10.

11   During the Gulf War, apart from the need for licenses, the television networks were in the midst of an effort to get the Federal Communications Commission (FCC) to allow them to participate in syndication profits, from which they were barred by FCC rules. Opposing government policy during the Gulf War would have been very risky from a profit-maximizing perspective. See Danny Schechter, "Gulf War Coverage," *Z Magazine* (December 1991), 22–25.

12 On the constraining power of advertising, see Erik Barnouw, *The Sponsor* (New York: Oxford University Press, 1978); Baker, *Advertising and a Democratic Press.*

13 See Leonard Silk and David Vogel, *Ethics and Profits: The Crisis of Confidence in American Business* (New York: Simon and Schuster, 1976); A. Kent MacDougall, *Ninety Seconds To Tell All: Big Business and the News Media* (Homewood, IL: Dow Jones-Irwin, 1981). MacDougall tells the story of a *Los Angeles Times* reporter who called an oil company president to clarify a news release. He was told:"Just run it the way I sent it in, sonny" (p. 36). On the corporate system's funding of oppositional forces, see John Saloma, *Ominous Politics: The New Conservative Labyrinth* (New York: Hill & Wang, 1984); and Herman and Chomsky, *Manufacturing Consent*, 26–28.

14 Ledeen, *Grave New World*, 111.

15 Braestrup, *Big Story*, vol.1, 158ff.

16 See his remarks on Crossfire, Transcript #245, 13 February 1991.

17 Bill Keller, "Soviet Official Says Press Harms Army," *New York Times*, 21 January 1988.

18 Walter Lippmann, *Public Opinion* (London: Allen & Unwin, 1932 [1921]), 31–32, 248.

19 Bernard C. Cohen, *The Press and Foreign Policy* (Princeton, NJ: Princeton University Press, 1963), chapter 5.

20 On the prewar appeasement of Saddam Hussein, see Murray Wass, "Who Lost Kuwait?," *Village Voice* (January 16–22, 1991), 60ff.

21 Basic sources cited here are Douglas Kellner, *The Persian Gulf TV War* (Boulder: Westview Press, 1992); Hamid Mowlana, George Gerbner, and Herbert I. Schiller, eds., *Triumph of the Image: The Media's War in the Persian Gulf—A Global Perspective* (Boulder: Westview Press, 1992); John McArthur, *Second Front: Censorship and Propaganda in the Gulf War* (New York: Hill and Wang, 1992).

22 Kellner, *Persian Gulf TV War*, especially 89–97.

23 See Noam Chomsky, "The Media and the War: What War" in Mowlana et al., *Triumph of the Image*, 60–61.

24 On earlier media apologetics for Noriega, see Noam Chomsky, *Deterring Democracy*, 150–58; on the earlier whitewash of Saddam Hussein, Scott Armstrong referred to him as "the man who charmed the pants off many American leaders and journalists in the 1970s," and Armstrong gave supportive citations from Evans and Novak, the *New York Times* and *Washington Post*, in "Sixty-Four Questions in Search of an Answer," *Columbia Journalism Review* (November/December 1990), 23–24.

25 Kellner, *Persian Gulf TV War*, 67–71.

26   Ibid., 13–29; Pierre Salinger and Eric Laurent, *Secret Dossier: The Hidden Agenda Behind the Gulf War* (New York: Penguin, 1991), 110–47.

27   See Kellner, *Persian Gulf TV War*, 30–31; Salinger and Laurent, *Secret Dossier*, 110–14.

28   Kellner, *Persian Gulf TV War*, 31–37.

29   Ibid., 37, 318–35.

30   Ibid.; and Thomas Friedman, "Pax Americana: What the United States Has Taken on in the Gulf, Besides a War," *New York Times*, 20 January 1991. Friedman reported the urgent need for the administration to avoid diplomacy, as noted in the text above, then repeated later without qualification, in the January 20 article, the administration claim that it had exhausted all diplomatic options—"Now that diplomacy has failed and it has come to war . . ."—a wonderful illustration of a reporter's doublethink capability.

31   This poll is discussed in Chomsky's chapter in Mowlana et al., eds., *Triumph of the Image*, 58–59.

32   This opposition vigorously criticized the Bush war policy. The Bush administration, however, was not interested in and did not encourage or even talk with the Iraqi opposition; and the media followed in line. Ibid., 55–56.

33   The process of integration is thoroughly discussed in McArthur, *Second Front*.

34   Alex Jones, "War in the Gulf," *New York Times*, 15 February 1991.

35   Kellner, *Persian Gulf TV War*, 421.

36   Ibid., chaps. 3, 4, and 5.

37   Ibid., 203–206.

38   Ibid., chap. 9. After the war was over, it was also disclosed that the U.S. military had buried alive hundreds or even thousands of Iraqi soldiers by covering over their trenches with sand by bulldozer—another episode of doubtful legality and morality. The U.S. mainstream media, which had failed to pick up this process as war news, gave it minimal attention and an apologetic twist when disclosure finally arrived in September 1991. See Nancy Watt Rosenfeld, "Buried Alive," *Lies of Our Times* (October 1991), 12–13.

39   Kellner, *Persian Gulf TV War*, 381.

40   Ibid., 399–404, 429–30.

41   See Patrick Tyler, "U.S. Officials Believe Iraq Will Take Years to Rebuild," *New York Times*, 3 June 1991.

Chapter 13

Legitimization by Fraudulent Elections

In a recent editorial on "Election Risks in Cambodia," the *New York Times* warned that "flawed elections are worse than none," and that "the international community must proceed cautiously, lest a rigged election give Mr. Hun Sen a veneer of legitimacy."[1] Similarly, in writing on "Kenya's Flawed Election," the *Times* editors noted that "holding elections is not enough to assure democratic government," and they point specifically to the need for "an independent electoral commission less bound to political parties" and "independent broadcast media, allowing opposition voices to be heard outside election periods."[2]

These are very good points, but regrettably the *Times* applies them selectively, only calling into question flawed elections when their legitimacy is challenged by the State Department. In the case of flawed elections that are sponsored by the U.S. government, the *Times*—and the rest of the mainstream media—invariably find them to be an encouraging "step toward democracy" and hence legitimizing. Furthermore, flawed (or no) elections, in "constructively engaged" authoritarian states tend to be ignored, downplayed, or subject to gentle chiding by the *Times* and its media cohorts. The contrast between the urgent official attention to Cuba's electoral failings, and the official complaisance at the absence of elections in Saudi Arabia and rigged elections in Indonesia, is not discussed.

Poland versus Vietnam

This double standard has a long history. Back in 1947, under pressure from the West, the Soviet Union organized an election in Soviet-occupied Poland, which the Soviet-sponsored government won handily. The U.S. media were indignant, and denounced the incompatibility of a free election with external sponsorship, the threatening presence of Soviet and

Polish military forces, and other abuses. The high turnout was derided as based on coercion.[3]

However, in the cases of the Dominican Republic in 1966 and Vietnam in 1966 and 1967, where elections were U.S.-sponsored, despite the massive presence of U.S. and indigenous security forces during elections held following, or in the midst of, considerable violence against the local population, the media found no problem of a coercive threat and presented the large voter turnouts as democratic triumphs. In the case of Vietnam, the *Times* lauded the high turnout and the fact that thousands of villagers were "willing to risk participating in elections held by the Saigon regime," which showed "popular support." The editors stressed the fact that "most observers believe that on the whole the voting was fairly conducted."[4] For the *Times*, the exclusion of not only the main opposition, the National Liberation Front, but all "neutralists," and the presence of vast numbers of foreign troops as well as the Saigon army, did not reduce the value of *this* election—here flawed elections were better than none.

Central American Laboratory

Central America provided an excellent laboratory for testing media bias in election reporting from 1982 to 1990, as the Reagan and Bush administrations sponsored and massively intervened in elections in El Salvador in 1982, 1984, and 1989; supported the 1984 and 1985 elections in Guatemala; but took strong exception to the Sandinista-organized election in Nicaragua in 1984 and aggressively intervened in both the 1984 and 1990 Nicaraguan elections. The U.S. administrations wanted electoral legitimization of the governments of El Salvador and Guatemala, but not of the Nicaraguan government. What makes this test particularly telling is that in El Salvador and Guatemala *none* of the conditions for a free election—free speech and a free press, freedom of candidates to run, intermediate support groups able to mobilize people, and absence of fear and state terror—were met, and both states were controlled and traumatized by army terror. This was not true in Nicaragua, and its 1984 election, though hardly perfect, was found by the Latin America Studies Association (LASA) observer team and British Lord Chitnis to be satisfactory and superior to that of El Salvador in 1982.[5]

But just as it had done in the U.S.-sponsored elections in the Dominican Republic and Vietnam, the *Times* featured the turnout and even put a positive gloss on the role of the murderous armies of El Salvador and

Guatemala. As regards turnout, the *Times* found "most remarkable . . . the evident determination of so many Salvadorans to participate."[6] The paper failed to mention that voting was obligatory, that national identity cards (*cedulas*) had to be stamped recording a vote, and that the defense minister had asserted in the Salvadoran press that non-voting was an "act of treason."[7]

With respect to the role of the Salvadoran army, Warren Hoge asked, "Is the military playing any role in the elections?" and he answered: "Members of the military are not allowed to vote, and the armed forces are pledged to protect voters from violence and to respect the outcome of the contest."[8] Hoge failed to mention the terror of the prior 30 months that killed opposition leaders, demobilized and destroyed virtually all popular organizations, and kept the "main opposition" off the ballot. In U.S. sponsored elections, security forces "protect elections."[9] In the case of Kenya, the *Times* speaks of the need for opposition forces to be heard (and presumably to be allowed to exist) "outside election periods,"[10] but for the Salvadoran election only the election day promises of the army and voter turnout were featured.

In the case of Guatemala also, Stephen Kinzer hardly mentioned state terror, the unfree press, or that the left opposition was off the ballot. He cited the report of the International Human Rights Law Group election observers saying that the 1984 election was "procedurally correct," but he failed to quote their statement that "the greater part of the people live in permanent fear."[11]

The *Times* gave substantial weight to the censorship of *La Prensa* in evaluating the Nicaraguan election, but the far more severe attacks on journalists and the press in El Salvador and Guatemala were given no attention or weight. Similarly, Arturo Cruz's voluntary refusal to run in Nicaragua in 1984 discredited that election for the *Times*, but the exclusion of the left in El Salvador and Guatemala failed to do the same in its analysis of those elections.

In the end, the *Times* found that while the 1984 Nicaraguan election was a "sham," in Guatemala the military "has honored its promise to permit the free election of a civilian president."[12] And in El Salvador "an impressive majority" went to the polls in 1982, in "El Salvador's freest election in 50 years";[13] while in 1984, Duarte's victory represented a "transfer of power to a centrist committed to human rights, reform and reconciliation."[14] In short, the *Times* contributed to the electoral legitimization of two regimes of terror and helped delegitimize a non-terror regime pursuing what the LASA observer team referred to as the "logic of the majority." This was done by the use of a blatant double standard of evaluation and by serious dishonesty in using evidence.

Other Approved Elections

Examination of other elections shows that the *New York Times* frequently exonerates or overlooks serious electoral failings in those elections supported by U.S. policymakers.

—Uruguay held an election in 1984, under a military regime that was giving up limited power to civilian rule, but that kept disapproved candidates off the ballot. The leading opposition figure, Wilson Ferreira Aldunate, was jailed by the army, and a second major candidate, General Liber Seregni, was barred from participating in the election, along with an estimated 5,000 other individuals. These exclusions allowed a conservative opportunist, Julio Maria Sanguinetti, supported by the Reagan administration, to win. U.S. officials made no protest at the jailing of Ferreira, and the *Times*, which had labeled the Nicaraguan election a sham when Arturo Cruz had voluntarily refused to run, found the election to be legitimate in a case where a *real* main opposition candidate was jailed. "Uruguay is resuming its democratic vocation . . . the generals are yielding to the infectious resurgence of democracy in much of Latin America," editorialized the *Times*.[15]

—Turkey held an election under military rule in 1983, characterized by harsh press censorship, 21,000 *officially* acknowledged political prisoners, and with only the three parties "led by politicians sympathetic to the military government" allowed to run.[16] Twelve others parties, including several with a mass base, were denied eligibility. Nevertheless, the *Times* found that "Turkey Approaches Democracy," on the ground that the party "least favored by the generals" won![17] The *Times* stressed the exonerating factor of the "troubled history" of terrorism that "has been contained since the 1980 military coup." The editors were not concerned about the state terrorism carried out thereafter by the generals that was regularly assailed by Amnesty International and Human Rights Watch, but perhaps here again the fact that Turkey was a U.S. client state and an immobile U.S. aircraft carrier and was given "unconditional support" by the State Department,[18] once again explains why this election was encouraging rather than a sham.

—South Africa held an election in September 1989 that was limited to the white electorate, which means that 80 percent of the population was disenfranchised and that the main opposition, the African National Congress, was not an election participant. Black protests at this exclusion were vigorous, and the police repression needed to keep it in check involved scores of deaths. The *Times* coverage of the repression was low-key; positive acts that favored South Africa's image were featured. The issue of how an election could be meaningful when a majority was excluded from participation was simply not addressed, and election-period coverage gave the apartheid government an aura of moderateness and legitimacy. The *Times* editorial on the election cited the State Department's view of the election as positive, a "mandate for change," and the editors found the election not a sham, but a challenge.[19]

—Mexico has long been ruled by a one party (PRI) clique closely linked to Mexican big business and consistently supported by the U.S. government. The *Times* has therefore always found the Mexican elections encouraging, in contrast with past fraudulent ones (which, at the time, the editors also contrasted favorably with those in the more distant past). It has featured expressions of benevolent intent and downplayed structural defects and abuses. Thus, in its first editorial on the 1988 election that brought Carlos Salinas to power, the *Times* noted that prior elections were corrupt (the PRI "manipulated patronage, the news media and the ballot box"), but it stressed that PRI candidate Salinas "contends" that political reform is urgent and "calls for clean elections."[20] The editors question whether "his party" will "heed his pleas," a process of distancing reminiscent of the *Times* suggestions in past years that Duarte in El Salvador and the generals in Argentina might not be able to "control" their subordinates doing the killing. In the postelection period, also, the *Times* was very positive that the PRI would "need to follow Mr. Salinas's pledge" and would have to engage in reform on things like "income distribution," which in fact regressed further and more seriously after 1988.[21]

In its 1988 editorials on the Mexican election, the *Times* did not suggest possible ongoing electoral fraud, "manipulated patronage," or media controls and bias. Just three years later, however, at the time of the 1991 election, the editors stated that "As long as anyone can remember, Mexican elections have been massively fraudulent" as it prepared readers for new promises of a cleanup.[22]

The *Times* recently berated Kenya because it lacked an independent electoral commission,[23] but although this was a notable characteristic of Mexico, and in 1988 produced the scandal of a "computer breakdown" followed by new numbers that gave Salinas 50.7 percent of the vote, the *Times* did not mention this factor in 1988, in 1991, or later. The *Times* has also played down the enormous sums raised by the PRI from its business allies that have been vastly in excess of what is legally permissible; and it consistently neglects "the vast political advantages made possible by Washington's support, and the related access to foreign credit, making discussion of effective political opposition to single party PRI rule an absurdity."[24] But to the *Times*, U.S. intervention is always justifiable and never makes for electoral unfairness, whether it be in Nicaragua, Mexico, or Russia.

Russia: Promoting a Fraudulent Election

The Yeltsin government has presided over a 50 percent fall in national output and large income declines for 90 percent of the population, while a hugely corrupt privatization process has provided windfalls to a small minority, including an important criminal class. There has been a collapse of the social welfare net and health care system that has contributed to a startling rise in infectious diseases and mortality rates. The military establishment has deteriorated to the verge of collapse. Just before the 1996 election campaign, Yeltsin's popularity rating was 8 percent. That he could win reelection in such circumstances suggests—and reflects—a seriously flawed election.

However, the Yeltsin regime was strongly supported by the U.S. government and its Western allies, and is now a de facto client state, even if its leaders pretend to independence and great power status. Yeltsin and the ruling elite are, in an important sense, joint venture partners of Western business interests and governments that benefit from the "reforms" that are immiserating the Russian majority.

In these circumstances, that the *New York Times* would find the 1996 election "A Victory for Russian Democracy" was a foregone conclusion, as was the promotional quality of its editorial and news coverage. Electoral flaws were slighted or ignored, and the paper declared the very fact of holding an "imperfect" election "a remarkable achievement."[25]

The *Times* did recognize that it was a "political miracle that Russians did not throw Mr. Yeltsin out of office" given his "corrupt" privatization program, the rise of crime and criminal mafia power, and the "incredible wealth" going "to a small fraction of people."[26] But neither here nor elsewhere does the *Times* give a credible explanation of why Yeltsin did win. Instead, it follows the Yeltsin and U.S. official line that he won because the Russian people voted for "reform" and "democracy" over a return to Communism; that "Russians made clear by their votes that they favored continuation of the economic reforms begun by Mr. Yeltsin."[27] But the "reforms" were what gave Yeltsin his 8 percent pre-election campaign rating, and no party proposed a return to "Communism." So how did Yeltsin do it?

—The Yeltsin strategy was to avoid debate and all substantive issues and run against Stalin. This hysterical Red Scare campaign was based on the false claim that Zyuganov and the Russian Communist party proposed or were likely to return Russia to Stalinism. But the Communist Party campaigned for what the *Times* editors said the Russian people really want, namely "a more deliberate, humane transition from Communism to capitalism," and given the institutional changes already in place and the absence of Communist Party control over the army, the likelihood of its returning Russia to Stalinism was negligible. The *Times* took the Yeltsin line on the Red Scare as a valid fear, not as a diversionary propaganda ploy.[28]

—If Yeltsin and the *Times* are right, that the Communist party threatened a return to Stalinism, then in reality the Russian people had *no* party that represented their interests and the election was a sham for that reason. The possible absence of an option that would meet the desires and needs of the Russian people was never mentioned in the *Times*.

—Because Yeltsin and his team were responsible for the inhumane capitalism brought about by the "reforms," which the U.S. State Department and the *Times* supported, Yeltsin also ran against his own record. He fired Anatoly Chubais, the minister who had enthusiastically pursued and was identified with reform, and he promised more humane policies. But on the very day after his election victory, he put Chubais back in charge, so that "what the Russian people really want" was not going to happen. The *Times* never commented on the meaning of the firing and immediate reinstallation of Chubais.

—The Russian mass media were dominated by the government and its close business allies who were the main beneficiaries of the "corrupt" privatization program. They carried out what the political reporter for Isvestia called "a propaganda campaign . . . [as] we are united in the face of a common threat."[29] The *New York Times* acknowledged this in passing: "The media were totally rigged in support of Yeltsin,"[30] but this did not affect its preordained positive assessment. This propaganda campaign was hysterical and dishonest—it passed along many wild claims of sinister Communist intentions—it avoided all substantive issues that bore on privatization and looting, and it was incompatible with a free election.

—The Yeltsin government used immense sums of government money, in violation of the law, to buy support and fund propaganda. This caused the Yeltsin government to fall into severe violations of International Monetary Fund loan conditions, but the IMF still provided an additional $10.2 billion loan in the midst of this abusive use of money. Some of the government money was also used to bribe those journalists who still needed bribing. Russian analyst Yelena Dikun estimated that the Yeltsin campaign spent $15 million, or five times the legal campaign limit, just to bribe journalists.

—The West intervened heavily in the election, with numerous visits to Yeltsin by Western political leaders, an international meeting on "terrorism" convened in Moscow—while Yeltsin was terrorizing Chechnya—supplying election management experts, issuing propaganda statements of support, as well as granting loans despite violations of loan agreements.

—None of the very serious abuses that characterized the 1996 election were given attention and weight by the *Times* in this election involving a Western-supported "reformer."

Conclusion

It is clear that when an election is designed to legitimize governments that are serving Western interests, as in El Salvador in the 1980s and Russia in the 1990s, the *Times* does not focus on flaws even when they are severe, but finds exceptional circumstances to justify the imperfections and stresses improvement from the sad past. In cases in which the State Department does not want the government legitimized, as in Nicaragua in 1984 and Cambodia in 1998, the *Times* becomes scrupulous about flaws, gives no weight to improvements from the past, and finds the disapproved elections to be shams and "worse than no elections." But this is accomplished at the expense of using a double standard and an abandonment of press integrity. So we may ask: is election coverage based on such a double standard better than no coverage at all?

Notes

1   Editorial, "Election Risks in Cambodia," *New York Times*, 28 November 1997.

2   Editorial, "Kenya's Flawed Election," *New York Times*, 31 December 1997.

3   A characteristic negative assessment was *Newsweek*'s article "Poland: Foregone Conclusion" (27 January 1947), 26. For other citations and details, see Edward Herman and Frank Brodhead, *Demonstration Elections* (Boston: South End Press, 1984), 173–80.

4   Editorial, *New York Times*, 4 September 1967.

5   Lord Chitnis observed both elections. For details, see Edward Herman and Noam Chomsky, *Manufacturing Consent* (New York: Pantheon, 1988), chap. 3.

6   Editorial, "Democracy's Hope in Central America," *New York Times*, 30 March 1982.

7   For details, see Herman and Brodhead, *Demonstration Elections*, 127–30.

8   Warren Hoge, "El Salvador's Election: Issues and Consequences," *New York Times*, 27 March 1982.

9   Lydia Chavez, "Salvadoran [General] Promises Safe Election," *New York Times*, 14 March 1984.

10 Editorial, "Kenya's Flawed Election."

11 Stephen Kinzer, "Guatemala Rulers Renew Vow on Today's Voting," *New York Times*, 8 November 1985.

12 Editorial, "New Chance in Guatemala," *New York Times*, 12 December 1985; Editorial, "Nobody Won in Nicaragua," *New York Times*, 7 November 1984.

13 Editorial, "Democracy's Hope in Central America."

14 Editorial, "Narrow Chance in El Salvador," *New York Times*, 8 May 1984. In fact, Duarte had joined the Salvadoran government in 1980 just as it began its greatest reign of terror, and he was a consistent army figurehead and apologist. See Mark Cooper, "Whitewashing Duarte," *NACLA Report on the Americas* (January/March 1986).

15 Editorial, "Victories for Voters in Latin America; Uruguay's Slow Boat to Democracy," *New York Times*, 1 December 1984.

16 Marvine Howe, "Turkey's Generals Keep Foes Out of Election," *New York Times*, 28 August 1983.

17 Editorial, "Turkey Approaches Democracy," *New York Times*, 11 November 1983.

18   Howe, "Turkey's Generals Keep Foes Out of Election."

19   Editorial, "Countdown in South Africa," *New York Times*, 8 July 1989.

20   Editorial, "Mexico's Radical Insider," *New York Times*, 3 July 1988.

21   "Mexico Shatters a Monolith," *New York Times*, 9 July 1988.

22   Editorial, "The Missing Reform in Mexico," *New York Times*, 24 August 1991.

23   Editorial, "Kenya's Flawed Election."

24   Christopher Whalen, Letter, *Financial Times*, 12 June 1992.

25   Editorial, "A Victory for Russian Democracy," *New York Times*, 4 July 1996.

26   Ibid.

27   Editorial, "A Muted Kremlin Inauguration," *New York Times*, 9 August 1996.

28   For example, see A. Stanley, "Red Scare: Gennadi Zyuganov threatens to take Russia back to the old days of Communists—and hacks," *New York Times Magazine*, 26 May 1996.

29   Sander Thoenes and John Thornhill, "Media place glasnost on ice," *Financial Times*, 14 June 1996.

30   Michael Specter, "Old Guard; Even in Slow Motion It's a Russian Revolution," *New York Times*, 23 June 1996.

Chapter 14

NAFTA, Mexican Meltdown, and the Propaganda System

The North American Free Trade Agreement (NAFTA), which became law in November 1993, was a clear "win-win" according to the unified phalanx of the U.S. establishment, which included Clinton administration officials, Mobil Oil and the other members of the Business Roundtable, mainstream economists, and the corporate media. The Mexican collapse and virtual surrender of sovereignty to the U.S. Treasury, only a year after the win-win legislation became operational, presented a public relations problem to spokespersons for the establishment. Examining today's apologetics in the context of the apologetics for NAFTA back in 1993 provides insight into how a propaganda system meets such a challenge.

First Defense: Disconnect, Blame Mexico

The phalanx uniformly denies (or ignores) any connection between the Mexican collapse and the enactment and implementation of NAFTA. This was to be expected, but it is still a bit droll. After all, a win-win shouldn't become a lose-lose quite so quickly; to unsophisticated minds the proximity of the introduction of NAFTA and the meltdown suggests a definite linkage. The establishment's favorite economic forecasters of NAFTA's positive impact, Gary Hufbauer and Jeffrey Schott of the Institute for International Economics, had predicted a sustained Mexican current account deficit lasting for at least a decade, a forecast which conveniently allowed for a U.S. export surplus and increase in NAFTA-related jobs.[1] Furthermore, all through the first year, as U.S. exports to Mexico increased, officials, the press, Will Marshall of the Progressive Policy Institute, and many other NAFTA enthusiasts did not hesitate to attribute short-term, export-related job increases to NAFTA (while failing to mention the jobs lost because of imports from, and job relocations to, Mexico). After the meltdown, however, the propagandists had to return to the drawing board to fashion ways to shift blame elsewhere.

One gambit has been to blame Mexican officials for mismanagement in overvaluing the peso, thereby encouraging imports and retarding exports, with the resultant deficit funded by capital inflows. But if the peso was overvalued, how could Mexico's Harvard- and Yale-trained technocrats have been so foolish? Could it be that they got locked in to an overvalued peso in the period when overvaluation stimulated U.S. exports, thereby rebutting the critics' suggestion that NAFTA would impose serious job losses on U.S. workers? Could they have been influenced by the threat made to Mexican authorities by a delegation of U.S. fund managers in June 1994 that they would liquidate their Mexican holdings in the absence of a promise not to devalue and/or to provide dollar-indexed bonds (the Tesebonos)?

More important, the great merit of Mexico's "liberalization" was supposed to be that it "makes a country subject to market discipline" (IMF economist Liliana Rojas-Suarez), so that market correctives should keep national policies under tight control and prevent excesses.[2] Where was the discipline? The problem is that the establishment gets carried away in such bonanza times and suspends rational judgment in the heat of euphoria and fondness for the local market favorites. Just a few months before the devaluation, IMF head Michel Camdessus issued an accolade to Mexico's economic policy: "Mexico has maintained a correct macro-economic policy, and I am convinced it will continue along that line."[3] Treasury Department official and economist Larry Summers pronounced Mexico's fundamentals "sound" as late as December 27, 1994.[4] And market participants still sought Mexican business up to the last moment. A CS First Boston Ltd. analyst, Stefano Natella, who decided to urge his clients to move some of their assets out of Mexico five days before the devaluation, was harshly chastised by his boss, David Mulford, who was just leaving for a sales call to Mexico's finance minister!

The fact is that the market will surely discipline and contain any efforts by governments under its sway that try to serve poor people. But the market often fails to correct speculative bubbles engaged in by the rich, until the bubbles collapse of their own internal contradictions. (As market analyst James Grant puts it, "Wall Street is not in favor of free markets. It is in favor of free bull markets.")[5] Countries can be easily victimized by such bubbles when market forces are given command over their development processes.

Another defense of NAFTA, made by Larry Summers, among others, is that the Mexican debacle would have been worse without NAFTA.[6] This is not susceptible to proof, but it is implausible, because the speculative bubble was built on the euphoria generated by the enactment of NAFTA. The argument also begs a deeper question. NAFTA followed a decade or more of a semi-coerced integration of Mexico into the global system and into export-oriented and debt-driven growth. Mexico became more vulnerable to volatile capital market movements as well as changes in export market conditions and therefore potentially much more unstable (and vastly more unegalitarian) as a result of this increased market orientation, of which NAFTA was merely the crowning achievement. So insofar as the meltdown was not attributable to NAFTA it rested on the wonderful job the Mexican leadership and its foreign banker and intellectual mentors had done over the prior years.

Second-Order Defense: Mexico "Locked-In"

A further very important line of defense of NAFTA, both at the time of its enactment and following the onset of the recent Mexican crisis, runs to this effect: that a great merit of the agreement was that it "locked Mexico in" to free market policies, so that even with the current setback, in the long run benefits would flow because of the inherent properties of free markets. This argument is repeated by virtually all of the mainstream economists, and by the media, in lockstep. Six of the 10 New York Times editorials on NAFTA in 1993 mentioned its merit of locking Mexico in to "reforms."

In connection with the recent crisis, economist Jeffrey Schott points out that before NAFTA, Mexico might have blocked imports and restricted access to foreign currency; instead, Mexicans are not only adhering to the free market path, they are even "undertaking reforms that negotiators tried to get in NAFTA but couldn't," like wider privatization and openings to foreign investment.[7] Bush NAFTA negotiator Julian Katz pointed out with obvious approval that "if they were considering other options, they were foreclosed by NAFTA."[8] The bailout is necessary, however, to keep Mexico locked-in and to protect the image of a successful neoliberal experiment. As Treasury Secretary Robert Rubin told Congress, Mexico is "a prototype for countries that are striving to put inward-looking, state-controlled models of economic development behind them."[9] MIT economist Rudiger Dornbusch noted in testimony before the senate in January that "a failure to back up our model risks giving the advantage to the retrograde camp: Cardenas, Mexico's unreconstructed leftwing leader is already on the march."[10] (How bailing out fleeing investors and imposing huge new burdens on ordinary Mexicans will give an advantage to "our" model and its supporters, Dornbusch failed to make clear.)

The argument for assured long-run benefits to the "locked-in" Mexico is purely ideological. The win-win forecasts were not looking impressive after only one year, so the ideologists moved automatically to the long-run, where results are untestable. Whether late developing countries will ever do well in free market regimes in an age of high technology and powerful and aggressive transnational corporations (TNCs), and whether any gains from "free trade" will trickle down to the lower 60 percent, is debatable at best. The free market ideologues consistently ignore the fact that both the early and late "modernizers" (including, the U.S., Japan, and South Korea) relied heavily on the dread "protectionism" and "government intervention" in their critical eras of growth.

A second and even more important problem with the lock-in argument is its profoundly antidemocratic character. If Mexico was "locked-in" to the "market reforms" isn't this another way of saying that the Mexican people were denied their right to choose a development path and to control their own economic policies? Economist Paul Krugman said that NAFTA should be supported *mainly* because it will "help to keep free-market reformers in power in Mexico."[11] It never occurs (or is irrelevant) to Krugman, Larry Summers, the editors of the *New York Times*, and the U.S. establishment in general that their accolade to the lock-in policy represents a straightforward attack on Mexican democracy, sovereignty, and its citizens "right to choose." This is imperial arrogance at its most blatant.

This point is reinforced by the fact that Salinas represented illegitimate authority, having won the 1988 election by fraud, as was sometimes acknowleged even by the mainstream media. That Salinas negotiated the agreement locking Mexico in to a highly constrained policy path means that undemocratic means were employed to achieve the highly undemocratic result. It may be recalled that the U.S. media delegitimized Nicaragua's Daniel Ortega as "unelected" in 1984 after an election far cleaner than the Mexican election of 1988. Nicaragua's leadership was pursuing a development path opposed by the Western establishment; their project was oriented toward serving ordinary citizens, a "logic of the majority"; the Salinas-IMF path served an elite and minority interest. Delegitimizing Ortega in 1984 helped justify continued U.S. economic and military warfare against Nicaragua. Both the Nicaragua case and the failure to delegitimize Salinas after 1988, in fact making him into a courageous statesman, show dramatically the close attunement of media and economists' service to the needs of the state and dominant economic interests.

In the face of this antidemocratic reality, consider the common claim that one of the great things about NAFTA and the associated "reforms" is that they will reinforce "democracy"! The hypocrisy here is breathtaking. The Mexican right to choose was eliminated by collaboration with illegitimate authority. During the process of removing choice, a corrupt privatization program vastly increased the wealth of an elite who worked hand-in-hand with the fraudulently elected leader, income distribution became more unequal, and media concentration grew, all of which weakened the substantive base of democracy. The idea that the increased U.S. presence would help bring democracy to Mexico was already contradicted by U.S. support for the fraudulently elected and corrupt Salinas after 1988 and cooperating with him to lock Mexicans *out* of free choice of a development path. The argument ignores the dominant U.S. interest in a "favorable climate of investment," which is frequently provided by joint venture partners like Salinas, or Suharto, or the family dictatorships of the Arabian peninsula, rather than by democrats who may be "populists" and "inward-looking."

Media Hostility to Democracy at Home

The establishment's contempt for the Mexican people's right to choose was closely paralleled by their attitudes toward the U.S. public's right to participate in the NAFTA decision at home. Once the important people who represent the "national interest" had said yes to NAFTA, the matter was settled for mainstream institutions and experts. The task was to get enough unimportant people to accept it.

It was an awkward fact that ordinary citizens didn't like NAFTA. A series of polls during 1992 and 1993 showed that, despite the propaganda onslaught by the Bush and Clinton administrations, business, and the media, a majority of the public remained hostile to NAFTA—for example, in September 1992, 57 percent con, 33 percent pro, 10 percent no opinion (*National Journal*); in March 1993, 63 percent con, 31 percent pro, 6 percent no opinion (Gallup/CNN); in July 1993, 65 percent con, 28 percent pro, 7 percent no opinion (Gallup). Broken down, poll data showed a sharp class division in the appraisal of NAFTA—the higher the income and greater the education, the more positive the attitudes toward NAFTA. Thus, a November 1993 Gallup poll showed that middle-income families ($20,000 to $50,000) opposed NAFTA by 47 percent to 32 percent; affluent families ($50,000+) favored NAFTA by 51 percent to 36 percent. The mainstream media and economists spoke unequivocally for the affluent.

The mainstream media generally ignored the fact of majority opposition. In their 16 editorials on NAFTA, neither the *New York Times* nor the *Philadelphia Inquirer* mentioned such public opinion poll findings. When they did get close to ordinary citizen opinion they brushed it aside with suggestions that worker "anguish was misdirected," based on the public's lack of information, the false appeals of demagogues, and on the existence of a higher "national interest" that was served by NAFTA that ordinary folk did not understand.[12] It was a coincidence not worth mentioning that what was good for the national interest was also good for members of the Business Roundtable. (Remember when Charles Wilson's claim that "what was good for GM was good for America" was thought to be self-serving nonsense? That was during the superliberal years of the Eisenhower adminstration.)

The mainstream media, following Clinton's lead, also criticized labor for using "muscle" in trying to influence legislators. Editorials in both the *Times* and the *Washington Post* listed anti-NAFTA legislators and published the amount of their contributions from labor unions, suggesting bought votes. Clinton and the press also repeatedly suggested that anti-NAFTA votes were based on labor's illegitimate threats, rather than the normal exercise of interest group and voter rights. Clinton's own frenzied logrolling, business's massive lobbying and financial contributions, and even the $30 million plus lobbying campaign of the Mexican government in the United States elicited no comparable media comment. The point was clear: labor and the working class have no right to participate in the political process in opposition to policies favored by their betters. It would be hard to find a more explicit expression of the media's class bias.

Bailout Versus Democracy

As in the case of the passage of NAFTA, the Mexican bailout was opposed by the great majority of the public (approximately 70 percent in an ABC News/CNN poll) but was favored by the monied class and the political-intellectual-media elite. The public's opposition was once again irrelevant in the face of unified elite support, an elite which, in the midst of frenzied efforts to reduce spending for social needs still rushed to commit $40 billion to bailing out investors in Mexican securities. The IMF did the same, offering the unprecedented sum of $18 billion, in gross violation of Article 6 of the IMF Articles of Agreement, which requires the IMF to intervene to *prevent* members from using IMF credits to finance capital flight (whereas the bailout package facilitates it). It also violates the agreement requirement that the IMF strive to advance the welfare of *all* member countries, because the loan agreements compel Mexico to pursue a tight money policy aimed solely at getting peso interest rates high enough to induce investors to hold peso paper, at the cost of crushing the domestic economy in a process Mexicans call "fiscal terrorism."

The pro-NAFTA elite, of course, claimed that the emergency was dire, threatening falling dominoes in a systemic crisis, but this was fraudulent. As economist Robert Dunn pointed out, "Mexico faces a debt problem which is similar to that faced by Latin America countries many times in the past, and . . . the people most threatened by the difficulty, and who would therefore benefit from the proposed arrangement, are primarily in New York (and to a lesser extent Tokyo and elsewhere) rather than Mexico."[13] In the absence of the coercion by foreign monied interests, Mexico would have suspended payments, renegotiated financial terms, and avoided a huge, forced contraction that seriously damaged Mexican interests.

If the suffering ordinary citizens of the United States (and Mexico) believe that there is an elite conspiracy that serves elite interests at their expense, the NAFTA-Mexican bailout cases suggest that they are on to something. It may not be the UN, Jews, and assorted other villains, or even any explicit conspiracy, but the class-based bias of policy is evident, as is the supportive propaganda of mainstream intellectuals and media.

Media Boosterism

In their editorials on NAFTA in 1993, and in their news sections as well, the media not only marginalized the opposition, they also served as NAFTA boosters. They quickly took the position that the benefits of NAFTA were obvious, were agreed to by all qualified authorities, and that only demagogues and "special interests" opposed it. Among their booster tricks were the following:

1. Rhetorical Appeals

While they decried the NAFTA opposition's demagoguery, the mainstream media outcompeted the opposition on this score. In repeated editorials, the *Philadelphia Inquirer* castigated an alleged "demonizing" of NAFTA and portrayed the vote on NAFTA as "a barometer of America's faith in itself."[14] The use of "demonizing" in reference to criticisms of NAFTA was name-calling, and the *Inquirer* and other mainstream media kept criticisms of NAFTA to a minimum. The reference to "America's faith" is crude rhetoric. If America had faith in itself would it have to integrate with its neighbors? Wouldn't it maintain its distance and autonomy? The editors were asking for faith in the internationalizing project being pushed by the TNCs, whose interests were implicitly identified with those of "America." The editors also argued that defeating NAFTA would be a setback for Clinton, a foreign policy defeat for America, and would jeopardize Clinton's other programs such as health care reform. These were purely opportunistic gambits that deflected attention from NAFTA's merits and demerits.

2. Perot as the Opposition

In a further rhetorical trick, the press latched on to Ross Perot as the anti-NAFTA spokesperson of choice and repeatedly cited (and contested) his views. (Six of 10 *New York Times* editorials cited Perot.) Ralph Nader is a national figure who spoke out strongly and competently against NAFTA, but he was a less convenient target, so he was ignored in favor of a man who could be more easily dismissed as a demagogue. In one editorial, the *Times* cited a public opinion poll that gave Gore the nod over Perot in their TV debate. As noted earlier, the *Times* carefully avoided editorial mention of the polls that indicated the general public's rejection of NAFTA, a vastly more consequential point than whether Gore or Perot had "won" a debate. The *Times* carefully chooses opinion polls fit to print.

3. Limiting the Boundaries of Debate

Meg Greenfield, *Washington Post* opinion page editor, stated that "On the rare occasion when columnists of the left, right and middle are all in agreement . . . I don't believe it is right to create an artificial balance where none exists."[15] On TV, also, Rush Limbaugh and Michael Kinsley were in agreement on NAFTA's merits. But with a majority of the public opposing NAFTA, the pro-NAFTA unity among the pundits simply highlights the huge class bias of mainstream punditry.

In accord with Greenfield's recognition of an elite consensus, the *Post*'s editorial page ratio for and against NAFTA was 6 to 1, and in its 1993 Veteran's Day Special it had 10 unopposed pro-NAFTA opinion pieces. In the four months before Labor Day, 1993, 68 percent of the sources used in the news columns of the *Post* and *New York Times* were pro-NAFTA, 20 percent were opposed.

4. Economists Fit to Cite

The mainstream media used economic opinion with similarly biased selectivity. Although it ignored economist Edward Leamer's estimate that the wages of "low-skilled" workers would decline by $1000, the *Inquirer* did see fit to quote Leamer to the effect that "factory workers [who are mainly not "low skilled"] worried about falling wages . . . would be better off picketing their school board than pro-NAFTA pols."[16] As noted earlier, Gary Hufbauer and Jeffrey Schott, both of whom are affiliated with a pro-free trade think tank, and who predicted a Mexican trade deficit that would last for many years, and hence a U.S. export surplus that would increase U.S. jobs, were the media's economists of choice. Models that yielded conflicting results, by Clyde Prestowitz, Edward Leamer, Tim Koechlin, Mehrene Larudee, Sam Bowles, Gerry Epstein, and James Cypher were ignored.

With the Mexican collapse and the end of the U.S. export surplus in one year instead of a decade or more, the Hufbauer and Schott model and forecasts were quickly confuted by history, and Hufbauer was quoted in the *Wall Street Journal* in April 1995 as saying that he was going out of the forecasting business.[17] But his badly flawed model had served the purpose—like the inflated CIA claims of greatly increased Soviet military expenditures in the late 1970s and early 1980s—of advancing an establishment agenda, even if by intellectual error or fraud. And the mainstream media gullibly regurgitated both.

5. Win-win, but Magnitude of Effects Unclear

The media boosters were sure that both the United States and Mexico would benefit from NAFTA, but they couldn't make up their minds about the magnitude of the gains. On balance, the boosters stressed that the impact of NAFTA would be quite small (following economists Krugman and Dornbusch and the Congressional Budget Office), but that Mexico would be the surer and larger beneficiary. Given the small effects, the inference drawn was—why worry? But if NAFTA would have such a tiny impact, why the frenzied boosterism?

6. Downplaying Class-based Distribution of Benefits and Losses

The media sometimes acknowledged that there would be winners and losers, with "predominantly women, blacks and hispanics" and "semi-skilled production workers" (i.e., a large majority) possible losers,[18] but they did not dwell on this. Nor did they insist that the losers be compensated, that expansionary macro policies be installed to offset job losses, or that labor law be strengthened in the United States and Mexico to offset the new bargaining advantage of capital. The editorials never mentioned the diminished bargaining position of labor. They just assumed that new and better jobs would be available for those thrown out of work. Leamer's estimate that NAFTA would cause an average $1000 decline in the income of low-skilled U.S. workers was never cited in the *Times* or *Inquirer* editorials or news articles.

7. Mantra: Free Trade Good

The editorials and vast bulk of "news" articles postulated that free trade was good for all, always. The *New York Times*, both editorially and in news articles by Sylvia Nasar, simply rewrote economic history to make it appear that government intervention was antithetical to growth.[19] The effect of advanced technology and globalization on the distribution of benefits and losses between and within countries was simply glossed over.

8. Playing Down Investor Rights and the Absence of Labor Rights

A very sizable part of the NAFTA agreement was devoted to spelling out the rights of investors, in an attempt to lock-in a favorable climate of investment in Mexico. The media ignored this, pretending that the agreement was only about "free trade," which resonates better than "investor rights." Meanwhile, the several thousand pages of the NAFTA agreement said nothing about labor rights. This was consistent with the view that Mexico's cheap labor and government controlled unions were among the attractions of investment in Mexico and that the intent of the interests pushing NAFTA was *downward* harmonization of wages and working conditions.

Criticism of this exceptional one-sidedness led eventually to a "side agreement" that supposedly protected labor (and the environment). It was of course revealing that labor rights entered through a side agreement, as an afterthought, and under pressure. It is therefore no surprise that the side agreements are a joke. Under NAFTA the rights of investors are clearly defined, are harmonized *upward*, and are protected by the threat of trade sanctions. In contrast, there is no attempt in the side agreements to harmonize labor or environmental standards upward; the agreements require only that each country enforce its own laws. Even then, only a narrow subset of labor laws are subject to possible trade sanctions (child labor, minimum wage, and health and safety laws). Egregious violations of the right to strike or freedom of association would be punished—at most—

by a "consultation" between the ministers of labor of the affected countries. When trade sanctions do apply, enforcement is subject to numerous procedural obstacles that do not encumber investors. Mexico's top trade negotiator, Jaime Serra Puche, stated that "The time frame of the process makes it very improbable that the stage of sanctions could be reached."[20] This was not cited in the mainstream media; they were satisfied with the labor protection offered.[21]

9. Impressive Environmental Protection

Environmental protection also entered the NAFTA process belatedly, in a toothless side agreement, with provisions similar to those applicable to labor. There is no upward harmonization, and sanctions require a "persistent pattern of failure to enforce the law" by the country in which violations occur; it is not enough to show that the law was violated. As in the case of labor protection, the layered enforcement procedures make it "very improbable that the stage of sanctions could be reached." But the media were impressed. The *New York Times* maintained that NAFTA was more environmentally oriented than any previous trade agreement ("No previous trade agreement tackles as many pollution issues as NAFTA does")[22]— that is, the nominal is greater than nothing whatever. The media never suggested that the side agreements might be cosmetic only, or that business might *like* the poor environmental protection in Mexico and lobby to keep it, and use Mexico's poor protection as a lever in this country.

The Economists as NAFTA Boosters

A very large fraction of the economics profession supported NAFTA, and the proportion was probably highest among the notables. This reflects the class bias of the profession—which increases with degree of notability and financial and other ties to the corporate establishment—and the powerful grip that neoliberal ideology has on a profession that is itself ever more closely integrated into the market.[23]

Quite a few notables work for institutions like the World Bank and the IMF, which serve a clientele that seeks to implement a neoliberal agenda, with resultant built-in constraints on economic thought. Others, like Jeffrey Sachs and Rudiger Dornbusch, are paid consultants and advisers to governments that seek entry into the global market system, whose business is to promote transitions from socialism and social democracy to maximally private economic orders. They are ideological servants and technicians of the neoliberal and TNC project.

A large fraction of the notables were among the 300 economists who signed a September 1993 letter that supported NAFTA.[24] The letter gave the case for NAFTA as following from past gains from Mexican trade, a CBO study that suggested that NAFTA would bring small net gains to both Mexico and the United States, and the fact that "an open trade relationship directly benefits all consumers." The superficiality of the economics, the economists' neglect of the imbalance in economic development and power between Mexico and the United States, the skewed class benefits and costs of Mexican growth, and the problems of the distribution of gains and losses in the United States itself in the new global system, is striking. The political naiveté underlying the letter can be seen in the penultimate sentence: "Working with our neighbors to build a strong partnership in North America is a desirable parallel track to multilateral efforts for an open world trading system." The economists had no problem with Mexico's illegitimate authority as a partner in negotiations, with massive corruption and inequality, or with the removal of any Mexican people's democratic right to choose their policy. (They might be "irresponsible," as the Chilean people were before Pinochet saved them from themselves, in Kissinger's famous argument.)

The classic example of economic boosterism was Rudiger Dornbusch's letter in the *Financial Times* on "Lessons that Brazil can learn from Mexico" (Oct. 16, 1991), that portrayed the Salinas government as a model of probity (his changes "go far beyond rooting out corruption"; privatization is "left to the professionals," etc.) and a model of courage for supporting the antipopulist and antidemocratic demands of the global capital market. This article was itself a "model": of ignorance and crude apologetics for authoritarianism that served the TNC project. In a revealing sequel, Dornbusch gave a speech to Mexican businessmen in March 1995, telling them that Salinas was "the Nick Leeson of Mexico."[25] The earlier unlimited apologetics for Salinas was reversed in favor of a gimmick that shifted blame for the debacle from the "reforms" to the *prior* Mexican leadership.

The notables were almost all supportive of the Clinton bailout, finding it necessary to prevent the spread of the contagion to other "emerging markets." But what about the further shifting of the burden of "reform" from wealthy foreign investors to poor Mexicans? Wouldn't the bailout cause investors in other emerging markets to expect future bailouts for themselves? And doesn't a bailout undermine the protective role of risktaking, which supposedly underlies the merits of free markets? (Let's not talk about these matters, or if we do, let's stress the urgency of the special case. The ultimate apologist-opportunist, Dornbusch, testified in favor of the bailout on January 31, then published an article in *Business Week* six weeks later explaining that bailouts were intolerable.[26] (The article did not mention his earlier support for the Mexican bailout.) Didn't the settlement seriously undermine Mexico's sovereignty by turning its revenues over to foreign authorities, as in the days of the banana republics? Martin Feldstein, head of the National Bureau of Economic Research, contended that the actual bailout was superb because it did *not* interfere with Mexican sovereignty: "It is good that we have done this in concert with other leading nations and without trying to impose conditions on Mexico that would hurt its economy and offend its sovereignty."[27]

Note also Feldstein's stress on "the economy," reminiscent of Brazilian police state head General Emilio Medici's 1971 distinction between "the economy" and "the people": the former, he said, is doing fine, the people are unfortunately doing badly. General Medici's spirit prevails among the U.S. elite. The economists are earning their pay as spokespersons for "the economy" and the "national interest."

Notes

1   Gary Hufbauer and Jeffrey Schott, *NAFTA: An Assessment* (Washington, D.C.: Institute for International Economics, 1993), 13.

2   Sheila Meehan, "Panelists Explore Interplay Between Policies and Expectations in Mexico's Economic Turnaround," *IMF Survey* (6 July 1992), 214–15.

3   "IMF Chief Expresses Confidence in Mexican Economy Despite Political Turmoil," *Associated Press*, 29 September 1994.

4   Editorial, "Asleep on Mexico," *Wall Street Journal*, 28 December 1994.

5   James Grant, of *Grant's Interest Rate Observer*, quoted in Floyd Norris, "How Foreigners Invest, and Lose Their Shirts," *New York Times*, 29 January 1995.

6   In his January 20, 1995, remarks before the George Washington University Law Center, *Treasury News*, Office of Public Affairs, Department of the Treasury, January 20, 1995.

7   Bob Davis, "Nafta Is Key to Mexico's Rescue of Peso; U.S. Exporters May Not See Tariff Help," *Wall Street Journal*, 4 January 1995.

8   Ibid.

9   Statement of Robert Rubin before the Senate Foreign Relations Committee (January 26, 1995), 2.

10 "The Mexican Crisis and U.S. Loan Guarantees," Testimony before the Senate Banking Committee, January 31, 1995.

11 Quoted in Sylvia Nasar, "A Primer: Why Economists Favor Free Trade Agreement," *New York Times*, 17 September 1993.

12 Editorial, "Nafta's True Importance," *New York Times*, 14 November 1993.

13 Robert Dunn, "$40 Billion for Wall Street," *Washington Post*, 24 January 1995.

14 Editorials, "A time for courage," *Philadelphia Inquirer*, 14 November 1993; "Back to NAFTA's basics," 16 November 1993.

15 Quoted in Howard Kurtz, "The NAFTA Pundit Pack; Sure, They Backed It. How Could They Lose?," *Washington Post*, 19 November 1993.

16 Editorial, "After NAFTA," *Philadelphia Inquirer*, 19 November 1993.

17 Bob Davis, "Free Trade Is Headed For More Hot Debate," *Wall Street Journal*, 17 April 1995.

18 Thomas Lueck, "The Free Trade Accord: The New York Region," *New York Times*, 18 November 1993.

19   Editorial, "One Specious Argument for Nafta," *New York Times*, 23 September 1993; Sylvia Nasar, "Industrial Policy The Korean Way," *New York Times*, 12 July 1991.

20   *Journal of Commerce*, 20 August 1993, quoted in Thea Lee and Mark Weisbrot, "The Political Economy of NAFTA: Economics, Ideology, and the Media," Economic Policy Institute (undated), 13.

21   For an excellent analysis of the almost nonexistent actual enforcement of the labor side agreement, and other matters discussed here, see Thea Lee, "False Prophets: The Selling of NAFTA," Briefing Paper, Economic Policy Institute, 1995.

22   Editorial, "Nafta and the Environment," *New York Times*, 27 September 1993.

23   See Mark Blaug, "Disturbing Currents in Modern Economics," *Challenge* (May/June 1998); also, Edward Herman, "The Institutionalization of Bias in Economics," *Media Culture & Society* (July 1982).

24   See Nasar, "A Primer; Why Economists Favor Free-Trade Agreement."

25   Barbara Belejack, "Mexican Soap Opera," *The Texas Observer*, 24 March 1995. Nick Leeson was a 27 year old broker for the British merchant bank Barings, whose very large hidden and illegal speculations led to losses that caused the bank to fail in 1996.

26   Rudi Dornbusch, "Bailouts Are Bad Medicine—In Mexico Or Elsewhere," *Business Week*, 13 March 1995.

27   Martin Feldstein, "The Right Policy for Mexico and the U.S.," *Wall Street Journal*, 1 February 1995.

Chapter 15

Carlos and Posada: Their Terrorists and Ours

On July 12 and 13, 1998, the *New York Times* ran successive front-page articles on the career of Luis Carriles Posada, a world class terrorist who had been trained by the CIA in the 1950s in preparation for the Bay of Pigs invasion, and who thereafter devoted his life to terrorist actions against Cuba. As a U.S.-sponsored terrorist, who for many years was in direct U.S. service, and who continued to terrorize a country subject to U.S. economic and other forms of warfare, Posada remained under effective U.S. protection for over 30 years. This protection was paralleled by a treatment by terrorism "experts" and the U.S. media that differed sharply from that accorded terrorists like Carlos the Jackal. The *Times* articles of July 12 and 13 represented a partial break from the past, in which a potent double standard for "their" terrorists and our terrorists had been consistently maintained.

In fact, nowhere is the bias and propaganda service of the mainstream media more dramatically evident than in their treatment of terrorism. This is a virulent word of defamation that the powerful regularly use to advance their political agendas: their enemies are "terrorists" or "sponsors" of terrorism, whereas the powerful and their allies and agents, who do the same or worse things, are "freedom fighters" or engage in "retaliation" or "counterterror."

In 1988, the Pentagon listed the African National Congress as one of the "more notorious terrorist groups" in the world, but it did not list Savimbi's Unita, nor the Israel-sponsored proxy army in South Lebanon, nor the U.S.-organized Nicaraguan contras. Libya has long been declared a sponsor of international terrorism, but never South Africa, which in the 1980s was supporting not only Unita in Angola and Renamo in Mozambique, but whose assassination attempts abroad extended to London, Paris, and Sweden (in 1996, the former head of a covert South African hit squad claimed that Swedish Prime Minister Olof Palme had been murdered in 1986 by South African agents). In its recent report on "Patterns of Global Terrorism," issued on April 30, 1998, the State Department lists Cuba as a sponsor of international terrorism, solely on the ground that it "harbors" alleged terrorists. But that Saudi Arabia gave safe haven to Idi Amin is different, and the U.S. provision of refuge to Haitian killers General Raoul Cedras and Emmanuel Constant, Salvadoran military officers Jose Guillermo Garcia and Carlos Vides Casanova—both recently named by the released soldiers who murdered four U.S. religious women in 1980 as the ones who gave the orders to kill—and numerous Cuban refugee terrorists, does not interfere for a moment with this country's right to name the world's terrorists!

The Politics of Terrorism

The use of accusations of "terrorism" as a propaganda weapon reached its zenith in the Reagan era (1981 to 1988), during which Claire Sterling's *Terror Network* became the administration's bible and Sterling the media's expert of choice. According to Sterling, the Soviet Union was the planning and organizational center of terrorism, exporting it through any left or oppositional groups disfavored by Western power, who were all Soviet agents. As Reagan was renewing the arms race to war against the Evil Empire, and was supporting terrorist counterrevolutionary forces everywhere—southern Africa, Central America, Argentina, Chile, the Philippines, and elsewhere—this was a perfect propaganda instrument.[1]

The Reaganite thrust meshed well with the plans of Israeli prime minister Menachim Begin. Israel had been under growing pressure to grant civil and national rights to the Palestinians in the late 1970s. Begin responded by organizing a meeting of the Jonathan Institute in Jerusalem in 1979, to gather together political/media supporters to declare the PLO a terrorist organization and tie it to the Soviet Union. One does not have to grant rights to, or negotiate with, "terrorists." Present at the Israeli gathering were Claire Sterling, George Will, George Bush, Norman Podhoretz, Ben Wattenberg, Senators John Danforth and Henry Jackson from the United States, and representatives from Britain, France, and elsewhere, who carried forth the Begin message with great effectiveness in succeeding years.

In addition to the politicians and pundits, a virtual industry of "experts" helped to convey the terrorism message.[2] These experts were funded by business and government, in institutes and think tanks like the Rand Corporation, the Georgetown Center for Strategic and International Studies, and the Hoover Institution, and had revolving door relations with government bodies like the CIA, the State Department, and the Pentagon. The system of institutes and experts extended throughout the Free World, and close and collegial links existed between those in the United States, Canada, Britain, France, Israel, and, in the 1980s, apartheid South Africa. These experts all followed a Free World party line, according to which dissidents, rebels, and governments that fought against and were opposed by Western governments and their client states were invariably "terrorists," and all Western and allied forces were freedom fighters and counterterrorists, by rule of affiliation alone. For example, all the experts found Libya to be a terrorist state worthy of much attention, but none of them so designated South Africa, which fit the definition far better than Libya. (South Africa had its own Terrorism Research Center, which had warm relations with Western, especially British, institutes and experts.)

All of the experts paid great attention to Carlos the Jackal and Abu Nidal, but the major works by Claire Sterling, Paul Wilkinson, Walter Laqueur, and others didn't even mention comparable rightwing terrorists such as Stephano Delle Chiaie (Italy) and Luis Posada Carriles. This spectacular bias of the establishment experts has never fazed the mainstream media one bit: these experts are accredited by their closeness to power; their resultant conflict of interest as information sources is invisible to the mainstream media.

Carlos versus Posada

Ilich Ramirez Sanchez, popularly known as Carlos the Jackal, carried out many terroristic acts against Israel, other Western states (including France), and Arabs who cooperated with Israel and the West (one of his most notable ventures was kidnapping a group of Arab oil officials from a high level conference). The Western media have credited him with some 83 killings over his career. Taken into custody by France in a deal with Sudan where he was in hiding, Carlos was recently tried and convicted of murder in Paris. For the Western media and Western experts, Carlos is the model terrorist and is portrayed without qualification as evil incarnate.

Luis Posada Carriles, on the other hand, was trained by the CIA as part of the Bay of Pigs invasion project, and has been a long-standing member of the Cuban refugee terrorist network. This network has been one of the most active and durable anywhere, because it was given legiti-macy by U.S. sponsorship, has served U.S. aims, and has in consequence been under U.S. protection.[3] The U.S. official and media treatment of Posada has reflected this protection and the role of this terrorist network.

Posada came to public notice when a Cuban airliner was blown up in October 1976, killing 73 people. Two Cubans were apprehended, con-fessed, and implicated Posada and Orlando Bosch as fellow participants. Posada was caught and tried three times in Venezuela, but was acquitted on technicalities. Before a further trial could be held, he escaped prison. He next came into notice when Eugene Hasenfus's contra supply plane was shot down over Nicaragua in 1986, and evidence surfaced that Posada was an operative in the contra supply network, working for the Reagan administration at Ilopango airbase in El Salvador.

The mainstream media's treatment of this disclosure was extremely muted. I believe that if Carlos had turned up as a literal employee of Bulgaria or the Soviet Union in some military-terrorist function, the me-dia would have expressed outrage, and would have cited this as definitive evidence of a Soviet terror network. In fact, when it was disclosed in 1990 that Carlos had been given refuge in Hungary, the *New York Times* gave the story front-page coverage[4]—and it distorted the news in the pro-cess, by suppressing the facts, available in the European media, that Carlos's refuge was conditional on his suspending all terrorist activities and that he was expelled in 1982. In the case of Posada, an escaped and wanted terrorist was not only protected against prosecution for serious terrorist crimes, he was also being used in U.S. terrorist operations against Nica-ragua. But as he was our terrorist, the media were virtually silent, thereby collaborating as "news" organizations in facilitating what the World Court declared to be the "unlawful use of force" by the United States as well as U.S. sponsorship of contra terrorism.

The U.S. media always search diligently for links to high officials in the case of enemy misdeeds.[5] With Posada, there was a very definite link to the top: he was a good friend of Felix Rodriguez, a fellow right-wing Cuban, who was Vice President George Bush's liaison to the contra ter-rorist campaign against Nicaragua in the 1980s. But in this case, in a long-standing mode of propaganda and double standards, the media showed no interest whatever in the connections of this terrorist to the political leadership. There were also other differences from the treatment of Carlos. Whereas the *New York Times* had at least 14 separate articles featuring Carlos, there was only a single *Times* article that focused on Posada and discussed him in any detail, prior to the two part series on July 12 and 13, 1998. That article was on page 21, and was entitled

"Accused Terrorist Helping to Supply Contras."[6] Even U.S. officials acknowledged that Posada had been involved in the Cuban airliner bombing and was a real terrorist, but unlike Carlos, Posada was only an "accused" terrorist in the *Times*. Although it reported the accusation that he had participated in a terrorist bombing that had killed 73 people, the paper didn't mention that two colleagues had quickly incriminated him, and that he was still wanted for crimes in Venezuela. Also, the article stressed his anticommunism, his long fight against Castro, and his devotion to his family, a form of humanization and exoneration not extended to Carlos.

Posada Terrorizes Cuba and Honduras

Posada has been living in Honduras and El Salvador since 1986. His exact location has long been known to U.S. authorities (as was acknowledged to the *Miami Herald*),[7] and he could easily have been extradited or seized by U.S. forces in these client states; this would have been easier than France's recovery of Carlos from the Sudan. But Posada is our terrorist, who has worked for us directly and indirectly, and thus has remained free to continue his activities. The contrast between our failure to apprehend this world-class terrorist and the French treatment of Carlos is not discussed in the mainstream media.

In 1994 and 1995 Posada joined with a group of right-wing army officers in Honduras to destabilize the government of Carlos Roberto Reina. Reina had angered the officers by cutting the military budget and curbing their kickbacks on arms purchases, and the Cuban right-wing felt that he was too soft on Castro and might interfere with plans to use Honduras as another secret base for anti-Cuban operations. This terrorist program involved a dozen or more bombings in late 1994 and early 1995, during which at least six Hondurans were killed and 26 were injured.[8] Neither the terrorist operation in Honduras nor Posada's involvement were reported in the leading U.S. newspapers or TV newscasts.

On November 16, 1997, a lengthy article in the *Miami Herald* by Juan O. Tamayo traced the spate of 11 bombings of hotels and restaurants in Cuba during 1997 to a "ring of Salvadoran car thieves and armed robbers directed and financed by Cuban exiles in El Salvador and Miami . . . And it was Luis Posada Carriles . . . who was the key link between El Salvador and the South Florida exiles who raised $15,000 for the operation." The Cuban bombings killed one tourist and wounded six other people.

The *Miami Herald* article on the Cuban bombings was based on "dozens of interviews with security officials, friends of the bombers, Cuban exiles and others in El Salvador, Miami, Guatemala and Honduras." Carried out by a distinguished group of reporters, led by Tamayo, this story had great credibility. But it was neither reproduced nor were its findings summarized in the *New York Times*, the *Washington Post*, the *Los Angeles Times*, or on the TV network broadcasts. In fact, in the puny stories covering these terrorist attacks none of these papers ever mentioned Posada.

Nor were the important revelations of a subsequent investigative report by the *Miami Herald* picked up in any of the major media forums. "One of the most ambitious" of Posada's adventures, the *Herald* reports, "appears to have been a plot to assassinate Castro at a 1994 summit of Ibero-American heads of government in the Colombian port city of Cartegena." But although Posada and his five accomplices "managed to smuggle arms into Cartegena," the report continues, "Columbian security cordons kept them too far away to take a good shot at Castro." "If there is no publicity, the work is not useful," the *Herald* reporter quotes Posada himself as having written to a fellow "conspirator." "The U.S. newspapers don't publish anything unless it is confirmed."[9] Posada was wrong—stories that fit newspapers' biases require minimal confirmation; those that don't, like Posada's terrorist activities, will get minimal publicity despite compelling evidence.

The *New York Times*'s method of keeping the story of Posada's connection to the Cuban bombings out of the public eye in 1997 is enlightening. The killing of the tourist was covered in the World News Briefs section on page A13, and got 3.5 inches of space.[10] In the case of the other bombings, the *Times* quoted generalities from Cuban reports and accusations, always on the back pages.[11] After a Salvadoran was captured, confessed, and linked the bombings to the Cuban-American National Foundation (CANF), the *Times* sub-head was that "Havana tries to link a suspect to an exile group in Miami."[12] The confession didn't make the link real for the *Times*, and it was offset by denials from the CANF and statements by the State Department that Cuba hasn't given them solid evidence. But Tamayo and his colleagues did more, and the *Times* trick is to cite only Cuban officials—easily dismissed as biased—and to avoid a serious source that is more credible. (This method, of using the less credible witness to make the case you oppose, is widely used by the *Times* and other media; e.g., in its letters column the *Times* often publishes a weak offering that provides nominal balance while rejecting others that contain unwanted critical substance.) It is also notable that the *Times* failed to do any investigative research of its own on the anti-Cuban terrorism. It didn't want to know, or to have the public know, of the escapades of our terrorist.

Posada Surfaces in the Times

However, on July 12 and 13, 1998, the *Times* ran two lengthy front-page articles on Posada, by Ann Louise Bardach and Larry Rohter, based on interviews with him at his secret Caribbean hideout, as well as on borrowings (unacknowledged) from the *Miami Herald*.[13] What caused the *Times* to alter its news judgment and give Posada such attention? One reason was the recent softening in administration policy toward Cuba, manifested in the reopening of direct air travel between Cuba and the United States, the tightening of restraints on exile forays into Cuban waters, and a crackdown on the smuggling of refugees from Cuba. The *Times* has long "followed the flag" in reporting on foreign policy, so that when a bipartisan hard-line policy is in place the paper protects "our terrorists" and downplays the U.S. terror campaign in which a Posada (or a D'Aubuisson, or a Savimbi) plays his part. Although the *Times* performed this protective service in relation to Posada through 1997, it had not been entirely happy with U.S. policy toward Cuba; it denounced the Helms-Burton Act and called for a more humane mode of opposition to the Castro regime.[14] The softening of policy that preceded the July 12 and 13 articles was therefore surely welcomed; this editorial position undoubtedly contributed to making Posada, at long last, newsworthy.

The moderation of policy itself has been a reflection of changing political forces bearing on Cuban policy, including the effect of the Pope's visit to Cuba, the growing interest of U.S. business in Cuban markets, and the desire to move away from the damaging confrontation with allies over the Helms-Burton Act and the U.S. policy of destructive engagement.

Another important factor was the November 1997 death of Jorge Mas Canosa, the influential head of the CANF, and the consequent disarray and weakening of his hard-line faction (displayed in part by the willingness of Posada to implicate CANF in his activities, and thereby damage its legal and moral status in the United States). The July 12 and 13 articles featured Posada's close relationship with Mas Canosa and the longtime and regular funding Posada received from him and the CANF. Posada made it clear that the money was provided with the understanding that it was underwriting his general terrorist activities, including the 1997 bombing campaign in Cuba. In short, he was a terrorist arm of the tax-exempt CANF, which had been organized at the recommendation of the Reagan administration.

In early August 1998, Posada retracted his claims about support from Mas Canosa and the CANF,[15] almost surely under pressure from the still-powerful hard-line elements in the exile community, some of whom, "angry with Posada, began speaking openly about [and immediately under-mining] his Dominican plot," to assassinate Castro at the meeting of Caribbean leaders in Santo Domingo on August 20–25.[16] But, apart from the unpersuasiveness of the retraction itself, some of the claims Posada retracted had already been confirmed in CIA documents and in Posada's published autobiography.

The July 12 and 13 articles also focus on Posada's long relationship with the CIA as an agent and informant, and it quotes Posada time and again explaining how his friendly relations with CIA and FBI personnel and long service as a U.S. operative protected him and allowed him to continue his life and "work." The *Times* describes in detail the experience of a Cuban-America businessman in Guatemala, who discovered Posada's (and his partners') assemblage of bombs and a planned assassination attempt against Castro, and notified the FBI, which apparently made no investigation and took no action on the case. Posada himself told the interviewer that the FBI had never questioned him in connection with this incident. It was made clear throughout the series that the rule of law has long been inoperative in dealing with the CANF, Posada, and the approved terrorism that they represent.

Although much of this information is neither new nor surprising, it is useful to have it confirmed from the terrorist's mouth and be given a *Times* news imprimatur. It should be noted, however, that significant biases are still evident in these articles. In the use of words, for example, Posada is not referred to as a terrorist; in fact, the authors note that *Cuba* calls Posada a terrorist, but they themselves repeatedly describe him as a "Cuba foe" and as a man who has "devoted his life to trying to bring down Castro," or even as a "fugitive." They state that when Hasenfus's plane was shot down in Nicaragua in 1986, the world soon learned that "Ramon Medina was actually Luis Posada Carriles, the international fugitive." The *Times* never called Carlos a mere "fugitive," nor did it ever identify Carlos by his self-designated objectives (anti-Israel, anti-imperialist); unlike Posada, his acts and methods made him an unqualified terrorist.

The series is kind to Posada in other ways. The authors state that Posada "opposed the dictatorship of Fulgencio Batista," without offering any evidence. Almost as much space is devoted to the injuries Posada suffered in a 1990 assassination attempt as to his terrorist acts and the damage inflicted on his victims. As in the past, the *Times* does not mention the fact that the two terrorists apprehended after the 1976 Cuban airliner bombing quickly named Posada as an accomplice. This bloody killer is humanized and asked no difficult or harsh questions. His history and linkages are spelled out by him on his own terms and his own rationales are unchallenged.

The articles also fail to make connections and draw conclusions. His close relationship with Felix Rodriguez, with whom he worked at the Ilopango air base in El Salvador in the 1980s, is mentioned without noting that Rodriguez was Vice President George Bush's liaison to the contra war, which ties the employment of this terrorist to the highest echelons of the U.S. government. More important, the authors nowhere ask whether or not the close relationship between the "fugitive" and U.S. government makes the United States a sponsor of international terrorism, and its leaders and mainstream intellectuals and journalists—who regularly denounce the scourge of terrorism—world class hypocrites.

Concluding Note

When Cuba shot down an overflying Cuban refugee network plane in 1996, the *Times* gave the story front page and intense coverage, and expressed the greatest indignation.[17] This is the same refugee network that Posada has tapped for his terrorist activities, and one under U.S. protection. The relative treatment of the shootdown, and the intense and indignant coverage of Carlos, versus the earlier "don't-want-to-know" treatment of Posada, and the recent surfacing and moderate critique of Posada in a time of softening policy, exemplifies well the *Times*'s bias, role, and propaganda service.

Notes

1   For a critique of Sterling, see Diana Johnstone, "The 'fright story' of Claire Sterling's tales of terrorism," *In These Times*, 20–26 May 1981; Edward Herman, *The Real Terror Network* (Boston: South End Press, 1982), chap. 2.

2   For a description of this industry, see Edward Herman and Gerry O'Sullivan, *The "Terrorism" Industry: The Experts and Institutions That Shape Our View of Terror* (New York: Pantheon, 1990).

3   For a description of this network and its history, see Herman, *Real Terror Network*, 65–69.

4   Celestine Bohlen, "Aide Says Hungary Gave Refuge in '79 to Terrorist Carlos," *New York Times*, 28 June 1990.

5   See Herman and Chomsky, *Manufacturing Consent*, 42–44, 64–66.

6   Joseph Treaster, "Accused Terrorist Helping to Supply the Contras," *New York Times*, 10 December 1986.

7   Juan Tamayo and Gerardo Reyes, "An Exiles's Relentless Aim: Oust Castro," *Miami Herald*, 7 June 1998.

8   Juan Tamayo, "'94 Bombings Against Honduran Leader May Be Linked to Anti-Castro Plot," *Miami Herald*, 28 September 1997.

9   Tamayo, "An exile's relentless aim: oust Castro."

10 "Man Killed in Havana As Blasts Hit 3 Hotels," *New York Times*, 5 September 1997.

11 For example, Steve Erlanger, "Cubans Blame Exiles in U.S. for 4 Bombings in a Single Day," *New York Times*, 6 September 1997.

12 Larry Rohter, "Cuba Arrests Salvadoran in Hotel Blasts," *New York Times*, 12 September 1997.

13 Ann Louise Bardach and Larry Rohter, "Life in the Shadows, Trying to Bring Down Castro," *New York Times*, 12 July 1998: "Key Cuba Foe Claims Exiles' Backing," 13 July 1998.

14 Editorial, "Turning a Page in Cuba," *New York Times*, 25 November 1997.

15 "Cuba Exile Says He Lied to Times About Financial Support," *New York Times*, 4 August 1998 (no byline).

16 Juan Tamayo, "Plot to assassinate Castro leaked," *Miami Herald*, 9 August 1998.

17 Barbara Crossette, "U.S. Says Cuban Pilots Knew Their Targets Were Civilians," *New York Times*, 28 February 1996; editorial, "The Cuban Shootdown," *New York Times*, 27 February 1996.

Chapter 16

Suharto:
The Fall of a Good Genocidist

The fall of Suharto, and the media's coverage of his exit, reveal once again, and with startling clarity, the ideological biases and propaganda role of the mainstream media. Suharto was a mass killer, with at least as many victims as Pol Pot, a dictator far more ruthless than Castro, and a grand larcenist in the Mobutu class. But as he served U.S. economic and geopolitical interests, he was helped into power and his dictatorial rule was warmly supported for 32 years by the U.S. economic and political establishment. The U.S. was still training the most repressive elements of Indonesia's security forces as Suharto's rule was collapsing in 1998, and the Clinton administration had established especially close relations with the dictator ("our kind of guy," according to a senior administration official).[1]

Making of a Good Genocidist

Suharto's overthrow of the Sukarno government in 1965 turned Indonesia from Cold War "neutralism" into fervent anticommunism and destroyed the Indonesian Communist Party—exterminating a sizable part of its mass base in the process. Robert McNamara referred to the transfer of power, accompanied by mass extermination, as one of the "dividends" of the U.S. military aid and training programs in Indonesia. And the U.S. establishment's enthusiasm for the coup-cum-mass murder was ecstatic. *Time* magazine called it "The West's best news for years in Asia."[2]

Suharto also quickly transformed Indonesia into an "investor's paradise," only slightly qualified by the steep bribery charge for entry (the corruption drain was estimated by an Indonesian National Audit Board official in the 1980s to be 30 to 40 percent of the national budget).[3]

Beyond the corruption, it was another awkward fact that from 1965 into 1998 an important part of the lure to foreign investors—and the basis of the much-vaunted "growth"—was the ability of the dictatorship to assure favorable entry terms, unrestricted repatriation of profits, and the forcible prevention of independent unions, which helped keep wages very low. Investors flocked in to exploit the timber, mineral, and oil resources, as well as the cheap labor, often in joint ventures with Suharto family members and cronies. Investor enthusiasm for this favorable climate of investment was expressed in political support and even in public advertisements; for example, the full page ad in the *New York Times* by Chevron and Texaco entitled "Indonesia: a model for economic development" (September 24, 1992), and ads lauding Suharto by Mobil and Arco that also appeared in the same year.

Another awkward fact for the media was Suharto's invasion and occupation of East Timor from 1975, which resulted in the death of an estimated 200,000 in a population of only 700,000. Combined with the 500,000–1,000,000 or more slaughtered within Indonesia in 1965–66, and the 150,00–200,000 deaths resulting from the Indonesian occupation of West Papua,[4] this triple genocide would seem to put Suharto in a more advanced class of mass murderers than Pol Pot. Adding in his corruption and ruthless dictatorial rule, the Suharto record should have elicited intense coverage and repeated and indignant calls for withdrawal of U.S. support and other remedial action, on the assumption that the mainstream media are objective, eschew double standards, and give primary weight to democratic and humane values. If, on the other hand, the media are essentially servants of the state, the fondness of their government and Fortune 500 companies for the Suharto regime would cause them to look the other way, find excuses for its crimes, and maintain a firm double standard as between Suharto, on the one hand, and Pol Pot and other demonized "enemies" (Castro, Saddam Hussein, Daniel Ortega), on the other hand.

The media's record in dealing with Indonesia, regrettably, supports the second hypothesis. They featured the 1965–1966 holocaust as an outburst of collective irrationality rather than a deliberate and centrally orchestrated operation that was executed with U.S. encouragement and support. Not only was the mass killing not condemned in the mainstream media, it was often treated as happy news and welcomed as a geopolitical victory, a "positive achievement" and one of "the most hopeful political developments" in Asia.[5] Long-term and large-scale imprisonment without trial and under terrible conditions was mainly ignored; official statements that prisoners would be released were taken at face value and failed to provoke further questions.[6]

Similar media apologetics accompanied the mass slaughter in East Timor, which was given the go-ahead by Kissinger and Ford in 1975, was protected against an effective international response by U.S. policy in the UN—Ambassador Moynihan bragged in his autobiography that the task of making the UN "utterly ineffective" in responding to Indonesian aggression "I carried . . . forward with no inconsiderable success"[7]—and was implemented with weapons supplied by Presidents Ford and Carter. The media treatment was muted, relied heavily on Indonesian officials for news and (mis)interpretation, almost never tapped East Timorese sources, provided minimal details of the suffering by the victims, and displayed no indignation and issued no calls for remedial action.[8] The bias of the media may be illustrated by *Times* reporter Barbara Crossette's statement that Indonesia refused to let reporters visit East Timor "because of the Government's belief that they will not be objective."[9] Crossette mentioned no other possible reason for exclusion.

Henry Kamm also explained that "Because of continuing insecurity, the former colony remains a restricted area."[10] Again, no other possible motive was suggested and the claim of an Indonesian official was not questioned. Note also how Kamm put East Timor's colonial status in the past, implying that the Indonesian occupation was not a continuation (and worsening) of such status. As a further spectacular illustration of bias, Crossette several times described the predecessor Sukarno government as "a military threat to its neighbors and an international bully," whereas under Suharto "Indonesia has become a stabilizing influence."[11] Crossette did not find the invasion and occupation of East Timor a *realized* "military threat" or case of bullying of Indonesia's neighbors.

In 1979, Noam Chomsky and I pointed out that the *New York Times* news coverage of East Timor fell to zero in 1977 as Indonesian violence reached its peak.[12] (*Times* editors nevertheless have repeatedly pointed out that "most of the world wasn't looking" when Indonesia invaded East Timor, that "there has been little international outcry," and that East Timor "was largely ignored until last Nov. 12, when Indonesian troops killed 50 Timorese,"[13] as if they had not contributed to this result by their own news choices.) We also stressed the huge contrast with the media's treatment of Pol Pot in Cambodia, in the same time frame; in that case indignation was great, the sourcing was of the victims, not the Pol Pot government, and the coverage never slackened. There were also vague hints that the Cambodian killings should be stopped by international action, but specific proposals for action were rare; intervention would have been difficult in Cambodia, but was potentially much easier in East Timor because the United States was supplying the weapons. The idea that Suharto should be punished for mass murder, or that force should be threatened or used to get him out of East Timor, was never suggested in the mainstream media.

In short, for several decades the mainstream media underplayed Suharto's crimes and "normalized" Indonesian conditions, which helped prevent the U.S. public from getting very much concerned, thereby insulating the dictatorship, and its U.S. corporate beneficiaries, from effective democratic pressure.

But with his sudden decline and fall in 1997 and 1998, Suharto became highly newsworthy, which presented a challenge to the mainstream media, who had treated him so kindly while he had served the Western establishment. Let us examine how the media dealt with the good genocidist and dictator in the period of his fall, in comparison with their treatment of the bad genocidist Pol Pot and other leaders of enemy states; how they explained and justified their country's role in helping Suharto obtain and maintain his power; and how they worked it out that the "market" brought Suharto down.

Good Versus Bad Genocidists in the Media

Suharto's killings of 1965 and 1966 were what Chomsky and I called "constructive terror," with results viewed as favorable to Western interests. His mass killings in East Timor were "benign terror," carried out by a valued client and therefore tolerable. Pol Pot's killings, in contrast, were "nefarious terror," done by an enemy and therefore appalling and to be severely condemned. Pol Pot's victims were "worthy," Suharto's "unworthy."

Biased language derived from this politicized classification system was unfailingly employed by the media in the period of Suharto's decline and fall (1997 and 1998). When Pol Pot died in April 1998, the media were unstinting in condemnation, calling him "wicked," "loathsome," "monumentally evil," a "lethal mass killer," "war criminal," "blood-soaked," and an "egregious mass murderer."[14] His rule was repeatedly described as a "reign of terror" and he was guilty of "genocide." Although he inherited a devastated country with starvation rampant, all excess deaths during his rule were attributed to him, and he was evaluated on the basis of those deaths.

With Suharto, although his regime was responsible for a comparable number of deaths in Indonesia, along with many thousands in West Papua and more than a quarter of the population of East Timor, the media never used the word "genocide" to refer to him or to his rule. Earlier, in a rare case in which the word was brought up in discussing East Timor, Henry Kamm referred to it as "hyperbole—accusations of 'genocide' rather than mass deaths from cruel warfare and the starvation that accompanies it on this historically food short island . . ."[15] So, no "hyperbole" for a good genocidist; and one looks in vain for any description of him as bloodsoaked or a murderer. In the months of his exit, he was referred to as Indonesia's "soft-spoken, enigmatic President,"[16] a "profoundly spiritual man,"[17] and a "reforming autocrat."[18] His motives were described as benign: "It was not simply personal ambition that led Mr.Suharto to clamp down so hard for so long; it was a fear, shared by many in this country of 210 million people, of chaos," and he "failed to comprehend the intensity of his people's discontent," otherwise he undoubtedly would have stepped down earlier.[19] He was sometimes described as "authoritarian," occasionally as a "dictator," but never as a mass murderer. Suharto's mass killings were referred to—if at all—in a brief and antiseptic paragraph.

It is interesting to see how the same reporters move between Pol Pot and Suharto, indignant at the former's killings, somehow unconcerned by the killings of the good genocidist. Seth Mydans, the New York Times's principal reporter on the two leaders during the past two years, calls Pol Pot "one of the century's great mass killers . . . who drove Cambodia to ruin, causing the deaths of more than a million people," who "launched one of the world's most terrifying attempts at utopia."[20] But in reference to Suharto, this same Mydans says that "More than 500,000 Indonesians are estimated to have died in a purge of leftists in 1965, the year Mr. Suharto came to power."[21] Note that Suharto is not even the killer, let alone a "great mass killer," and this "purge [not "murder" or "slaughter"] of leftists" was not "terrifying," nor allocated to any particular agency. The use of the passive voice is common in dealing with Suharto's victims; they "died" instead of being killed ("the violence left a reported 500,000 people dead,"[22] or "were killed" without reference to the author of the killings).[23] In referring to East Timor, Mydans speaks of protestors shouting grievances about "the suppression of opposition in East Timor and Irian Jaya."[24] This is perhaps an understatement in describing an invasion and occupation that eliminated 200,000 out of 700,000 people.

The good and bad genocidists are handled differently in other ways. For Suharto, the numbers killed always tend toward the 500,000 official

Indonesian estimate or below, although independent estimates run as high as 2 million.[25] For Pol Pot the media numbers usually range from 1 to 2 million, although the best estimates of numbers executed run from 100,000 to 400,000, with excess deaths from all causes (including residual effects of the prior devastation) ranging upward from 750,000.[26]

Pol Pot's killings are always attributed to him personally—Shenon refers to him as "the man responsible for the deaths of more than a million Cambodians," and the editors call him the person "who *ordered* [emphasis added] more than a million people killed."[27] Although analysts of the Khmer Rouge claim that their suffering under the intense U.S. bombing made them vengeful, and although the conditions they inherited were disastrous, for the media nothing mitigates Pol Pot's responsibility. The only allowable "context" that explains his killing is his "crazed maoist-inspiration," his Marxist ideological training in France, and his desire to create a "utopia of equality."[28]

Suharto, by contrast, is not only not made responsible for the mass killings, the killings are rationalized by a mitigating circumstance: namely, a failed leftist or Communist coup, or "onslaught from the left,"[29] that "touched off a wave of violence."[30] In the *New York Times*' historical summary: "General Suharto routs communist forces who killed six senior generals in an alleged coup attempt. Estimated 500,000 people killed in backlash against Communists."[31] This formula is repeated in virtually every mainstream media account of the 1965–1966 slaughter. Some mention that the "communist plot" was "alleged," but none try to examine its truth or falsehood, even though it was the propaganda rationalization of a military group seizing power.[32] Note also the phrase "routs communist forces," which suggests a fight rather than a vast slaughter of unarmed civilians. The crucial army role in the killing, which generally "did not begin until elite military units had arrived in a locality," and featured army units as "the main killers" in the worst massacres in the countryside,[33] was ignored in the media presentations. By suggesting a provocation, using words like "backlash" and "touching off a wave of violence," and by suppressing awkward facts, the media justify and diffuse responsibility for the good genocide.

The good genocidist is also repeatedly allowed credit for having encouraged economic growth, which provides the regular offset for his repression and undemocratic rule as well as for the mass killing. In virtually every article Seth Mydans wrote on Indonesia, the fact that Suharto brought rising incomes is featured; the mass killings and other negatives Mydans relegated to side issues. Joseph Stalin also presided over a remarkable development and growth process, but the mainstream media have never been inclined to overlook his crimes on that basis. Only "constructive" terror merits such contextualization in the media.

East Timor

With East Timor, also, the media have found it difficult to locate anybody responsible for the killing, and they stress the inexplicable sadness and complexity of it all and Indonesia's valiant efforts to cope with a difficult situation. As Thomas Friedman says, "Indonesia is too complex to be a pariah," and he goes on to quote an Indonesian official that East Timor "is a complex issue with a long history that we are trying to resolve."[34] "Complexity" is a signature word of apologetics.

Earlier, Steven Erlanger had reported that "This is one of the world's sadder places, where 100,000 to 200,000 people died from 1974 in a brutal civil war and the consequent invasion through combat, execution, disease and starvation."[35] The lack of a clear agent and the use of the passive voice once again protect the good genocidist. The misrepresentation of facts is also standard: the civil war was short and left at most 3,000 dead; the invasion was not "consequent" on the civil war, but came after it was clearly over.

The readiness with which reporters accept without question the sincerity of Indonesian expressions of regret and truthfulness of claims of reform is another manifestation of an apologetic bent. Erlanger says that prodded by international criticism "the tone of official behavior has changed, with an emphasis on reconciliation, development and progress."[36] In 1988, Erlanger found that "Jakarta's Human Rights Record Is Said to Improve," based on an Asia Watch study, causing the organization's executive director to write a scathing accusation of misrepresentation and apologetics.[37] After the Dili massacre of November 1991, Philip Shenon's retrospective, which gives disproportionate space to official Indonesian views, is entitled "Indonesia Seeks to Atone for a Massacre in Timor," although the article contains nothing suggesting any regret or policy change on the part of the Indonesian government.[38]

Although the Indonesian occupation and annexation has never been recognized by the UN, it has been recognized by the *New York Times*, whose reporters for years, even into 1998, referred to the continued Timorese resistance as "separatist," thereby legitimizing the aggression and occupation, just as friends of Saddam Hussein might have labeled the ousted government of Kuwait in 1990 as "separatist." Seth Mydans notes that the UN "regards Portugal as the administrative power," but that doesn't stop him from referring repeatedly to a "separatist insurgency" and Jose Ramos-Horta as "the separatist leader."[39] This of course fits Clinton administration policy and thought—Clinton reportedly would not see Ramos-Horta after his Nobel Peace Prize award on the ground that he "has been associated with groups promoting violence" (i.e., the East Timorese "separatists"), and Mr. Clinton and his friend Suharto are averse to the use of violence.[40]

As Suharto's position weakened in 1997 and 1998, the mainstream media did not permit East Timor to become a major issue. They reported the changing stance of Indonesian leaders, from initial refusal to consider any change to willingness to consider "special administrative status," but the media did not allow Timorese voices or human rights spokespersons to spell out a critical answer or propose solutions.[41] William Branigin described East Timor as a "challenge that the Indonesian military . . . may yet have to face."[42] Media editorialists did not call for Indonesian withdrawal nor did they urge international action if the East Timorese were not granted self-determination. During this period, the United States was pressing Serbia to withdraw its forces from Kosovo and cease its attacks on the rebellious Albanians. But although the ethnic cleansing in East Timor has been vastly more extensive and savage than that of Serbia in Kosovo—which is also part of the Serbian state and not a victim of foreign aggression—the media support the pressure on Serbia, but refrain from suggesting any pressure on Indonesia to withdraw from East Timor. The *Times* urges Indonesia to allow a Timorese vote and possible autonomy; the *Washington Post* leaves matters to the new democratic government of Indonesia ("no democratic government can sustain his [Habibie's] no-negotiation stance"); the *Financial Times*, openly acknowledging that Suharto killed a larger fraction of Timorese than Pol Pot did Cambodians, still urges only that talks be begun that would lead to a Timorese vote.[43]

Corruption

"Herman's Law" states that when the dictator of a shakedown state loses control and ceases to be useful to the United States, the mainstream media suddenly discover that he is a crook and focus intently on his corruption. This was the case with Marcos and Mobutu, and fits well the recent treatment of Suharto. There were, of course, a fair number of references to corruption prior to the collapse in each of these cases, but the mainstream media rarely if ever offered in-depth analyses of the massive structures of looting and asset holdings of the dictators and their families and cronies while the dictators were still in power.

In Suharto's case the data were there and were published in out of the way sources (e.g., Richard Robison, "Class Analysis of the Indonesian Military State," *Indonesia*, April 1978), but the mainstream media were not interested, even though the topic would seem extremely newsworthy. The *New York Times* reported that in Indonesia "Newly liberated newspapers competed to display ever-bolder headlines about the 'Suharto trillions'."[44] But U.S. media were under no coercive restraint as they failed to do what the liberated Indonesian papers are now doing. My hypothesis is that Suharto was too valuable an ally and joint venture partner of Fortune 500 companies; serious exposes would have produced costly flak. Only as he lost power, just as his own people could finally express their anger at his looting and terror, so too the mainstream media's reporters obtained more freedom of action.

In fact, at a certain point in Suharto's period of exit, the dismantling of his (and his cronies) business and financial empires even became a policy priority. Once it appeared that his rule was no longer assured and sustainable, the United States and the IMF sought "reforms" that would enlarge transnational corporate opportunities in Indonesia. Media critiques of Indonesian corruption became more than acceptable: they fit the changing needs of the Western establishment and they demonstrated, even if belatedly, the West's and media's aversion to corruption!

The Suharto family's 30 to 40 billion dollars in assets and the Indonesian structures of privilege have thus become highly newsworthy, although details about the linkages with, and gains of, Western business from these privileged networks remain sparse.[45]

Repression and the Absence of Democracy

The mainstream media have always acknowledged that Suharto's regime was undemocratic and repressive, but they have never focused intently on these matters or pressed for an "Indonesian Democracy Act" that would parallel the "Cuban Democracy Act." Although Suharto's rule has fitted the definition of totalitarian, with a one-party regime, an official ideology, and control by terror, the word has never been applied to Indonesia.

The media often explain away repression and the absence of democracy in Indonesia with a two-pronged apologetic: the need for "stability" in the face of an alleged "security threat" and the benefits of growth.

There have been constant references over the years to the "stability" Suharto brought to Indonesia, following the Sukarno era of upheaval. According to the ineffable Crossette, "Many critics of the Government [unidentified], recalling the years of racial and political violence [Suharto's mass killings don't qualify as "political violence"] and economic disaster, do not quarrel with President Suharto's rationale in forging restraints with firmness."[46] This formula continued in 1998. Kristof points to the "turmoil of the last political transition [1965–1966] . . . reminding people of the dangers of instability."[47] Mydans also explains the repression as a product of "a fear shared by many in this country of 210 million people, of chaos."[48] Kamm writes that the army is also devoted to stability and has "always strived to save the country from suspected designs on state power from left and right."[49]

This projection to the Indonesian people of the devotion to "stability" of Suharto, the army, the U.S. government, and reporters for the mainstream media, led these reporters to underrate public dissatisfaction and readiness for revolt. Only three months before Suharto's resignation, Keith Richburg wrote in the *Washington Post* that "Suharto is at the peak of his power," with critics conceding that "they can think of no credible alternative," so that change "will not come from the streets . . . but from the powerful armed forces."[50] Four months before Suharto's exit, David Sanger and Seth Mydans contended that, given his willingness to use force, and the "remarkable prosperity . . . that has cemented his control," Suharto was likely to hang in there.[51]

After the uprising in May, however, Mydans was compelled to acknowledge that "virtually the entire nation turned against him [Suharto]."[52] And after the uprising, in explaining the long lag in its arrival in Indonesia, Kristof finally acknowledged that "Indonesians are more scared of their Government than Filipinos were of theirs. Indonesia is haunted by the brutal political repression that began in the fall of 1965 and ended with some 500,000 deaths." Kristof even quoted an elderly man hesitant to join protestors, who whispered to him: "Who has the courage to stand up now except the students?"[53] In this revised but perhaps more honest version, it appears that the citizenry didn't support Suharto because of their devotion to "stability," but out of fear of state terror.

It should also be noted that the rigged elections under the dictatorship have been treated lightly by the mainstream media. These elections were acknowledged to be a formality that "holds little suspense," but this was not regarded as a serious matter.[54] This contrasts sharply with the media's treatment of the unrigged election in Nicaragua in 1984, which was derided as a sham and a serious failure that delegitimized the government. No such questions about legitimacy followed the truly sham electoral successes of Suharto.

Repression for Growth

During the period of Suharto's fall, as in earlier years, repression and lack of democracy were always juxtaposed with the fact of economic growth, and thus were partially exonerated and justified. A major article by Philip Shenon featured this tradeoff explicitly: "As Indonesia Crushes Its Critics, It Helps Millions Escape Poverty," although the article was devoted mainly to the growth and prosperity rather than to the facts of repression.[55] While very shy about giving details on the major beneficiaries of Indonesian-style growth (Suharto, cronies, transnational corporations), the mainstream media have repeatedly claimed that benefits have been widely diffused and that poverty has been reduced. Shenon gives the World Bank figure of a reduction in "abject poverty" from 60 to 15 percent over twenty years, and the *Washington Post*, probably relying on the same source, notes the "remarkable achievement" that "only one in seven Indonesians lives in poverty, as officially defined."[56]

But the World Bank is not an objective source, and its biases and blunders are notorious (most recently, it was caught in press with a book claiming that Indonesia's macrostability was greatly improved, just as the country plunged into the basket).[57] Furthermore, the claims of poverty reduction don't mesh well with other facts sometimes reported in the same news article. Shenon, for example, says that "the average Indonesian was the recipient of only $2 to $3 a day." In 1996, the Indonesian government acknowledged that the minimum wage of $2.26 a day was below subsistence for one person.[58] If the average wage is $2 to 3 a day, given the huge inequality of income distribution, there is no way that the numbers in poverty or even "abject poverty" can have fallen to 15 percent.

Furthermore, a pathbreaking *Wall Street Journal* article of July 14, 1998, dealt a devastating blow to the World Bank's (and mainstream media's) claims of poverty reduction. It is contended there that the bank, in collusion with the Suharto government, "softened reports on Indonesia's economy, reports that helped the government win better ratings and draw capital in . . . To the government, the World Bank reports became a smokescreen."[59] In its claims about poverty reduction, the bank accepted the Indonesian government's definition of poverty, which in fact "has been less than the globally accepted poverty line of $1 a day. Until the crisis, it was only about half that in Indonesia's cities, and less in the countryside." The *Journal* quotes former vice minister of planning, Mubyarto, who "flatly says the reported dramatic lowering of poverty rates was 'false,' and he accuses the World Bank of going along with it." Jeffrey Winter, a Northwestern University professor and former AID consultant in Jakarta, says the claimed reduction of poor numbers to 30 million "was a huge collusive effort . . . The number has been reported over and over, but it is a lie."[60]

This *Journal* article was rare indeed. The media have generally taken Indonesia's growth at face value, not only not questioning the possibly doctored numbers, but also never looking below the surface at the sources, costs, and distribution of benefits of that growth. Australian analyst Clive Hamilton says: "Can Indonesian growth have been a mirage? There is no denying the enormous dividends generated by Indonesia's oil reserves, and the extraordinary increases in agricultural yields due to the green revolution. These were pieces of luck the benefits of which even the massive inefficiency of the system of corruption could not entirely erode. In more recent years, the boom has been sustained by mining and logging on the one hand, and foreign investors in search of the other lucrative resource, cheap labor."[61] The media rarely discuss Indonesia's environmental destruction or rapid depletion of irreplaceable natural resources;[62] unmentioned in the accolades to growth were the huge fires of the past year, a manifestation of serious environmental abuse.

Would the media have allowed Pol Pot an offset if growth had taken place in Cambodia? Not too likely. In the case of Cuba there was significant growth for many years, and notable accomplishments in the provision of health care and a drop in mortality rates. But media reports on Cuba's human rights deficiencies rarely if ever mentioned these accomplishments as a counterbalance to the negatives. "Balance" seems to occur only with dictators who provide a favorable climate of investment.

Worthy Army

The Indonesian army has been ruthless, sometimes genocidal, specializing in the slaughter of unarmed civilians. It has also been notoriously corrupt, and has been heavily involved in economic ventures, bribery, and the buying and selling of office.[63] But it has long been trained and supplied by the United States and has served U.S. interests, a service that has included protecting the dictatorship from internal "security threats" (i.e., democratic forces).

It is not surprising, therefore, that the media have treated the Indonesian military, and U.S. relations with them, gently and uncritically. According to Steven Erlanger, the role of the Indonesian armed forces "includes political responsibilities, enshrined in national doctrine as the military's 'dual function': to defend the country from all threats, external and internal, and to take part directly in domestic political life and development." He added that although some in the military wanted Suharto to step down, they "do not wish to act unconstitutionally to encourage or accomplish that end."[64] With no comments on these statements affording even nominal balance, Erlanger legitimized the military role, the constitution, and the army's respect for a rule of law that was inoperative in a dictatorship. Seth Mydans did the same in 1998, noting without comment that "the armed forces have an explicit legal role as part of Indonesia's Government and administration."[65]

Mydans also repeatedly alleged that the army was "the one institution that enjoys broad support among most Indonesians," is "seen by most people as organized and efficient," and "not as a threat but as a promise of stability," so that "many Indonesians might welcome a seizure of power by the military."[66] Only a "leading editor" is cited on what "most people" feel, and because ascertaining their true feelings in a fear-ridden dictatorship would be difficult, the generalizations are clearly a projection of Mydans's pro-Indonesian army bias. Finally admitting in 1998 that Suharto's control was based "mostly on the fear he was able to instill,"[67] Mydans never explained how he determined that the public's hostility toward Suharto—an army man whose power was based on the army—did not extend to the army itself.

Much of the reporting about the military in 1998 concerned their actions against protesters, U.S. and other appeals for "restraint," reports of continued U.S. training of the Indonesian army, and the jockeying for position among the Indonesian generals. In the numerous articles devoted to the power struggle among the generals, there was little questioning of the propriety of army rule.[68] Shenon assured readers that General Wiranto is "described by associates as a thoughtful soldier who would ultimately put the interests of the nation and the military [apparently what is good for one is good for the other] ahead of the interests of the Indonesian president."[69] Catherine Dalpino, a former Clinton administration official who is now at the Brookings Institution, warns us to "refrain from demonizing the military,"[70] clearly a real threat from the U.S. establishment.

It was Allan Nairn, writing in *The Nation*, who first disclosed that the U.S. military was still training Kopassus, the most abusive and violent element of Indonesia's military forces (ABRI), in 1998.[71] Describing the close and increasing relations between U.S. and ABRI officials, Nairn argued that the U.S. was clearly counting on ABRI to continue to assure by its traditional modes of violence that U.S. aims in Indonesia were met. The United States had nurtured ABRI through the 1965–1966 massacres and 32 years of repression, and still "loves the army" (Nairn, quoting a U.S. official). The mainstream media picked up a part of this story, passing along without comment the U.S. army claim that its objective was to gain influence and bring a democratic and human rights perspective to the Indonesian military.[72] But the media ignored entirely Nairn's analysis of the sinister meaning of "gaining influence" in light of the historical role of the army and undeviating U.S. support of the army-based Suharto dictatorship. The argument of democratic intent, repeatedly advanced in defense of U.S. military aid to a stream of repressive governments, not only ignores history, it also fails to recognize that the decision to aid is necessarily supportive and strengthens the aid recipient. The media invariably fail to ask why U.S. military aid flows so regularly to repressive regimes and whether this might result from the fact that such governments serve U.S. imperial goals.

To its credit the *New York Times* acknowledged in a notable editorial that "The record of American training in repressive military cultures like Indonesia's is bleak."[73] The paper also reported Indonesian dissident Megawarti Sukarnopurti's criticism of U.S. military aid: "Noting that her country faces no foreign threat she suggested that the troops' real targets were Indonesians protesting against their Government."[74] But apart from this article there was virtually no critical analysis of the role U.S. military aid had played in consolidating the dictatorship and helping it fend off democratic threats. Nor was there any suggestion that the close and supportive relation between the United States and ABRI poses any threat to Indonesia's democratic prospects.

The *Times* did run several editorials that called upon the Indonesian military to withdraw from politics,[75] but none of them approach the severity of its editorial opinion on the Sandinista army of Nicaragua, which called for disarming the army.[76] The Sandinista army was a revolutionary army that supported what the Latin American Studies Association called "the logic of the majority"; the Indonesian army, far more deadly, has served the logic of transnational corporations, the Indonesian military, and the elite economic minority. The Indonesian army is therefore a "worthy" army, with a continuing role to play, in the view of the Western establishment, of which the mainstream media is a part.

The U.S.-Suharto Love Fest

Dealing with the U.S.-Suharto connection has always been a problem for the media, as we are supposedly opposed to mass murder, dictatorship, and looting. The problem has been handled by low-key and antiseptic treatment, failures to investigate, and by an unwillingness to acknowledge the importance of U.S. support in consolidating the dictatorship and keeping democratic forces and tendencies at bay. It was Kathy Kadane, working out of the small and local South Carolina *Herald-Journal*, who disclosed details on the U.S. participation in the 1965–1966 massacres,[77] not the major media. In fact, as with Gary Webb's reports on the CIA involvement in the contra-drug connection, the *New York Times* treated Kadane's work with hostility and in a defensive mode.[78] And as noted, it was Allan Nairn in *The Nation* who first reported the ongoing U.S. training of ABRI in 1998.

During the period of Suharto decline and fall the media could hardly fail to acknowledge that the U.S. "had maintained generally cordial relations with Indonesia" during the 32 year dictatorship.[79] That cordiality extended to support of Suharto himself virtually to the day of his resignation. The administration put its stress on "economic stability," not democracy, and the media noted that "Mr. Clinton's advisers do not deny that in stabilizing the Indonesian economy, they may also be stabilizing Mr. Suharto's hold on power,"[80] but first things first. The administration's claim that political developments should be judged on the basis of "inclusiveness, dialogue, and restraint by the military" (State Department's James Rubin), even elicited a touch of sarcasm: "While Rubin did not say so, critics of the former Indonesian leader say those principles were almost totally lacking during Suharto's 32 years in power.[81]

But for the most part, the media reported straight the administration claims of devotion to helping Indonesia "build a stable democracy" (Clinton), ignoring the record of support of "our kind of guy" and ABRI. The media continued to fail to analyze the 32-year love fest between the U.S. leadership and Suharto, the advantages of the dictatorship to U.S.-based companies, and its costs to the Indonesian people.

Explaining the Crisis

The mainstream media's explanations of the crisis that brought Suharto down closely followed the official line. The crisis was a result of Indonesia's failure to "reform" adequately, its lack of "transparency," and its corruption and privileged monopolies. This led the *Times*'s Thomas Friedman, Nicholas Kristof, and Anthony Lewis to proclaim that it was the "market" that ended Suharto's rule as it proceeded on its march toward democratizing the world. In Friedman's words, "When market forces concluded that Indonesia's economic growth was unsustainable without more democratic reform, they stampeded."[82]

A problem, however, is that "the market" loved Suharto through 32 years of dictatorship and poured huge investment resources into his undemocratic regime; and its repressive quality was clearly the basis of some of its most attractive features to the transnational corporate community. The 30 years of lavish lending to Suharto's regime by the World Bank never entailed any requirement on his part to democratize; nor was democracy on the list of IMF reforms when the crisis struck Indonesia in 1997. These market-loving institutions have never been fazed by dictatorship and terror, only by limits on the openness of markets to transnational corporations. Suharto's economic policies have also "long drawn praise from the World Bank and other institutions of economic orthodoxy,"[83] so that their ex post facto claims of serious failings in Indonesian policy don't ring true.

The market did help bring Suharto down, but inadvertently, and as a result of its own failures. Although the market is supposed to behave rationally, it was so enthused over the Suharto regime that it poured speculative funds into Indonesia, which were then withdrawn. Further lending ended in the financial debacle of 1997–1998, partly in recognition of serious market misjudgment. This brought down a dictator who the market had long prized, not because it recognized his defects, but because of overenthusiasm at the opportunities in his corrupt investors paradise, and the fact that the market is inherently unstable and can bring down its friends in its cyclical gyrations.

New World Order Justice

Speaking of Pol Pot, the *Times* says: "Time cannot erase the criminal responsibility of Pol Pot, whose murderous rule of Cambodia in the late 1970s brought death to about a million people, or one out of seven Cambodians. Trying him before an international tribunal would advance justice, promote healing in Cambodia and give pause to any fanatic tempted to follow his example."[84] But for the *Times*, and its media confreres, Suharto's killings in East Timor and West Papua—and the huge slaughter of 1965–1966—are not crimes and do not call for retribution or any kind of justice to the victims. Reporter David Sanger differentiates Suharto from Saddam Hussein, saying that "Mr. Suharto is not hoarding anthrax or threatening to invade Australia."[85] The fact that he killed 500,000 or more at home and invaded East Timor killing another 200,000 has disappeared from view. That is because this was constructive and benign terror carried out by a "good" genocidist.

Notes

1   David Sanger, "Real Politics: Why Suharto Is In and Castro Is Out," *New York Times*, 31 October 1995.

2   "Vengeance with a smile," *Time* (July 15, 1966), 26. For other expressions of establishment approval, see Noam Chomsky and Edward Herman, *The Washington Connection and Third World Fascism* (Boston: South End Press, 1979), 215–17.

3   Jane Mayer, "Indonesian Corruption Seen as Obstacle To Stronger Economic Ties With U.S.," *Wall Street Journal*, 1 May 1986.

4   Indonesia took over control of West Papua (or Irian Jaya) in 1962, and achieved United Nations recognition of this occupation in 1969. The Free Papua Movement estimates the number of deaths since 1962 at 150,000, most of them since the Suharto takeover. In 1983, the Anti-Slavery society in London put the possible death toll at around 200,000. See R. Osborne, *Indonesia's Secret War: The Guerrilla Struggle in Irian Jaya* (Sydney: Allen and Unwin, 1985, 146; C. Budiardjo and L.S. Liang, *West Papua: The Obliteration of a People* (Surrey: Tapol, 1988), 78–79.

5   The quotations are from Cyrus Sulzberger, "Foreign Affairs; As the Shadow Lengthens," *New York Times*, 3 December 1965, and James Reston, "Washington: A Gleam of Light," *New York Times*, 19 June, 1966. For further details on the warm reception given this holocaust, see Noam Chomsky, *Year 501* (Boston: South End Press, 1992), 126–31.

6   Henry Kamm, "Jakarta Says Most Political Prisoners Will Be Free in '79," *New York Times*, 12 April 1978.

7   Patrick Daniel Moynihan, *A Dangerous Place* (Boston: Little Brown, 1978), 247.

8   For some details, Chomsky and Herman, *The Washington Connection and Third World Fascism*, chap. 3.

9   Barbara Crossette, "East Timor Seeks To Open Its Doors," *New York Times*, 20 March 1988.

10 Henry Kamm, "Guerillas In Timor Still Fight Indonesia," *New York Times*, 19 April 1978.

11 Barbara Crossette, "For Suharto, A Whisper Of Defiance," *New York Times*, 13 March 1988; "East and West Are Knocking on Indonesia's Door," *New York Times*, 20 April 1986.

12 Ibid., 151.

13   Editorials, "Tears for Timor," *New York Times*, 25 July 1980; "The Tiananmen
     in East Timor," *New York Times*, 21 April 1992.

14   Editorial, "No Rest, Please, For the Wicked Pol Pot," *Chicago Tribune*, 18 April
     1998; Editorial, "'Killing Fields' Are Unavenged," *Los Angeles Times*, 17 April
     1998; Marvin Ott, "Khmer Rouge by Any Other Name Is Still Evil," *Washington
     Post*, 17 April 1998.

15   Henry Kamm, "The Silent Suffering of East Timor," *New York Times Magazine*,
     15 February 1981.

16   "Economic despair turns protests violent," *USA Today*, 14 May 1998.

17   Nicholas Kristof, "Suharto, a King of Java Past, Confronts Indonesia's Future,"
     New York Times, 17 May 1998.

18   Steven Erlanger, "Suharto Fostered Rapid Economic Growth, and Staggering
     Graft," *New York Times*, 22 May 1998.

19   Seth Mydans, "Indonesia, in Drama's Grip, Warily Awaits Finale," *New York
     Times*, 2 June 1998; Mydans, "Suharto, Besieged, Steps Down After 32–Year
     Rule in Indonesia," *New York Times*, 21 May 1998.

20   Seth Mydans, "Pol Pot Cremated; No Tears Are Shed," *New York Times*, 19
     April, 1998; Mydans, "For Pol Pot, An Endgame," 13 April 1998.

21   Mydans, "Suharto Besieged, Steps Down."

22   Stephen Myers, "Amid Turmoil, Pentgon Chief Visits Suharto," *New York Times*,
     15 January 1998.

23   See Keith Richburg, "Suharto's Ace: He's the Only Game in Town," *Washington
     Post*, 23 February 1998; Cindy Shiner, "Cries of Freedom Sound in Jakarta,"
     Washington Post, 26 May 1998.

24   Seth Mydans, "Protesters Angered by Raid Battle Police in Indonesia," *Wall Street
     Journal*, 28 July 1996.

25   See Robert Cribb, ed., *The Indonesian Killings 1965–1966* (Clayton Victoria,
     Australia: Monash University, 1990), 8–14; Chomsky and Herman, *Washington
     Connection*, 206–209.

26   See especially, Michael Vickery, *Cambodia: 1975–1982* (Boston: South End
     Press, 1982), 184–88.

27   Philip Shenon, "U.S. Seeks China's Help In Arranging Pol Pot Trial," *New York
     Times*, 11 April 1998; Editorial, "A Trial for Pol Pot," 24 June 1997.

28   Philip Shenon, "After the Reign of Terror, Safe Harbor," *New York Times*, 19
     April 1998; Editorial, "Death of an executioner," *Boston Globe*, 17 April 1998.

29   Henry Kamm, "Indonesia Looks Warily Toward Iran For Lessons," *New York
     Times*, 17 June 1979.

30   Seth Mydans, "Indonesia Moves Quickly to Suppress a Budding Opposition," *New York Times*, 7 August 1996.

31   "Suharto: After 30 Years, A Swift End," *New York Times*, 21 May 1998.

32   For an alternative view, see the statement of Ben Anderson and Ruth McVey in *Human Rights in Indonesia and the Philippines*, House Hearings of the Committee on International Relations, 94th cong., Dec. 18, 1976, 49–54.

33   Cribb, *The Indonesian Killings*, 21, 26.

34   Thomas Friedman, "Living Dangerously," *New York Times*, 10 July 1998.

35   Steven Erlanger, "East Timor, Reopened by Indonesia, Remains a Sad and Terrifying Place," *New York Times*, 21 October 1990.

36   Ibid.

37   Steven Erlanger, *New York Times*, 21 November 1988; Aryeh Neier, "Indonesia's Human Rights Record Worse," *New York Times*, 28 December 1988.

38   Philip Shenon, "Indonesia Seeks to Atone for a Massacre in Timor," *New York Times*, 17 September 1992.

39   Seth Mydans, "Indonesian Leader Softens Stand on the Status of East Timor," *New York Times*, 11 June 1998.

40   Thomas Lippman, "No White House Meeting for East Timor Advocate; Nobel Peace Prize Winner Fails to Gain a Cabinet-Level Audience," *Washington Post*, 28 May 1997.

41   Mydans, "Indonesian Leader Softens Stand on the Status of East Timor."

42   Willian Branigan, "Nepotism, Cronyism, Undercut President," *Washington Post*, 21 May 1998.

43   Editorial, "For a Vote in East Timor," *New York Times*, 8 July 1998; Editorial, "Opportunity in Indonesia," *Washington Post*, 8 June 1998; Editorial, "Timor time," *Financial Times*, 30 May 1998.

44   Seth Mydans, "Suharto's Fortune Drawing New Fire," *New York Times*, 30 May 1998.

45   See especially, Philip Shenon, "For Asian Nation's First Family, Financial Empire Is in Peril," *New York Times*, 16 January 1998; Seth Mydans, "Sukarno [sic] & Company: Out, Yes, but Still Hugely Rich," *New York Times*, 25 May 1998; Joseph Kahn, "Kin Earned Riches, Says New Leader Of Indonesia," *New York Times*, 3 June 1998; Keith Richburg, "Cashing in on Years in Power; The Suharto Fortune," *Washington Post*, 22 May 1998.

46   Barbara Crossette, "In Indonesia, a Lull Without a Storm," *New York Times*, 2 February 1987.

47   Nicholas Kristof, "Indonesia Is Not the Philippines, Yet," *New York Times*, 17 May 1998.

48   Mydans, "Indonesia, in Drama's Grip, Warily Awaits Finale."

49   Kamm, "Indonesia Looks Warily Toward Iran For Lessons."

50   Keith Richburg, "Suharto's Ace: He's the Only Game in Town," *Washington Post*, 23 February 1998.

51   David Sanger and Seth Mydans, "Sudden Weakness Aside, Suharto Looks to Outlast Economic Crisis," *New York Times*, 18 January 1998.

52   Seth Mydans, "Suharto, Besieged, Steps Down After 32-Year Rule in Indonesia," *New York Times*, 21 May 1998.

53   Kristof, "Indonesia Is Not The Philippines, Yet."

54   Keith Richburg, "Long-Ruling Indonesian Faces Signs of Discontent," *Washington Post*, 24 May 1997; Seth Mydans, "Indonesian Governing Party Wins Yet Another Landslide," *New York Times*, 30 May 1997.

55   Philip Shenon, "As Indonesia Crushes Its Critics, it Helps Millions Escape Poverty," *New York Times*, 27 August 1993.

56   Editorial, "Indonesia: A Chance to Breathe," *Washington Post*, 16 May 1997.

57   For an account of this Bank publication, see David Felix, "Asia and the Crisis of Financial Globalization," mimeo, Economics Department, Washington University in St. Louis, 1998.

58   Edward Gargan, "One Indonesian Asset is also a Liability," *New York Times*, 16 March 1996.

59   Marcus Brauchli, "Speak No Evil: Why the World Bank Failed to Anticipate Indonesia's Crisis," *Wall Street Journal*, 14 July 1998.

60   Ibid.

61   Clive Hamilton, "IMF Stuck in Soeharto's Mire," *Australian Financial Review* (March 18, 1998).

62   See however, Keith Richburg, "Captive Of a Boom Gone Bust," *Washington Post*, 12 October 1997.

63   See Richard Robison, "Class Analysis of the Indonesian Military State, *Indonesia* (April 1978).

64   Steven Erlanger. "Indonesia Military Weighing Its Roles," *New York Times*, 11 October 1990.

65   Seth Mydans, "Many Indonesians See Military as Rock of Stability," *New York Times*, 16 February 1998.

66   Ibid.; Mydans, "Unrest in Indonesia: the Generals," *New York Times*, 15 May 1998; Mydans, "Indonesia, in Drama's Grip, Warily Awaits Finale."

67   Seth Mydans, "Suharto Finds Friends Are Few Now That He's Just an Ex-V.I.P.," *New York Times*, 9 June 1998.

68   Keith Richburg, "Armed Forces Could Back Regime and Suppress Protests, Or Pressure President," *Washington Post*, 10 May 1998; Mark Landler, "In Indonesia, the Grab for Power May Hinge on the Rivaly of Two Generals," *New York Times*, 18 May 1998.

69   Philip Shenon, "U.S. to Appeal to Indonesia Military to Stop Crackdown," *New York Times*, 14 May 1998.

70   Catherine Dalpino, "Indonesia: A New Approach," *Washington Post*, 28 May 1998.

71   Allan Nairn, "Indonesia's Killers," *The Nation* (March 30, 1998).

72   Dana Priest, "Indonesia and U.S. Military," *Washington Post*, 15 May 1998.

73   Editorial, "Military Mischief in Indonesia," *New York Times*, 23 March 1998.

74   Tim Weiner,"Jakarta Dissident Questions U.S. Military Aid," *New York Times*, 25 March 1998.

75   See Editorials, "Military Mischief in Indonesia," *New York Times*, 23 May 1998; "The Duty of Indonesia's Generals," 1 June 1998.

76   Editorial, "Disarm Nicaragua," *New York Times*, 7 March 1990.

77   Kathy Kadane, "US aided '65 massacre of Indonesian left, ex-officials say," *Boston Globe*, 23 May 1990.

78   Michael Wines, "CIA Tie Asserted in Indonesia Purge," *New York Times*, 12 July, 1990.

79   Norman Kempster and Art Pine, "Clinton Welcomes Decision by Suharto, Calls for Reform," *Los Angeles Times*, 22 May 1998.

80   David Sanger, "The Indonesian Tangle: How It Enmeshes the U.S.," *New York Times*, 6 May 1998.

81   Kempster and Pine, "Clinton Welcomes Decision by Suharto."

82   Thomas Friedman, "Where's The Crisis," *New York Times*, 23 May 1998; Nicholas Kristof, "Suharto's Stealth Foe: Globalizing Capitalism," *New York Times*, 20 May 1998; Anthony Lewis, "Their Suharto and Ours," *New York Times*, 25 May 1998.

83   Paul Blustein, "Indonesia's Rupiah Continues to Stumble; Southeast Asia's Currency Crisis Worsens,' *Washington Post*, 7 October 1997.

84   Editorial, "Bringing Pol Pot to Justice," *New York Times*, 10 April 1998.

85 David Sanger, "Indonesia Faceoff; Drawing Blood Without Bombs," *New York Times*, 8 March 1998.

Chapter 17

Corporate Junk Science in the Media

One of the ideological rationales of capitalism is that consumers are sovereign, their demands ultimately ruling the system, with producers only responding to consumer needs and wants. In reality, by virtue of their immense resources and power, producers, not consumers, are sovereign.

Producer Sovereignty and the Rule of Corporate Convenience

This is dramatically evident in the recent history of the chemical industry, in which "the corporation's convenience has been allowed to rule national policy," as was acknowledged in an exceptional President's Science Advisory Committee report on *Restoring the Quality of Environment* back in 1965,[1] produced in the wake of Rachel Carson's 1962 classic, *Silent Spring*. In accord with corporate convenience, chemicals may be marketed without proof of safety, and the onus is on consumers and the public to prove otherwise. Those suffering injury or death in consequence, or their heirs, may sue for damages; however, not only is the burden of proof unfairly located, but damaged individuals are at a huge disadvantage when they seek relief because of difficulties in proving cause and the imbalance in the resources of plaintiffs and producers. These difficulties are compounded by the informational and legal strategies of producers, and form part of the basis on which producers make their business decisions.

If consumers were sovereign, or if this were a truly democratic community, the principles applicable to rights and obligations in production would be *precautionary* and there would be *reverse onus*. That is, goods would not be put into the market unless they were assuredly safe, based on full and adequate testing (the precautionary principle); and the responsibility for failures to assure safety would fall on the producers (the reverse onus principle). Under producer sovereignty these are rejected in favor of the principle of caveat emptor (buyer beware), the selection of applicable principle resting on the ability of the powerful to institutionalize rights that serve themselves.

The producers of chemicals must of course meet a market test—that the goods be salable—but chemicals may do the job for which they are designed (e.g., kill mosquitos) while producing side effects that are extremely harmful. Obviously, if workers or consumers using a product were to fall over dead upon contact the product would not sell, but if damaging effects on users, and on outsiders and the general environment, are not immediately evident, producers may be able to sell profitably for a lengthy period, and with an effective use of corporate junk science, political power, and litigation they may be able to maintain profitability in excess of legal damage costs indefinitely.

Corporate Junk Science

"Junk science," defined as the science geared toward serving political and propaganda ends, plays an extremely important role in the public relations and regulatory strategies of the chemical industry. It aims, first, to reassure the public that pesticides and other chemicals are not a public health threat and are essential to economic growth and welfare. But it is also designed to create enough confusion and uncertainty among legislators and regulators, as well as the public, to preserve the industry's freedom to pour chemicals into the environment. The industry has been highly successful in pursuit of this two-pronged strategy, based in large measure on its resources and numerous scientists on the corporate payroll and consequent power over politicians, regulators, and the media.

Although the chemical industry regularly claims a devotion to "good science," and does surely apply strictly scientific standards in developing its products, the record shows that in its political and propaganda outreach the industry's criterion is strictly pragmatic: Good science is that which yields congenial results, irrespective of scientific quality. The industry's opportunism here is remarkable. In one case involving the testing of the health effects of saccharin, although the methodology used in the study had been approved in advance by the industry and preliminary "favorable" results were greeted enthusiastically, as the final results did not meet industry desires the testing methodology was immediately under attack.[2] The industry regularly points to animal tests as proof that products are safe for humans, but when they yield unfavorable results the use of animals in drawing inferences on human effects ceases to be good science.[3]

Numerous false purportedly scientific statements have been made by the industry, directly or through closely controlled proxies. This goes back a long way. In 1925, shortly after a conference at which numerous public health authorities and scientists gave evidence on the poisonous effects of the use of lead in gasoline, Dr. Emery Hayhurst, a paid consultant to Ethyl Corporation, wrote that scientific evidence showed that leaded gasoline afforded "complete safety as far as the public health is concerned."[4] The cigarette company leaders have sworn under oath that they believe cigarettes are not addictive, whereas internal documents state that "We are . . . in the business of selling nicotine, an addictive drug."[5] In 1996, Borden stated, falsely, that "Various studies over a period of years demonstrate that formaldehyde neither causes asthma nor has an effect on asthmatics different from its effects on persons who are not asthmatics."[6]

More serious than individual lies is the fact that the rich chemical industry can dominate science important to its interests by buying up most of the experts. Of scientists working on insecticides, 85 percent of them work for industry, 4 percent for the government, and 11 percent in universities without industry contracts.[7] This allows industry to define what is worked on, and much of that work is to find defenses for what industry wants to sell. To a remarkable degree, industry-hired scientists come to conclusions sought by their employers. Even vinyl chloride (VC) was found safe by an industry-funded study by the University of Louisville's Vinyl Chloride Project.[8] Fagin and Lavelle show that of 43 studies of the safety of four major insecticides financed by industry, in 32 (74 percent) they were found safe, whereas in 118 studies of the same chemicals not so funded only 27 (23 percent) had similarly favorable results (71, or 60 percent were distinctly unfavorable).[9] A 1997 Canadian study of research on calcium channel blockers, a hypertension and angina drug, found a very strong correlation between an industry financial connection and a finding that the drug was beneficial.[10]

The chemical industry, like tobacco, has established its own research institutes to produce good science. One, the Environmental Sensitivities Research Institute (ESRI), was founded to deal with multiple chemical sensitivity (MCS), an ailment afflicting great numbers and brought into prominence because of its possible applicability to the symptoms of Gulf War veterans and women with silicone breast implants. One theory regarding MCS is that severe toxic exposure leads to a loss of chemical tolerance.[11] Another view is that the evidence "strongly suggests behav-

ioral and psychogenic explanations for symptoms."[12] It should be no surprise that the last view is the "good science" espoused by ESRI.

In an important case of doctored evidence in research, Monsanto's
1979–1980 study of workers who had been exposed to dioxin while
making Agent Orange found no link to worker deaths. But during a worker
lawsuit against Monsanto in 1984, defense lawyers discovered that four
workers classified as "unexposed" in the dioxin study had been classed as
"exposed" in another Monsanto study. This shift, confirmed by one of the
authors under oath, affected the results—when corrected, the dioxin link
had significant effects on worker deaths.[13] Industry research has also
employed other dirty tricks, such as using too few animals; allowing too
little time to elapse for symptoms to appear; and testing for only one of
numerous possible negative effects (as in silicone breast implants testing),
pretending that the test of this single effect gives the definitive answer.[14]
Back in 1969, a commission on pesticides, reviewing 17 industry-spon-
sored studies of the carcinogenicity of DDT, concluded "that fourteen of
these studies were so inherently defective as to preclude any determination of carcinogenicity."[15] But such studies serve the industry well.

Control Over the Media's Agenda

In addition to its political power and domination of research, the chemical
industry's success has depended on its ability to influence the media and
set the agenda by which the issues are discussed (or ignored). Industry
success here has not been total, but it has been remarkable given the
public health consequences of virtually unconstrained chemical industry
growth and the resultant "epidemic in slow motion" that continues un-
abated.[16] The industry has succeeded in controlling the deeper agenda,
which takes for granted the industry's right to produce and sell chemicals
not fully tested for hazards by any independent agency; its right to do this
without any clear industry responsibility for negative outcomes; and its
right to chemicalize the environment without full disclosure. These basic
assumptions, and the grossly inadequate regulatory process that supposedly protects the public, are not subject to ongoing debate.

A Silent Spring, a Love Canal or Bhopal disaster, a reported decline
in male sperm count, or a regulatory scandal can cause a brief flurry, but
the flurry is brief, the media fail to dig deeply and press the issue, and
more important issues—anti-U.S. terrorism, monitoring Iraq's weapons,
Clinton's sex life, stock market movements—quickly take over. These more
important matters can obtain intensive coverage that is sustained long

enough to affect public attitudes; the epidemic in slow motion does not. The media even tend to feature and institutionalize industry junk science claims (e.g., on Alar and dioxin, discussed below) while entirely ignoring numerous major findings on chemical damage and cases of regulatory failure.

A key piece of evidence of fundamental media bias is found in the media's usage of the phrase "junk science." The chemical industry applies the phrase to the science advanced by environmentalists, progressive critics of industry, and lawyers suing the industry for poisoning people; they contrast it with "good science," which, as noted, is any science that supports industry positions. And the mainstream media follow the corporate lead, like watchdogs of property rather than of any public interest. In the years 1996 through September 1998, of 258 articles in mainstream newspapers that used the phrase "junk science," only 21, or 8 percent, used it to refer to corporate junk science—these mainly referring to cigarette industry disclosures—whereas 160, or 62 percent, applied it to the science used by environmentalists, other corporate critics, or tort lawyers suing corporations (77, or 30 percent, did not fit any of these categories).[17] The news magazines have been equally biased. Newsweek, for example, finding Dow-Corning's 1998 breast implant settlement "a victory for junk science," goes on to say that "O.J. can hire scientists to cast doubt on those DNA matches; a drunken driver can hire scientists to explain away his blood-alcohol content as a metabolic anomaly, or to question testing methods."[18] That's all. The magazine never suggests that any chemical company might hire a scientist to give a twisted version of scientific evidence. It has internalized industry usage.

The Rachel Carson Exception

The publication of Rachel Carson's Silent Spring in 1962,[19] preceded by a derived series of articles in the New Yorker, temporarily broke the chemical industry's command over the flow of information on pesticides and other chemicals. There had been critical articles and letters of protest over the broadscale use of DDT and other poisons, but these were only occasional and hardly disturbed the industry's informational hegemony.

As was pointed out by Frank Graham Jr., Carson's book "marked the end of closed debate in the field. Rachel Carson uncovered the hiding places of facts that should have been disclosed to the public long before; she broke the information barrier."[20] Her book came into public view shortly after the revelations of the devastating effects of thalidomide, which reinforced her message's stress on inadequate controls over the use of chemicals. Eloquently written and well-documented, Carson's book struck a chord and provided a coherent justification for public fears that had been suppressed by industry informational domination. A serious alternative viewpoint was suddenly placed on the public agenda. With the Kennedy administration also relatively receptive to the new message, it came across to the public with exceptional force. A major *CBS Reports* broadcast of April 3, 1963, seen by 10 to 15 million people, was organized around Carson and her book and message. The sympathetic program "allowed her and not her critics to define the issue."[21]

Carson was able to attack the deeper agenda and question whether we should allow "poisoning us first, then policing the result." Although she assailed the testing and regulatory process, Carson's main focus was on the long-term and ecological effects of heavy chemical use and the need for a concerted effort to find alternatives to chemicals. The raising of basic questions frightened the industry and it struck back wildly, with emotional cries about Carson's emotionalism as well as crude efforts at censorship (threatening libel suits, getting three of five advertisers to withdraw from sponsoring the CBS report, among other tactics). But while the industry failed to discredit Carson, and she undoubtedly gave great impetus to an emerging environmental movement, her ability to attack the deeper agenda in the mainstream media was exceptional. Thereafter, the industry, having learned a lesson in public relations, and with ever enlarging resources and a basically friendly corporate media, would deal more effectively with challenges to its informational hegemony. It quickly regained control of the deep agenda, and although it has lost many small battles, its domination of the agenda is almost as great now as in the pre-Carson era.

The Continuing Right to Poison Us First

After the furor over *Silent Spring* in the early 1960s, there was no slackening in the production and use of pesticides either here or abroad. Although the 1965 President's Science Advisory Committee report on *Restoring the Quality of the Environment* had called for the "orderly reduction in the use of persistent pesticides" as a policy goal, there was never any attempt to realize this goal. Pesticide use doubled in this country over the next 30 years, from 540 million pounds in 1964 to well over a billion pounds in 1993; intensity of application per acre of farmland more than doubled; and pesticide use in households and home lawn care skyrocketed. Some poisons such as DDT and PCBs were eventually banned but others took their place, and dozens of chemicals that are carcinogens or have known damaging effects on neurological and immune systems remain in widespread use.

Atrazine, a suspected human carcinogen, is one of the most widely used pesticides in U.S. agriculture and has contaminated ground water supplies over virtually the entire country. In *Toxic Deception*, Fagin and Lavelle describe how Ciba-Geigy (now called Novartis) has been able to keep atrazine in the market for 30 years, despite the accumulating evidence of its dangers, by manipulating science, the Environmental Protection Agency (EPA), the political system, and the media. This is a major story of political-regulatory-scientific corruption with serious public health consequences. But the mainstream media have not been interested. As members of the corporate system the media's role has been to protect the powerful chemical industry's rights, to avoid and deflect fundamental criticism, and to normalize the ongoing arrangements. As in the case of the military budget, we sometimes get brief, usually back-page, pieces of information on damage and scandals, but a great deal of information is blacked out, and serious and extended analyses and debates about the industry's abuses, modes of self-protection, social costs, and alternatives to poisoning are off the agenda.

Industry's ongoing right to poison first has been dramatically illustrated in recent years by the introduction of Monsanto's recombinant bovine hormone drug rBGH and some two dozen genetically engineered food crops. As in the case of chemicals, this has been done almost entirely on the basis of industry assurances of safety, without testing or serious independent evaluation of potential downstream effects. As Peter Montague says, "Putting genetically-engineered plants and animals into the natural environment is nothing more than a crap shoot—one with potential consequences far greater than Monsanto's previous calamitous experiments, polychlorinated biphenyls (PCBs) and Agent Orange."[22] Harvard geneticist Richard Lewontin says that "I would be surprised if we don't get one rude shock after another" under a regime of engineered plants.[23] It is already a concern of U.S. organic farmers that Monsanto's incorporation into its potato seed of a gene from the bacteria bacillus thuriengensis (Bt)—which kills Colorado potato beetles—will quickly bring forth resistant insects, thus harming organic farmers who use Bt sparingly.[24] A recent study of the effects of growing genetically modified crops on a commercial scale in Britain, commissioned by the British government, concluded that there were insufficient safeguards to prevent the creation of hybrid, multi-resistant plants, and that such a development posed major dangers to British hedgerows, birds, and indigenous plants.[25]

But Monsanto and its comrades have invested vast sums in biological research, and they want a market payoff now. Long-term ecological and safety effects have never been a prime concern of the chemical industry and Phil Angell, publicity director of Monsanto, acknowledged recently that safety is not his company's business or responsibility: "Our interest is in selling as much of it as possible. Assuring its safety is the F.D.A.'s job."[26] Of course, when the FDA [or EPA] is too aggressive about safety, the industry works hard to weaken or capture the agency to make it responsive to industry demands. If successful, as is often the case, the industry can produce and sell without much impediment based on possible safety threats, while claiming that the FDA [or EPA] is taking care of safety and the public interest!

rBGH has not been accepted for use in Canada because, among other reasons, no long-term toxicology studies were ever required of its manufacturer, and Canada's science evaluators concluded that the only short-term toxicology study was improperly reported by both Monsanto and the FDA to have found that the growth hormone "was not and could not be absorbed into the bloodstream." Thus, despite a reported $1 to $2 million bribe offer from Monsanto for an expedited approval and support for the company by the top officials of the Canadian health regulatory body, Monsanto's effort there remains stymied.[27]

Despite the Canadian setback, and the fact that European authorities and many scientists have grave doubts about the effects of genetic engineering on human health and ecology, it has moved ahead in the United States without serious regulatory impediment or public debate within the media. One exception was the critical article by Michael Pollan on "Playing God in the Garden,"[28] but this article stood alone in the major media. The Canadian dispute, which included the dramatic bribe effort by Monsanto and the recent disclosure of a highly critical British government-sponsored report on the risks of genetically engineered food, were both ignored by the mainstream U.S. media.

Another manifestation of industry control has been the media's selective treatment of books on the environment. Those that seriously challenge the industry tend to be ignored; those compatible with the industry's agenda and that attack the industry's enemies get more generous treatment. The *New York Times*, for example, has never reviewed Samuel Epstein's *Politics of Cancer* (1978), Marc Lappé's *Chemical Deception* (1991), Jennifer Curtis and Tim Profeta's *After Silent Spring* (1993), Fagin and Lavelle's *Toxic Deception* (1995), John Wargo's *Our Children's Toxic Legacy* (1996), or the eloquent personal-scientific memoir by Sandra Steingraber, *Living Downstream* (1996). Theo Colbourn, John Peterson

Myers, and Dianne Dumanoski's *Our Stolen Future* (1996) was given an extremely hostile review by Gina Kolata (discussed further below).

Joe Thornton's *Science For Sale* (1990), published by Greenpeace, which described Monsanto's abuse of science in its dioxin studies, was neither reviewed nor mentioned by the *New York Times*, *Washington Post*, or *Los Angeles Times*. On the other hand, *Galileo's Revenge* (1991), by Peter Huber of the Manhattan Institute, with an industry-friendly perspective, was reviewed in both the *New York Times* and *Los Angeles Times*. And Marcia Angell's *Science on Trial* (1996), which "portrays Dow-Corning as a near-innocent raped by scurrilous plaintiffs and lawyers,"[29] was reviewed twice in the *New York Times* (as well as in the *Washington Post* and widely elsewhere). Gregg Easterbrook's *A Moment on the Earth* (1995), which celebrated the successes of environmentalism, chided environmentalists as negativists, and suggested that things were under good control—a book described by scientist Peter Raven as offering "a Panglossian world view, in which he offers us a sugar-coated invitation to inaction"[30]—was greeted warmly in all the mainstream media. It was also welcomed by the chemical industry because it met their crucial demand of reassurance as well as offering minimal criticism of the industry or regulatory system.

Normalizing Damage from Chemicalization

In *Living Downstream*, Sandra Steingraber places great stress on the fact that although cancer rates have increased steadily in tandem with the chemicalization of the environment, and hundreds of micro-studies have shown the linkage in particular cases, the connection "has not been pursued in any systematic, exhaustive way. The environment . . . keeps falling off the cancer screen."[31] She illustrates this, among many other ways, by the fact that when an Illinois State Cancer Registry was established in 1984 to monitor health effects of hazardous substances, the cancer registry was funded but not the registry of hazardous substances (which industry strenuously opposed). She notes how regularly public authorities and public educational campaigns stress "lifestyle" causes of cancer, not environmental facts related to industry products and wastes.[32] She hints at what I believe is obvious: that the chemical industry, desiring that environmental causes be played down, has succeeded in getting governments and mainstream educators to do the same.

And so do the mainstream media, which have had hundreds of opportunities to open the Pandora's box—but with each report suggesting chemical damage, the media at best give the local facts, with "balance"; at worst, they ignore or misread such reports. And they don't allow the facts to provoke a larger investigation. Thus a typical news report tells us that the EPA has decided to permit the continued use of alachlor "despite its potential for causing cancer and contamination of the drinking water supplies in farm communities," because of the "substantial benefits" that "outweigh the risks." Environmentalists are angry at the decision, whereas Monsanto says that it reflects "good science"; and this superficial account and "balanced" debate was given a short article on page 25 of the *Washington Post* (December 16, 1987). Similarly, an AP dispatch in the *New York Times* of October 19, 1994, entitled "Midwesterners Getting Pesticides in Drinking Water, Study Says," featured the Environmental Working Group's claim that 3.5 million midwesterners faced a substantial cancer risk from the presence of numerous pesticides in their water. But the substance of the study was given with great brevity, with superficial history and context, and the study's claims were balanced by reassurances from the EPA and denials by industry. The article was placed on page A20, and had neither editorial support nor follow-up.

The International Joint Commission (IJC), a joint U.S. and Canadian venture dating back to 1978, was given the formidable task of trying to halt the flow of toxic chemicals into the Great Lakes. It reports each year that it has failed to stem the tide and that the toxic flow continues to increase and is seriously damaging to human health. From 1992 onward the annual reports of the IJC have called for an ending of the use of chlorine in manufacturing as the crucial requirement for meeting its assigned task. The commission finds, not surprisingly, that industry is not interested in curtailing the use of chlorine. But the national media also treat the IJC's annual reports with extreme brevity and no follow-up. The IJC's U.S. co-chairman Gordon Durnil has remarked that "we have a societal problem about how to deal with this, but 90 percent of the population doesn't even know there's anything to worry about."[33]

Normalizing Regulatory Failure

In accord with industry domination of the media's environmental perspective, the media portray the EPA as a powerhouse organization that is perhaps too aggressive and adversarial in its pursuit of the public interest. The reality—a seriously underfunded organization, unable to do its job properly, sometimes captured and often driven to industry-friendly compromises—can only be grasped, if at all, by a very close, often between-the-lines study of media reporting.[34] The media have normalized the fact that, contrary to the stated aim of the 1976 Toxic Substances Control Act, the EPA has not been able to cope with the toxic chemical flood, and an estimated 70 to 75 percent of the chemicals in wide use have still not been tested for toxicity.

Neither does the media focus on the evidence that the system of leaving safety-testing to industry has failed. For example, in the course of a struggle with Monsanto over the company's right to introduce Santogard between 1986 and 1990, the EPA discovered that some years back Monsanto had found negative effects of Santogard in a study that the company had failed to submit to the EPA, contrary to law. Monsanto was fined $196,000, although by law the fine should have been $19.7 million.[35] The company was then allowed to search for other delinquent toxicity studies, and turned up 164, for which it was fined another nominal $648,000. Realizing that the other chemical companies were also probably failing to submit studies the EPA arranged an "amnesty" with the industry, promising only nominal fines for the next three years in exchange for the industry coughing up previously hidden studies. Under this amnesty the industry produced some 11,000 documents![36] Although the nominal fines, and the demonstration of a massive industry failure to provide evidence of chemical effects as required by law, showed gross inadequacies in the ongoing methods of evaluating chemical risks, the media did not find this story of even passing interest.

Equally sensational, and even more revealing of EPA's regulatory weakness and frequent connivance with industry, was the sequence of events surrounding dioxin regulation between 1986 and 1993. The paper and pulp industry, which produces dioxin, became worried over the regulatory threat in the 1980s. In their book *No Margin of Safety*, published by Greenpeace in August 1987, Paul Merrell and Carol Van Strum showed how the EPA colluded with the paper industry to keep information out of the public domain, to characterize any information they were compelled to release as "preliminary," and to fix dioxin standards at politically acceptable levels. Following publication of the book, a paper industry official leaked 300 pages of documents to Greenpeace, which fully confirmed the claims in *No Margin of Safety*, demonstrating joint EPA-industry planning to lower the risk assessment of dioxin and to assuage public fears by reassurances of safety and by labeling study results as only preliminary.

Although AP and UPI each put out a news report based on the disclosures in *No Margin of Safety*, neither the *New York Times* nor the *Washington Post* picked them up or reported the story. The sensational paper industry inside material was first offered as an exclusive to the *New York Times*, and an article based on it was prepared, but was killed by higher authority. The *Times* article that eventually did appear merely noted that "industry executives were concerned about public responses when the contamination of paper products became known."[37] Not only was the evidence of industry-EPA collusion suppressed, the article also stated that the EPA had "found less contamination than officials had expected," which, given the suppressed internal documents' proof of the EPA's agreement to help soften the public impact of the findings, represents exceptionally dishonest journalism. The *Washington Post*, after publishing an article that reported the EPA's finding that dioxin levels were "seen as no threat to health,"[38] did finally devote a piece to the industry's public relations campaign and attempt to influence the EPA, with hints that this campaign was successful.[39] But the article, which was framed as a public relations problem for the paper industry, was placed on page 23 and had no follow-up.

Equally enlightening has been the media's treatment of evidence of industry falsification of data. The EPA's fixing of tolerances on dioxin was based in part on Monsanto and BASF studies of the effects of accidents involving dioxin. As noted earlier, these studies, which claimed no serious human damage, were both eventually shown to have been fatally compromised by data manipulation; when corrected for the tricks used (mainly inappropriate inclusions and exclusions of workers), there were significant negative health results. Monsanto's falsifications and their implications for dioxin regulation were brought to the attention of EPA officials—as well as environmentalists and veterans groups that had been adversely affected by the industry's junk science—by EPA chemist Cate Jenkins in 1991. EPA began a criminal investigation of Monsanto's fraud, which was quietly dropped following Monsanto pressure and private exchanges and assurances between the company and EPA officials. On the other hand, Cate Jenkins, the whistleblower, was subjected to harassment and a series of internal legal proceedings (all of which failed).[40]

Neither the *New York Times* nor the *Washington Post* ever mentioned the Monsanto/BASF frauds, the abortive EPA criminal investigation of Monsanto, Cate Jenkins and her memos on the dioxin frauds and regulation, or her persecution as a whistleblower. What makes this blackout especially important is the fact that both the *Post* and the *Times* lined up with the paper industry during this period in claiming that "good science" was showing the old dioxin nemesis to have been inflated. So just as Monsanto and BASF doctored evidence, so the major papers doctored the news, suppressed negative evidence on both the quality of industry's "good science" and EPA-industry collusion (with a partial exception in the *Post*'s treatment of the collusion scandal of 1986–1987), and scoffed at the dioxin "scare" (discussed further below).

In 1993 the National Research Council published a report on *Pesticides in the Diets of Infants and Children*, which showed that in establishing pesticide "tolerances" the EPA and FDA had used adults as the standard and failed to take into account the fact that children are far more vulnerable. The report called for a new health-based approach to pesticide tolerances with a focus on the biology of children. This study, which would seem important in its implications for public health and in demonstrating a pro-industry bias in regulatory standards, was given minimal attention by the mainstream media. More recently, Monsanto successfully petitioned the EPA to increase allowable residue levels for the chemical glyphosate, the active ingredient in its genetically reengineered soybean Roundup Ready, from 6 to 20 parts per million. As Marc Lappé and Britt Baily note, what was "safe" in 1987 "was considered 'safe' eight years later at three times the original tolerance."[41] This regulatory change was not discussed in the mainstream media.

Normalizing the Right Not-To-Know

For decades the chemical industry has fought against disclosure of the effects of its products on the grounds of "proprietary information" and the free speech right to be silent. Although full disclosure would seem especially urgent when products can harm and potential victims need to know as much as possible to deal with damage, the industry has been remarkably successful in preserving its right to silence and the public's right not-to-know. Worker knowledge of the effects of workplace chemicals came only by decades of struggle, and it wasn't until 1986, after Bhopal (and a leakage of the Bhopal death chemical in West Virginia), that Congress finally passed an Emergency Planning and Community Right-To-Know Act. The act was passed over furious industry opposition, many key provisions by one vote.

Under the act, the larger chemical-producing firms were obliged to make public information about their releases into the environment of some 654 named chemicals. The mainstream media did not find the industry's resistance to informing the public, or the passage of the act and the act itself or its effects, of great interest. Steingraber cites industry admissions that this enforced disclosure compelled industry members to pay attention to the chemicals they were pouring into the environment, a point that would seem of enormous significance to public health.[42] And the Toxic Release Inventory showed startling figures—several billion pounds of toxic chemicals released each year—even with the limited coverage of chemicals and companies, self-reporting, and many refusals to comply. But you will look in vain in the mainstream media for detailed reports of these releases, calls for better data, discussions of the health consequences of these releases, or indignation at a system permitting such large-scale emissions of poisons.

From 1993 onward, business has gotten 24 states to pass "Audit Privilege Laws," which give companies the right to make their own environmental audits, to report this information to state authorities along with promises to correct noted deficiencies, and then to be free of any requirement to disclose environmental information to the public or in court proceedings. EPA official Steven Herman states that such laws are "anti-law enforcement, impede public right-to-know, and can penalize employees who report illegal activities to law enforcement authorities. They interfere with government's ability to protect public health and safety. They prevent the public from obtaining potentially critical information about environmental hazards."[43] But once again the mainstream media have been exceedingly quiet about this regressive process, giving the topic a few back-page articles, but without featuring this development or giving it critical editorial attention.

There has also been a very important right-to-know issue connected with the new biotechnology products. Many consumers and environmentalists have insisted that the milk produced by cows given Monsanto's growth hormones, and soybeans and other farm products that are bioengineered, should be labeled as such. Vermont and other states have tried to legislate labeling, and a number of European countries have been concerned about allowing such products entry as well as sale without labeling. There are deeper problems at stake here than disclosure to consumers, including animal and human health and ecological effects, but it is notable that the mainstream media in the United States do not consider any of these issues of great importance. They have been given back-page treatment at best and no editorial criticism in the national media. The *New York Times* editorially condemned the "food disparagement" laws in the case of Oprah Winfrey versus the Texas cattle ranchers,[44] but neither it nor the other national papers have spoken out in favor of labeling bioengineered products (or against "audit privilege laws"). It would appear that in these cases producer sovereignty overwhelms any concern for either biological threats or the consumer's right to choose.

Triumph of Industry Junk Science-Based "Scares"

As noted earlier, the media use the phrase "junk science" mainly as the industry uses it, to refer to non-industry-friendly science, not DuPont-, Novartis-, or Monsanto-friendly science, despite the long record of the industry's scientific frauds and its use of science as a public relations tool. Similarly, the media tend to jump on each industry bandwagon claiming that a challenge to industry products is a "scare" based on bad science.

Alar

This was dramatically illustrated following a CBS *60 Minutes* broadcast in February 1989 that featured the cancer risk of Alar, a chemical used on apples to keep them from dropping early and to improve their color. The EPA had stalled in taking action on Alar for 16 years, following lab tests in 1973 that showed that Alar produced cancer in mice. Later tests confirmed this result. In May 1989 the EPA finally did ban Alar as posing a carcinogenic threat, and in 1992 the National Academy of Sciences confirmed the seriousness of this threat. Alar should have been banned in 1973 under the Delaney clause, which barred the use of any carcinogen in food. The lag reflected regulatory failure.[45]

Nevertheless, after the CBS program caused a sudden shrinkage of apple sales, the industry and its public relations and media allies, with initial support from the EPA, denounced an "Alar scare" allegedly based on junk science. This claim was quickly institutionalized in the mass media, and Jane Brody, Walter Goodman, Peter Passell, and Gina Kolata in the *New York Times* have referred to this scare repeatedly as established truth. Most recently, Brody's article on "Health Scares That Aren't So Scary" (August 18, 1998) cited Alar as the leading case in point. Brody used as her sole uncontested source on this and other scares a document put out by the American Council on Health, an industry-funded propaganda operation, identified by Brody only as "based in New York." She falsely stated that the EPA had not found Alar unacceptable as a carcinogen, and implied that the high dosages given mice in lab tests made the tests useless (a regular industry gambit when the tests do not yield the right conclusions). (On September 5, 1998, a "correction" in the *Times* acknowledged Brody's failure to properly identify the council and to admit that the EPA had found Alar carcinogenic and banned its use.)

The Dioxin Scare

As noted, the *New York Times* and the *Washington Post* both failed to mention the 1990–1991 disclosures that the dioxin studies of Monsanto and BASF were fraudulent, and the *Times* never reported the compelling 1987 evidence of collusion between the EPA and paper industry to downplay the dioxin threat. These suppressions set the stage for both papers, but especially the *Times*, aggressively taking the industry line in the 1990s that the dioxin threat was overrated, that in the words of *Times* reporter Keith Schneider, dioxin exposure "is now considered by some experts to be no more risky than spending a week sunbathing."[46]

In a devastating critique of Schneider's reporting in the *American Journalism Review*, Vicki Monks showed, first, that the sunbathing analogy was concocted by Schneider and was repudiated even by his favorite expert Vernon Houk.[47] In a later article, allegedly based on the findings of a panel of independent scientists assembled by the EPA, Schneider claimed that the panel found that "the risk to average Americans exposed to dioxin . . . is lower than previously believed."[48] Schneider cited no panel scientist to this effect, and Monks quoted several that say his conclusion had no basis in the panel's findings. Furthermore, the panel members and other scientific studies in the same period suggested that dioxin is even more dangerous than previously recognized; that it posed a threat to reproductive and immune systems at levels already occurring in people's bodies. Schneider never reported this important finding. When questioned by Monks about his subsequent March 21, 1993 statement that "new research indicates that dioxin may not be so dangerous after all,"[49] he told her that he was referring only to dioxin's cancer-causing potential, but his article never stated that qualification, and Monks showed that the scientific consensus contradicted his statement on dioxin's cancer threat as well.

In his March 21, 1993 article, Schneider claimed that there was a new "third wave" of more reasonable environmentalism based on "science" and not driven by "popular panics." He cited no scientist supporting the third wave, but did include the "wise use" movement in the vanguard (without mentioning its destructive character and heavy industry funding),[50] and he cited Monsanto head David Mahoney's observation that people were finally recognizing the truths that industry has been pushing. Throughout his writings on dioxin, Schneider's main—almost exclusive—scientist spokesperson was Vernon Houk, who in May 1991 gave his opinion that the Times Beach, Missouri, residents who had been evacuated from a dioxin-contaminated town in 1982 never should have been moved. Schneider and the *Times* played this up on the front page, and Schneider claimed that this "reversal" by Houk also reflected the new wave. But Houk hadn't reversed his position at all—and Vicki Monks showed that Schneider knew this from his own earlier reports. Houk had long been a dioxin defender, was responsible for the sabotaging of a study of the effects of Agent Orange on Vietnam veterans,[51] and eventually ended up as an open spokesperson for the paper industry (all unreported by the *Times*).

Schneider's terrible reporting was widely picked up in the media and was cycled and recycled—in both the *Times* and elsewhere. It was repeatedly stated that dioxins were no more harmful than sunbathing; the number of "scientists" who allegedly said this grew rapidly; and, as the *Chicago Tribune* editorialized, "dioxin has turned out to be something of a non-issue where humans are concerned."[52] This is the process whereby industry junk science becomes institutionalized and genuine chemical threats are transmuted into "alarms."

Our Stolen Future, Kolata, and *Times* Policy

Peter Montague has shown convincingly that Gina Kolata's hostile *Times* review of *Our Stolen Future* was not only extremely biased but was error laden.[53] Other *Times* reporters also disliked *Our Stolen Future*, with its message of possibly serious environmental damage attributable to the industrial status quo. In his detailed study of "What's Wrong With The New York Times's Science Reporting?", Mark Dowie reported that when Colbourn and her co-authors visited the *Times* to discuss their book, Nicholas Wade, Kolata's then-superior, flew into a rage, denouncing the authors as "creating an environmental scare without evidence."[54] Wade hadn't read the book, which was in fact very well documented, but his reaction to "bad [i.e., critical of industry] science" was automatic. It is evident that Kolata, who Dowie called "a faithful apologist for corporate science," reflects *New York Times* policy. Dowie pointed out that the paper has repeatedly refused to publish corrections of Kolata's misquotations and errors, and she has remained in place to do her industry service for a decade. Keith Schneider also lasted almost a decade as an environmental reporter, and according to Dowie, senior editors in New York called Schneider to congratulate him on his dioxin series. Meanwhile, Philip Shabecoff, Philip Hilts, and Richard Severo were pushed out of environmental reporting as too critical. Shabecoff recalled that his boss told him that "New York is complaining. You're too pro-environment and they say you're ignoring the economic costs of environmental protection."[55]

Other Alarms

Along with the Alar, dioxin, and immune system scares there have been toxic waste site scares, asbestos in schools scares, power line leukemia scares, silicone breast implant scares, and others. The mainstream media have picked these up with an enthusiasm they rarely display in pursuit of industry-imposed damage or regulatory malpractice, and with the same gullibility as in the Alar and dioxin scare cases. Industry public relations and junk science are designed to reassure, and the frequent media deriding of alleged scares and the public's supposedly excessive fears and unwarranted aversion to risk serves this industry need extremely well.[56]

The other side of the coin is keeping the lid on the real public health threats emanating from the chemicalization of the environment. The normalization processes described earlier do this effectively. When the *Times*'s Brody, Schneider, or Wade mention the asbestos in schools scare, they never refer to the long history of asbestos industry denial of harm from asbestos. They regularly fail to discuss how industry power constrains, influences, and sometimes dominates regulatory policy. And never in all of their accounts of scares, risks, and cost-benefit tradeoffs do they ever suggest that the precautionary principle should control or that risks and costs should be borne by those imposing a product on society. They have internalized the deep agenda that serves industry needs and push industry interests, often with enthusiasm and passion.

Applicability of the Propaganda Model

That the mainstream media should adopt the industry's usage of "junk science" and normalize the chemical industry's freedom to poison fits well the predictions of the propaganda model. For each of the five filters incorporated into that model—ownership, advertising, sourcing, flak, and ideology—the chemical industry's money and influence give it substantial impact. At the level of *ownership and control*, media owners have an elite solidarity, as well as numerous contacts, with the owners, managers, and bankers of the chemical industry. On the board of the *Washington Post*, for example, are a former CEO of the pharmaceutical giant Johnson & Johnson, three executives of banks or large investment companies, and an attorney attached to a national law firm. The Tribune Company (*Chicago Tribune*) board has two bank and two insurance company interlocks as well as representation by the CEOs of a major electric utility and a large pharmaceutical company. The bankers and corporate executives on corporate media boards share a common culture in which hostility to alleged regulatory excesses has become a powerful element.

The *advertising* community, which funds the media, is part of this same culture. By my count, 31 of the 100 largest national advertisers produce and sell chemicals, while many more, such as the automobile companies, are deeply concerned over the regulation of their operations that use and transform chemical products (oil, gasoline, batteries). The powerful oil industry is very much concerned with the regulation of oil, gas, and petrochemicals. Numerous other industries, including the entire food industry chain from farmers to retailers, are involved with chemicals and regulatory issues. The print media themselves, owning vast acreages of forests and pulp mills that produce a great deal of toxic waste, have a direct stake in regulatory policy.

That these corporate perspectives, emanating from media owners and boards of directors and the reiterated preferences and choices of advertisers, must greatly influence media programming and framing of issues, would seem a structural necessity. The treatment of environmental problems on TV has long been circumscribed by advertiser hostility to programs that put any serious blame for environmental damage on industry. As Erik Barnouw pointed out some years back, a major NBC series on the environment foundered for lack of advertising at a time when corporations were spending huge sums advertising on the subject, because the industry wanted "reassurance," not progam "balance."[57] The industry focus, also, has been on individual—"our"—rather than corporate responsibility for environmental damage. As Mobil Oil headlined a recent op-ed ad in the *New York Times*, "The environment: it's everyone's business."[58]

In *sourcing* on chemical industry issues, although government regulators and victims of chemical damage and their spokespersons are frequently tapped by the media, the industry often dominates debates or creates a stalemate that leaves the question of seriousness of damage and responsibility uncertain. The industry commands numerous experts—in-house and beyond—and it subsidizes their work and pushes them into prominence through its connections and large promotional resources. The industry promotes its views directly through its own contacts, press releases, advertisements, and letters and opinion columns—in addition to Mobil Oil's regular op-ed-page ad in the *Times* (and elsewhere), Daniel Popeo of the corporate-funded Washington Legal Foundation also buys regular column space in the *Times* to denounce noncorporate junk science. The industry also employs public relations firms to set up phony "grass roots" organizations and to infiltrate, gain information on, and sabotage the organizations and activities of dissidents.[59] Chemical industry views are also propagandized by means of its numerous trade associations and captive institutes—the Chlorine Chemistry Council, Vinyl Institute, International Fabricare Institute, National Institute for Chemical

Studies, and Environmental Sensitivities Research Institute, among others.

These propaganda efforts, which cost hundreds of million dollars a year, can overwhelm both regulators and the media. In the case of the media, the industry takes advantage of journalists' ignorance, laziness, desire to avoid flak, and not infrequent pro-industry bias. Those reporters without a pro-industry bias will be constrained by the threat of flak, the demand for "balance," and other pressures from above.[60]

The media frequently assume that information supplied by industry and the EPA (or another government agency) provides "both sides" on an issue, when in fact the two are often on the same side, supporting a backroom compromise damaging to the public interest. The captured or weak government body likes to put a good face on its actions, even when it has capitulated to industry, and the media commonly miss the point. Jim Sibbison, a former publicity officer of the EPA, was impressed with how reporters chronically feature good intentions rather than regulatory failures or structural deficiencies, and how consistently they fail to follow up stories. Speaking of Philip Shabecoff, the best of the *New York Times* reporters on the environment in the 1980s, Sibbison said that "He is more knowledgeable than most of his colleagues and enjoys access to EPA officials who provide him with exclusive stories. This symbiotic relationship may account for the unduly optimistic, even flattering, stories he writes about the EPA's performance."[61]

The chemical industry is also an aggressive producer of *flak*. When the Environmental Working Group was about to issue its report *Tap Blue Waters: Herbicides in Drinking Water* in 1994, the public relations firm for the American Crop Protection Association carried out a preemptive media campaign, including setting up interviews with "experts" chosen by industry. Although the critical report still received substantial news coverage, industry-arranged interviews were heard on two national news programs and on ABC's *Good Morning America*, and as the PR firm noted, the bottom line is that "because of the dearth of negative publicity, ACPA's member companies avoided additional regulation of their products."[62] And in case after case the industry finds out in advance about challenging programs and causes them to be altered or canceled, frequently by threatening a libel suit. The best-known recent example was Monsanto's successful effort in 1997 to quash the showing on a Fox TV station of the program developed by investigative reporters Jane Akre and Steve Wilson on some problematic features of Monsanto's recombinant bovine growth hormone rBGH.[63] There is every reason to believe that these kinds of preemptive interventions, which raise the costs of TV programming at stations and networks, have a seriously chilling effect on critical programming.

The industry also benefits from the strengthening of market *ideology* in the post-Soviet New World Order. Although chemicals and their side effects are a beautiful illustration of market failure, faith in the market and hostility to regulation and government have been effectively played up by industry, aiding it in the normalization and agenda-setting process. The stress on "market-based" solutions, "risk assessment," and "cost-benefit analysis" meshes well with market ideology. The media like these re-sounding phrases, which assume in advance the industry's right to pro-duce poisons, leaving the risks and costs to be evaluated later ("policing the results" in Carson's words). The imbalance in ability to fund science, the conflict of interest in giving industry primacy in doing the research on costs and benefits, the difficulty in putting numbers on costs and benefits of environmental poisons, and the problems of regulatory capture and underfunding in diminishing the usefulness of risk assessment and cost-benefit analysis rarely if ever strike environmental reporters.

In the *New York Times*, for example, Peter Passell, the paper's main house economist through most of the 1980s and 1990s, repeatedly cited cost-benefit and risk-benefit principles without delving into the issues that make these techniques of dubious value. He regularly claimed that the public irrationally overrates risk, but he never discussed the extensive history of industry coverups of actual risks. In "The American Sense of Peril: A Stifling Cost of Modern Life" (May 8, 1989), the title accurately expressed his bias that risk threats are exaggerated and "stifle" progress. He located a 1981 "landmark study" that attributes only 2 percent of cancer deaths to environmental exposure, but other nonlandmark studies give much higher values (and cancer deaths are not the only damage stemming from environmental contamination). His follow-up piece, "Mak-ing a Risky Life Bearable: Better Data, Clearer Choices" (May 9, 1989), pursued the same line; his prime source here was Peter Huber of the Manhattan Institute. He referred to the "scares" that take a pyschological toll, but not to the extensive and well-documented realities of worker dam-age and fatalities. He said "safety is never free," but he never suggested that when safety is threatened there should be independent advance test-ing and/or that the cost of testing and any subsequent damage should be borne by the party who wants to introduce the product. He also failed to give evidence of any serious effect on "progress." This same bias is illus-trated by another *Times* piece titled "Vermont Resists Some Progress in

Dairying" (Keith Schneider, Aug. 27, 1989), where it is presumed that the potentially risky growth hormone represents genuine progress. In summarizing the work of analysts such as Passell and Schneider, Eleanor Singer and Phyllis Endreny say that these writers simply "adopt the frames provided by dominant social institutions."[64]

Concluding Note

The environmental movement has brought important benefits, both educationally and in policy actions. However, it has not changed the industry's right to put chemicals into the environment without independent testing in advance of general use and with only limited provision of public information. There is currently even a strong regressive movement to reduce information availability by means of Audit Privilege Laws. In short, the rule is still caveat emptor, not precaution and reverse onus; the producers remain sovereign; and the mainstream media, by normalizing industry rights and the deep agenda, help preserve that producer sovereignty.

Notes

1 Quoted in Frank Graham Jr., *Since Silent Spring* (Boston: Houghton Mifflin, 1970), 185.

2 Samuel Epstein, *The Politics of Cancer* (San Francisco: Sierra Club, 1978), 196.

3 Many examples are given in Epstein, *The Politics of Cancer*, chaps. 3 and 8, and in Dan Fagin and Marianne Lavelle, *Toxic Deception: How the Chemical Industry Manipulates Science, Bends the Law, and Endangers Your Health* (Secaucas, N.J.: Birch Lane Press, 1996).

4 See "History of Precaution," *Rachel's Environment & Health Weekly*, #539–540, 27 March 1997 to 3 April 1997.

5 Statement of Addison Yeaman, vice president and general counsel of Brown and Williamson, in Stanton Glantz, John Slade, Lisa A. Bero, and Peter Hanauer, *The Cigarette Papers* (Berkeley: University of Californai Press, 1996), 15.

6 Fagin and Lavelle, *Toxic Deception*, 89.

7 Ibid., 52.

8 Epstein, *Politics of Cancer*, 108.

9 Fagin and Lavelle, *Toxic Deception*, 51.

10 Elyse Tanouye, "Does Corporate Funding Influence Research?," *Wall Street Journal*, 8 January 1998.

11 Nicholas Ashford and Claudia Miller, *Chemical Exposures: Low Levels and High Stakes* (New York: Van Nostrand, 1998).

12 Dr. Ronald Gots, head of ESRI, quoted in ibid., 280.

13 William Sanjour, *The Monsanto Investigation: Annals of the EPA: Part 4* (Annapolis, Md.: Environmental Research Foundation, 1996), 1–7.

14 See Fagin and Lavelle, *Toxic Deception*, chaps. 1–3.

15 Epstein, *Politics of Cancer*, 302–06.

16 The quoted phrase is the language of William Hueper and W.C. Conway, senior scientists at the National Cancer Institute, describing the steady growth of "cancers of all types and all causes," in a book published 35 years ago: *Chemical Carcinogens and Cancer* (Springfield, Ill.: Charles Thomas, 1964), 17.

17 This was based on a Lexis-Nexis search of U.S. newspapers for the use of the phrase "junk science" for the period stated in the text.

18 Daniel McGinn and Karen Springen, "Disorder in the Court," *Newsweek* (July 20, 1988).

19 Rachel Carson, *Silent Spring* (Boston: Houghton Mifflin, 1962).

20 Frank Graham Jr., *Since Silent Spring*, xiv.

21 Linda Lear, *Rachel Carson: Witness for Nature* (New York: Holt, 1997), 450.

22 *Rachel's Environment & Health Weekly*, #622, 29 October 1998.

23 Quoted in ibid.

24 Michael Pollan, "Playing God in the Garden," *New York Times Magazine*, 25 October 1998.

25 This report, which remains unpublished because of its "controversial" nature, is described in Marie Woolf, "Revealed: Risks of Genetic Food," *The Independent*, 12 December 1998.

26 Quoted in Pollan, "Playing God in the Garden."

27 Richard Lloyd, "Health Canada scientists told to serve drug companies," *CCPA Monitor* (Dec. 1998–Jan. 1999).

28 *New York Times Magazine*, 25 October 1998.

29 Michael Castleman, "Implanted evidence," *Mother Jones*, January 1998.

30 Review of *A Moment on the Earth*, in *The Amicus Journal* (Spring 1995), 44.

31 Sandra Steingraber, *Living Downstream* (Reading, MA.: Addison-Wesley, 1997), 43.

32 Ibid., 260–62.

33 Quoted in Susan Stanich, "Experts Are at a Loss How to Stem Toxic Flow Into Great Lakes," *Washington Post*, 5 October 1995.

34 The weakness of the EPA is made clear in books such as Fagin-Lavelle, *Toxic Deception* or Susan Steingraber, *Living Downstream*, or by reading issue after issue of *Rachel's Environment & Health Weekly*.

35 Jeff Reisner, "EPA Program Trades Leniency For Toxicity Data," *Journal of Commerce*, 14 January 1992.

36 Ibid.; see also, "On Regulation," *Rachel's Environment & Health Weekly*, #538, 20 March 1997.

37 Philip Shabecoff, "Traces of Dioxin Found in Range of Paper Products," *New York Times*, 24 September 1987.

38 Michael Weisskopf, "Dioxins Found in Some Paper Products," *Washington Post*, 25 September 1987.

39   Michael Weisskopf, "Paper Industry Campaign Defused Reaction to Dioxin Con-
     tamination," *Washington Post*, 25 October 1987.

40   Sanjour, *The Monsanto Investigation*, 1–21.

41   Marc Lappe and Britt Baily, *Against the Grain: Biotechnology and the Corpo-
     rate Takeover of Your Food* (Monroe, ME: Common Courage Press, 1998),
     125.

42   Steingraber, *Living Downstream*, 102.

43   Steven Herman, "EPA's 1998 Enforcement and Compliance Assurance Priori-
     ties," *National Environmental Enforcement Journal* (February 1998).

44   Editorial,"Free Speech About Food," *New York Times*, 19 January 1998.

45   See the valuable six-part series on "The True Story of Alar," *Rachel's Environ-
     ment & Health Weekly*, #530–535, 27 January to 27 February 1997.

46   Keith Schneider, "U.S. Backing Away From Saying Dioxin Is A Deadly Peril,"
     New York Times, 15 August 1991.

47   Vicki Monks, "See No Evil," *American Journalism Review*, June 1993.

48   Keith Schneider, "Panel of Scientists Finds Dioxin Does Not Pose Widespread
     Cancer Threat," *New York Times*, 26 September 1992.

49   Keith Schneider, "New View Calls Environmental Policy Misguided," *New York
     Times*, 21 March 1993.

50   See David Helvarg, *The War Against the Greens* (San Francisco: Sierra Club,
     1994).

51   See Lois Gibbs, *Dying From Dioxin* (Boston: South End Press, 1995), 15–17.

52   Quoted in Monks, "See No Evil."

53   "Our Stolen Future-Part 1," *Rachel's Environment & Health Weekly*, #486, 21
     March 1996.

54   Mark Dowie, "What's Wrong with the New York Times's Science Reporting,"
     The Nation (July 6, 1998).

55   Quoted in ibid.

56   For a discussion of the more general media focus on the public's excessive fears,
     see Kevin Carmody, "It's a jungle out there," *Columbia Journalism Review* (June/
     July 1995), 40–46.

57   Erik Barnouw, *The Sponsor* (New York: Oxford University Press, 1978), 135.

58   Mobil, "The environment: it's everyone's business," *New York Times*, 9 July
     1998.

59 For numerous illustrations of the widely used dubious tactics of public relations firms, see John Stauber and Sheldon Rampton, *Toxic Sludge Is Good For You!* (Monroe, ME: Common Courage Press, 1995).

60 For a forcible expression of the weakness of media performance and the fallacy of their search for "balance," see Gordon Durnil, *Making of a Conservative Environmentalist* (Bloomington, Ind.: Indiana University Press, 1995), 140–41.

61 Jim Sibbison, "The EPA Speaks," *Lies of Our Times* (June 1990), 4. For further material on the lack of enterprise and gullibility of environmental reporters, R. Smith, "Covering the EPA, or, Wake me up if anything happens," *Columbia Journalism Review* (September/October 1983).

62 See Fagin and Lavelle, *Toxic Deception*, 173–74.

63 See Sheldon Rampton, "This report brought to you by Monsanto," *The Progressive* (July 1998), 22–24.

64 Eleanor Singer and Phyllis Endreney, *Reporting on Risk* (New York: Russell Sage Foundation, 1993), 173.

Part 4

PROPAGANDA AND DEMOCRACY

Chapter 18

The Propaganda Model Revisited

In *Manufacturing Consent: The Political Economy of the Mass Media*, Noam Chomsky and I put forward a "propaganda model" as a framework for analysing and understanding how the mainstream U.S. media work and why they perform as they do.[1] We had long been impressed with the regularity with which the media operate within restricted assumptions, depend heavily and uncritically on elite information sources, and participate in propaganda campaigns helpful to elite interests. In trying to explain why they do this we looked for structural factors as the only possible root of systematic behavior and performance patterns.

The propaganda model was and is in distinct contrast to the prevailing mainstream explanations—both liberal and conservative—of media behavior and performance. These approaches downplay structural factors; they presuppose either their unimportance or the positive impact resulting from the multiplicity of agents. Both liberal and conservative analysts emphasize journalists' norms and conduct, public opinion, and news source initiatives as the main determining variables. These analysts are inconsistent in this regard, however. When they discuss media systems in communist or other authoritarian states, the idea that journalists or public opinion can override the power of those who own and control the media is dismissed as nonsense and even as apologetics for tyranny.

There is a distinct difference, too, between the political implications of the propaganda model and mainstream media analysis. For the former, because structural factors shape the broad contours of media performance, and that performance is incompatible with a truly democratic political culture, it follows that a basic change in media ownership, organization, and purpose is necessary for the achievement of genuine democracy. In mainstream analyses such a perspective is politically unacceptable, and its supportive arguments and evidence are rarely subject to debate.

In this chapter I will briefly describe the propaganda model, address some of the criticisms that have been leveled against it, and discuss how the model holds up a decade or so after its publication.[2] I will also provide some examples of how the propaganda model helps explain the nature of media coverage of important political topics at the turn of the century.

The Propaganda Model

What is the propaganda model and how does it work? Its crucial structural factors derive from the fact that the dominant media are firmly imbedded in the market system. They are profit-seeking businesses, owned by very wealthy people (or other companies); and they are funded largely by advertisers who are also profit-seeking entities, and who want their ads to appear in a supportive selling environment. The media are also dependent on government and major business firms as information sources, and both efficiency and political considerations, and, frequently, overlapping interests, cause a certain degree of solidarity to prevail among the government, major media, and other corporate businesses. Government and large nonmedia business firms are also best positioned (and sufficiently wealthy) to be able to pressure the media with threats of withdrawal of advertising or TV licenses, libel suits, and other direct and indirect modes of attack. The media are also constrained by the dominant ideology, which heavily featured anticommunism before and during the Cold War era, and was mobilized often to induce the media to refrain from criticizing U.S. attacks on small states that were labeled communist.

These factors are linked together, reflecting the multileveled capability of powerful business and government entities and collectives (e.g., the Business Roundtable; the U.S. Chamber of Commerce; industry lobbies and front groups) to exert power over the flow of information. We noted that the five factors involved—ownership, advertising, sourcing, flak, and anticommunist ideology—work as "filters" through which information must pass, and that individually and often in additive fashion they greatly influence media choices. We stressed that the filters work mainly by the independent action of many individuals and organizations; these frequently, but not always, have a common view of issues and similar interests. In short, the propaganda model describes a decentralized and nonconspiratorial market system of control and processing, although at times the government or one or more private actors may take initiatives and mobilize coordinated elite handling of an issue.

Propaganda campaigns can occur only when they are consistent with the interests of those controlling and managing the filters. For example, these managers all accepted the view that the Polish government's crack-down on the Solidarity union in 1980 and 1981 was extremely newsworthy and deserved severe condemnation; whereas the same interests did not find the Turkish military government's equally brutal crackdown on trade unions in Turkey at about the same time to be newsworthy or reprehensible. In the latter case the U.S. government and business community liked the military government's anticommunist stance and open door economic policy; the crackdown on Turkish unions had the merit of weakening the left and keeping wages down. In the Polish case, propaganda points could be scored against a Soviet-supported government, and concern could be expressed for workers whose wages were not paid by Free World employers! The fit of this dichotomization to corporate interests and anticommunist ideology is obvious.

We used the concepts of "worthy" and "unworthy" victims to describe this dichotomization, with a trace of irony as the differential treatment was clearly related to political and economic advantage rather than anything like actual worth. In fact, the Polish trade unionists quickly ceased to be worthy when communism was overthrown and the workers were struggling against a western-oriented neoliberal regime. The travails of today's Polish workers, like those of Turkish workers, don't pass through the propaganda model filters. *Both* groups are unworthy victims at this point.

We never claimed that the propaganda model explained everything or that it shows media omnipotence and complete effectiveness in manufacturing consent. It is a model of media *behavior and performance*, not of media *effects*. We explicitly pointed to alternative media, grassroots information sources, and public scepticism about media veracity as important limits on media effectiveness in propaganda service, and we urged the support and more effective use of these alternatives. Both Chomsky and I have often pointed to the general public's persistent refusal to fall into line with the media and elite over the morality of the Vietnam War and the desirability of the assault on Nicaragua in the 1980s (among other matters). The power of the U.S. propaganda system lies in its ability to mobilize an elite consensus, to give the appearance of democratic consent, and to create enough confusion, misunderstanding, and apathy in the general population to allow elite programs to go forward. We also emphasized the fact that there are often differences within the elite that open up space for some debate and even occasional (but very rare) attacks on the *intent* as well as the tactical means of achieving elite ends.

Although the propaganda model was generally well received on the left, some complained of an allegedly pessimistic thrust and implication of hopeless odds to be overcome. A closely related objection concerned its applicability to local conflicts where the possibility of effective resistance was greater. But the propaganda model does not suggest that local and even larger victories are impossible, especially where the elites are divided or have limited interest in an issue. For example, coverage of issues like gun control, school prayer, and abortion rights may well receive more varied treatment than, say, global trade, taxation, and economic policy. Moreover, well-organized campaigns by labor, human rights, or environmental organizations that are fighting against abusive local businesses can sometimes elicit positive media coverage. In fact, we would like to think that the propaganda model can help activists understand where they might best deploy their efforts to influence mainstream media coverage of issues.

The model does suggest that the mainstream media, as elite institutions, commonly frame news and allow debate only within the parameters of elite interests; and that when the elite is really concerned and unified, and/or when ordinary citizens are not aware of their own stake in an issue or are immobilized by effective propaganda, the media will serve elite interests uncompromisingly.

Mainstream Liberal and Academic "Left" Critiques

Many liberals and a number of academic media analysts of the left did not like the propaganda model. Some of them found repugnant a wholesale condemnation of a system in which they played a respected role. Some asked rhetorically where we got the information used to condemn the mainstream media if not from the media themselves (a tired apologetic point that we answered at length in our preface). To these critics the system is basically sound, its inequalities of access regrettable but tolerable, its pluralism and competition effectively responding to consumer demands. In the postmodernist mode, global analyses and global solutions are rejected and derided, and individual struggles and small victories are stressed, even by nominally left thinkers.

Many of the critiques displayed barely concealed anger; and in most critiques the propaganda model was dismissed with a few superficial cliches (conspiratorial, simplistic, etc.), without fair presentation or subjecting it to the test of evidence. Let me discuss briefly some of the main criticisms.

Conspiracy Theory

We explained in *Manufacturing Consent* that critical analyses like ours would inevitably elicit cries of conspiracy theory, and in a futile effort to prevent this we devoted several pages of the preface to show that the propaganda model is best described as a "guided market system," and to explicitly reject conspiracy. Mainstream critics still couldn't abandon the charge, partly because they are too lazy to read a complex work, partly because they know that falsely accusing a radical critique of conspiracy theory won't cost them anything, and partly because of their superficial assumption that, as the media comprise thousands of "independent" journalists and companies, any finding that they follow a "party line" that serves the state must rest on an assumed conspiracy. (In fact, it can result from a widespread gullible acceptance of official handouts, common internalized beliefs, fear of reprisal for critical analysis, etc.). The apologists can't abide the notion that institutional factors can cause a "free" media to act like lemmings in jointly disseminating false and even silly propaganda; such a charge must assume a conspiracy.

Sometimes the critics latched on to a word or phrase that suggests a collective purpose or function, occasionally ironically, to make their case. Communications professor Robert Entman, for example, stated that we damaged our case by alleging that media coverage of the 1973 Paris accord on Vietnam "was consciously 'designed by the loyal media to serve the needs of state power' . . . which comes close to endorsing a conspiracy theory, which the authors explicitly disavow early on."[3] The word "consciously" was Entman's, and he neglected numerous statements about the media's treatment of the Paris accord that didn't fit his effort to bring us "close to" a conspiracy theory. To say that we "disavow" a conspiracy theory is also misleading: we went to great pains to show that our view is closer to a free market model; we argued that the media comprise numerous independent entities that operate on the basis of common outlooks, incentives, and pressures from the market, government, and internal organizational forces.

The propaganda model explains media behavior and performance in structural terms, and intent is an unmeasurable red herring. All we know is that the media and journalists mislead in tandem—some no doubt internalize a propaganda line as true, some may know it is false, but the point is unknowable and irrelevant.

Chomskian Linguistics

Some of the criticisms of the propaganda model have been funny. Carlin Romano, in his review in *Tikkun*, located the problem in Chomskian linguistic theories that allegedly view everything as rooted in deep structures.[4] He was unaware that the rooting of corporate behavior and performance in structure is the core of modern industrial organization analysis, that I had already used it in a 1981 book, *Corporate Control, Corporate Power*, and that I was mainly responsible for the chapter in *Manufacturing Consent* that presented the propaganda model. Of course, whether traceable to Chomskian linguistics or industrial organization theory, the substantive issues are: Are the assumptions plausible? Does the model work? But showing a possible esoteric origin is a form of putdown that suggests remoteness from, and lack of touch with, real media people.

Failure to Touch Base with Reporters

Romano did in fact follow up with the admonition that we had failed to ask reporters why they did what they did. He implied, without offering any evidence, that the journalistic bias we criticized might have been revealed as for good cause, if we had only asked for an explanation. But, apart from the fact that we did speak with quite a few reporters, the criticism is inane. Are reporters even aware of the deeper sources of bias they may internalize? Won't they tend to rationalize their behavior? More important, if we find, for example, that in reporting on the Nicaraguan and Salvadoran elections of 1984, they asked different questions in the two elections, in exact accord with the propaganda line of the U.S. government, would asking journalists what went on in their minds serve any useful purpose? This line of criticism, like the insistence on inquiry into reporter-proprietor intentions, is a cop-out that essentially denies the legitimacy of a quantitative (or scientific) analysis of media performance.

Failure to Take Account of
Media Professionalism and Objectivity

A more sophisticated version of the last argument, put forward by communications professor Dan Hallin, is that we failed to take account of the maturing of journalist professionalism, which he claims to be "central to understanding how the media operate."[5] Hallin also states that in protecting and rehabilitating the public sphere "professionalism is surely part of the answer."[6]

But professionalism and objectivity rules are fuzzy, flexible, and superficial manifestations of deeper power and control relationships. Professionalism arose in journalism in the years when the newspaper business was becoming less competitive and more dependent on advertising. Professionalism was not an antagonistic movement by the workers against the press owners, but was actively encouraged by many of the latter. It gave a badge of legitimacy to journalism, ostensibly assuring readers that the news would not be influenced by the biases of owners, advertisers, or the journalists themselves. In certain circumstances it has provided a degree of autonomy, but professionalism has also internalized some of the commercial values that media owners hold most dear, like relying on inexpensive official sources as *the* credible news source. As Ben Bagdikian has noted, professionalism has made journalists oblivious to the compromises with authority they are constantly making.[7] And Hallin himself acknowledges that professional journalism can allow something close to complete government control through domination of sources.[8]

Although Hallin claims that the propaganda model cannot explain the case of media coverage of the Central American wars of the 1980s, when there was considerable domestic hostility to the Reagan policies, in fact the model works extremely well there, whereas Hallin's focus on "professionalism" fails abysmally. Hallin acknowledges that "the administration was able more often than not to prevail in the battle to determine the dominant frame of television coverage," "the broad patterns in the framing the story can be accounted for almost entirely by the evolution of policy and elite debate in Washington," and "coherent statements of alternative visions of the world order and U.S. policy rarely appeared in the news."[9] This is exactly what the propaganda model would forecast. And if, as Hallin contends, a majority of the public opposed the elite view, what kind of "professionalism" allows a virtually complete suppression of the issues as the majority perceives them?

Hallin mentions a "nascent alternative perspective" in reporting on El Salvador—a "human rights" framework—that "never caught hold." The propaganda model can explain why it never took hold; Hallin doesn't. Even though 700 journalists were present at the Salvadoran election of 1982, allegedly "often skeptical" of election integrity,[10] why did it yield a "public relations victory" for the administration and a major falsification of reality (as described in *Manufacturing Consent*)? Hallin doesn't explain this. He never mentions the Office of Public Diplomacy or the firing of reporter Raymond Bonner or the work of the flak machines.[11] He doesn't explain the failure of the media to report even a tiny fraction of the crimes of the contras in Nicaragua and the death machines in El Salvador and Guatemala, in contrast with media inflation of Sandinista misdeeds and the double standard in reporting on the Nicaraguan election of 1984. Given the elite divisions and public hostility to the Reagan policy, media subservience was phenomenal and arguably exceeded that which the propaganda model might have anticipated.[12]

Failure to Explain Continued Opposition and Resistance
Both Hallin and historian Walter LaFeber (in a review in the *New York Times*)[13] pointed to the continued opposition to Reagan's Central America

policy as somehow incompatible with the model. These critics failed to comprehend that the propaganda model is about how the media work, not how effective they are. Even the sophisticated and sympathetic Philip Schlesinger calls ours an "effects" model, that "assumes that dominant agendas are reproduced in public opinion," but he immediately quotes our statement that the "system is not all powerful . . . Government and the elite domination of the media have not succeeded in overcoming the Vietnam syndrome."[14] Nowhere does he cite us saying anything like his summary of our alleged views on effects. We also stated explicitly with regard to Central America that the elite was sufficiently divided over tactics to allow space and considerable debate. We did stress, however, that the parameters of debate did not extend to fundamental challenges to the U.S. intervention.[15]

By the logic of this form of criticism of the propaganda model, the fact that many Soviet citizens did not swallow the lines put forward by *Pravda* demonstrates that *Pravda* was not serving a state propaganda function.

Propaganda Model is too Mechanical and Functionalist and Ignores the Existence of Space, Contestation, and Interaction

This set of criticisms is at the heart of the negative reactions of the serious left-of-center media analysts such as Philip Schlesinger, James Curran, Peter Golding, Graham Murdock, and John Eldridge, as well as that of Dan Hallin. Of these critics, only Schlesinger both summarizes the elements of our model and discusses our evidence. He acknowledges that the case studies make telling points, but in the end he finds ours "a highly deterministic vision of how the media operate coupled with a straightforward functionalist conception of ideology."[16] Specifically, we failed to explain the weights to be given our five filters; we did not allow for external influences, nor did we offer a "thoroughgoing analysis of the ways in which economic dynamics operate to structure both the range and form of press presentations" (quoting Graham Murdock); and although we put forward "a powerful effects model" we admit that the system is not all powerful, which calls into question our determinism.

The criticism of the propaganda model for being deterministic ignores several important considerations. Any model involves deterministic elements, so that this criticism is a straw person unless the critics also show that the system is not logically consistent, operates on false premises, or that the predictive power of the determining variables is poor. The critics often acknowledge that the case studies we present are powerful, but they don't show where the alleged determinism leads to error nor do they offer or point to alternative models that would do a better job.[17]

The propaganda model deals with extraordinarily complex sets of events, and only claims to offer a broad framework of analysis that requires modification depending on many local and special factors, and that may be entirely inapplicable in some cases. But if it offers insight in numerous important cases that have large effects and cumulative ideological force, it is defensible unless a better model is provided. Usually the critics wisely stick to generalities and offer no critical detail or alternative model; when they do provide alternatives, the results are not impressive.[18]

The criticism of the propaganda model for functionalism is also dubious, and the critics sometimes seem to call for more functionalism. The model does describe a system in which the media serve the elite, but by complex processes incorporated into the model that involve means whereby the powerful protect their interests naturally and without overt conspiracy. This would seem one of the model's merits; it shows a dynamic and self-protecting system in operation. The same corporate community that influences the media through its power as owner, dominant funder (advertising), and as a major news source also underwrites the efforts of Accuracy in Media and the American Enterprise Institute to influence the media through harassment and the provision of right-thinking experts. Critics of propaganda model functionalism like Eldridge and Schlesinger contradictorily point to the merit of analyses that focus on "how sources organize media strategies" to achieve their ends. Apparently it is admirable to analyse corporate micro strategies to influence the media, but to focus on global corporate efforts to influence the media is illegitimate functionalism!

Golding and Murdock criticize the model for its focus on "strategic interventions" that allegedly cause us to "overlook the contradictions in the system. Owners, advertisers, and key political personnel cannot always do as they wish." Analyzing "the nature and sources of these limits" is a "key task" of critical political economy.[19] The Golding-Murdock claim that the propaganda model focuses on "strategic interventions" is a surprising misreading, as the model's filters are built-in and operate mainly through the internalized recognition and enforcement of constraints and choices based on the structure of power. Strategic interventions certainly occur, but are of distinctly secondary importance.

It is also untrue that the propaganda model implies no constraints on media owners and managers; we recognized and spelled out the circumstances under which the media will be relatively open—mainly, when there are elite disagreements and when other groups in society are interested in, informed about, and organized to fight about issues. But the propaganda model does start from the premise that a critical political economy will put front and center the analysis of the locus of media control and the mechanisms by which the powerful are able to dominate the flow of messages and limit the space of contesting parties. The limits on their power are certainly important, but why should these get first place, except as a means of minimizing the power of the dominant interests, inflating the elements of contestation, and pretending that the marginalized have more strength than they really possess?

Enhanced Relevance of the Propaganda Model

The dramatic changes in the economy, the communications industries, and politics over the past decade have tended on balance to enhance the applicability of the propaganda model. The first two filters—ownership and advertising—have become ever more important. The decline of public broadcasting, the increase in corporate power and global reach, and the mergers and centralization of the media have made bottom-line considerations more influential both in the United States and abroad. The competition for advertisers has become more intense and the boundaries between editorial and advertising departments have weakened further. Newsrooms have been more thoroughly incorporated into transnational corporate empires, with budget cuts and even less management enthusiasm for investigative journalism that would challenge the structure of power. In short, the professional autonomy of journalists has been reduced.

Some argue that the Internet and the new communication technologies are breaking the corporate stranglehold on journalism and opening an unprecedented era of interactive democratic media. There is no evidence to support this view as regards journalism and mass communication. In fact, one could argue that the new technologies are exacerbating the problem. They permit media firms to shrink staff even as they achieve greater outputs, and they make possible global distribution systems that reduce the number of media entities. Although the new technologies have great potential for democratic communication, there is little reason to expect the Internet to serve democratic ends if it is left to the market.[20]

The third and fourth filters—sourcing and flak—have also strengthened as mechanisms of elite influence. A reduction in the resources devoted to journalism means that those who subsidize the media by providing sources for copy gain greater leverage. Moreover, work by people like Alex Carey, John Stauber, and Sheldon Rampton has helped us see how the public relations industry has been able to manipulate press coverage of issues on behalf of corporate America.[21] This industry understands how to utilize journalistic conventions to serve its own ends. Studies of news sources reveal that a significant proportion of news originates in public relations releases. There are, by one conservative count, 20,000 more public relations agents working to doctor the news today than there are journalists writing it.

The fifth filter—anticommunist ideology—is possibly weakened by the collapse of the Soviet Union and global socialism, but this is easily offset by the greater ideological force of the belief in the "miracle of the market" (Reagan). There is now an almost religious faith in the market, at least among the elite, so that regardless of evidence, markets are assumed to be benevolent and nonmarket mechanisms are suspect. When the Soviet economy stagnated in the 1980s, it was attributed to the absence of markets; the disintegration of capitalist Russia in the 1990s is blamed on politicians and workers failing to let markets work their magic. Journalism has internalized this ideology. Adding it to the fifth filter in a world where the global power of market institutions makes nonmarket options seem utopian gives us an ideological package of immense strength.

Further Applications

The propaganda model fits exceedingly well the media's treatment of the passage of the North American Free Trade Agreement (NAFTA) and the subsequent Mexican crisis and meltdown of 1994–1995, as described in chapter 14. Once again there was a sharp split between the preferences of ordinary citizens and the elite and business community; polls consistently showed substantial majorities opposed to NAFTA—and to the bailout of investors in Mexican securities—but the elite in favor. Media news coverage, selection of "experts," and opinion columns were skewed accordingly; their judgment was that the benefits of NAFTA were obvious, were agreed to by all qualified authorities, and that only demagogues and "special interests" were opposed. The effort of labor to influence the outcome of the NAFTA debates was harshly criticized in both the *New York Times* and the *Washington Post*.

As is suggested by the treatment of NAFTA and of labor's right to participate in its debates, the propaganda model applies to domestic as well as foreign issues. Labor has been under siege in the United States for the past several decades, but you would hardly know this from the mainsteam media. A 1994 *Business Week* article noted that "over the past dozen years . . . U.S. industry has conducted one of the most successful union wars ever," helped by "illegally firing thousands of workers for exercising their right to organize," with unlawful firings occurring in "one-third of all representation elections in the late '80s."[22] But this successful war was carried out quietly, with media cooperation. The decertification of unions, use of replacement workers, and long and debilitating strikes like that involving Caterpillar were treated in very low key fashion, and in a notable illustration of the applicability of the propaganda model, the long Pittston miners strike was accorded much less attention than the strike of miners in the Soviet Union.[23] For years the media found the evidence that the majority of ordinary citizens were doing badly in the New Economic Order of marginal interest; they "discovered" this issue only under the impetus of Pat Buchanan's right-wing populist outcries during the 1996 presidential election campaign.

Another striking application of the propaganda model can be seen in the media's treatment of the chemical industry and its regulation. As described in chapter 17, because of the industry's power, the media have normalized a system described by Rachel Carson in *Silent Spring* as "deliberately poisoning us, then policing the results." Industry is permitted to produce and sell chemicals (and now also bioengineered foods) without independent proof of safety, and the "policing" by the Environmental Protection Agency has been badly compromised by underfunding and political limits on enforcement as well as testing. Although industry denials of harm from its products—from lead in gasoline to asbestos and Agent Orange—and fraudulent testing have been notorious for many years, the media still use the phrase "junk science" to refer to the science employed by environmentalists and lawyers suing the industry on behalf of its victims, not that sponsored by industry. They have internalized industry usage, just as they have normalized a status quo of caveat emptor (buyer beware) rather than of safety first.

In the health insurance controversy of 1992–1993, the media's refusal to take the single-payer option seriously, despite apparent widespread public support and the effectiveness of the system in Canada, served well the interests of the insurance and medical service complex.[24] The uncritical media reporting and commentary on the alleged urgency of fiscal restraint and a balanced budget in the years 1992–1996 fit well the business community's desire to reduce the social budget and weaken regulation. The applicability of the propaganda model in these and other cases, including the "drug wars," seems clear.[25]

Final Note

In retrospect, perhaps we should have made it clearer that the propaganda model was about media behavior and performance, with uncertain and variable effects. Maybe we should have spelled out in more detail the contesting forces both within and outside the media and the conditions under which these are likely to be influential. But we made these points, and it is quite possible that nothing we could have done would have prevented our being labeled conspiracy theorists, rigid determinists, and deniers of the possibility that people can resist (even as we called for resistance).

The propaganda model remains a very workable framework for analysing and understanding the mainstream media—perhaps even more so than in 1988. As noted earlier in reference to Central America, the media's performance often surpasses expectations of media subservience to government propaganda. And we are still waiting for our critics to provide a better model.

Notes

1   Edward Herman and Noam Chomsky, *Manufacturing Consent* (New York: Pantheon, 1988).

2   Noam Chomsky analyzes some of these criticisms in his *Necessary Illusions: Thought Control in Democratic Societies* (Boston: South End Press, 1989), Appendix 1.

3   Entman's review is in the *Journal of Communication* (Winter, 1990).

4   Carlin Romano, "Slouching Toward Pressology," *Tikkun* (May 1989).

5   Dan Hallin, *We Keep America On Top of the World* (London: Routledge, 1994), 13.

6   Ibid., 4.

7   Ben Bagdikian, *The Media Monopoly* (Boston: Beacon, 1987), 180.

8   Hallin, *We Keep America on Top of the World*, 64, 70.

9   Ibid., 64, 74, 77.

10 Ibid., 72.

11 On the firing of Bonner and the role of the *Wall Street Journal* as a media flak machine, see chapter 9.

12 For compelling documentation on this extraordinary subservience, see Chomsky, *Necessary Illusions*, 197–261.

13 Walter LaFeber, "Whose News," *New York Times Book Review*, 6 November 1988.

14 Philip Schlesinger, "From production to propaganda?," a Review Essay in *Media, Culture & Society* (July 1989), 301.

15 See *Manufacturing Consent*, xii–xiii.

16 Schlesinger, "From Production to Propaganda," 297.

17 I should note that the case studies in *Manufacturing Consent* are only a small proportion of those that Chomsky and I have done that support the analysis of the propaganda model. Special mention should be made of those covering the Middle East, Central America, and terrorism. See especially Chomsky's *Necessary Illusions*, *The Fateful Triangle*, and *Pirates & Emperors: International Terrorism in the Real World*, and my *The Real Terror Network* and (with Gerry O'Sullivan) *The Terrorism Industry*.

18   In fact, the only attempt to offer an alternative model was in Nicholas Lemann's review of *Manufacturing Consent* in the *New Republic* of January 9–16, 1989. For an analysis of this effort, see Chomsky's *Necessary Illusions*, 145–48.

19   Peter Golding and Graham Murdock, "Culture, Communications, and Political Economy," in James Curran and Michael Gurevitch, eds., *Mass Media and Society* (London: Edward Arnold, 1991), 19.

20   For a discussion of the role of the Internet, see Edward Herman and Robert McChesney, *The Global Media* (London: Cassell, 1997), 117–35.

21   See Alex Carey, *Taking the Risk Out of Democracy* (Sydney, Australia: University of New South Wales Press, 1995); John Stauber and Sheldon Rampton, *Toxic Sludge is Good for You!* (Monroe, ME: Common Courage Press, 1996).

22   Aaron Bernstein, "The Workplace," *Business Week* (May 23, 1994), 70.

23   "Lost in the Margins: Labor and the Media," *EXTRA!* (Summer 1990).

24   "Health Care Reform: Not Journalistically Viable," *EXTRA!* (July/August 1993); John Canham-Clyne, "When 'Both Sides' Aren't Enough: The Restricted Debate over Health Care Reform," *EXTRA!* (January/February 1994).

25   See Noam Chomsky, *Deterring Democracy* (London: Verso, 1991), 114–21.

Chapter 19

Postmodernism and the Active Audience

An important element of the intellectual trend called postmodernism is the repudiation of global models of social analysis and global solutions, and their replacement with a focus on local and group differences and the ways in which ordinary individuals adapt to and help reshape their environments. Its proponents often present themselves as populists who are hostile to the elitism of modernists, who, on the basis of "essentialist" and "totalizing" theories, suggest that ordinary people are being manipulated and victimized on an unlevel playing field.

Postmodernism has occupied significant terrain in academia in the field of "cultural studies," both in the humanities and social sciences, and it has brought forth a vast array of analyses of texts, words, and varying meanings associated with gender, race, ethnic grouping, and other identity differences. In media studies this approach has been most clearly manifested in analyses of an "active audience," whose members allegedly "interact with" and "read" TV programs in accord with their own ideologies and interests, thereby not only deriving pleasure and "empowering" themselves, but also nullifying any ideological management from above. For postmodernists, an active audience is strengthened in its subversive influence by new music and other art forms and messages, which seep into the commercial media as well as attack its themes from without. The lessons are: the world is one of constant struggle, not domination and manipulation; our task is to watch, record, and celebrate the numerous small micro-victories; and—not to worry.

There are undoubtedly important elements of truth and insights in active audience analysis and other sectors of postmodern thought, but the active audience studies (on which I concentrate here) have tended to be narrowly focused and politically conservative, by choice and by default.

Having abandoned "global" approaches, they take the status quo as given, fail to examine forms and structures of domination that underpin it, and provide no basis for analyzing or organizing to change the status quo. Their patina of progressivism as they celebrate individual accomplishments and "resistance" is therefore pollyanaish, and complements perfectly the individualism of the New Right, which also argues that individuals have more resources than liberals imagine and will do well if the heavy hand of government paternalism is removed from them.

The postmodernist celebration of the power of the individual and rejection of global models (and inferentially, global solutions to problems) has an even deeper perversity in that it reinforces individualism at a time when *collective* resistance to corporate domination is the central imperative. The market consists of numerous corporations that organize and plan to achieve their narrow goals, and which have been steadily growing in size, global reach, and power. At home, they and their political allies are well funded and active; externally, institutions like the International Monetary Fund, World Bank, World Trade Organization, and the world's governments, work on their behalf. Individual powerlessness grows in the face of this globalizing market; meanwhile, labor unions and other support organizations of ordinary citizens have been under siege and have weakened. Stemming the current market tide, and any future turnabout, will require organization, programs, and strategies from below. In this context, could anything be more perverse politically and intellectually than a retreat to micro-analysis, the celebration of minor individual triumphs, and reliance on solutions based on individual actions alone?

Roots of Postmodern Ideology

There is surely a shared underpinning between the massive accommodation to the demands of the market by the elite of the economics profession and the rise of active audience and other postmodern modes of thought. The British literary theorist Terry Eagleton notes that "every central feature of postmodern theory can be deduced, read off as it were, from the assumption of a major political defeat."[1] With the increasing authority of the market, and associated erosion of democracy, radical change has seemed more and more utopian and taking existing arrangements as given a mere exercise in necessary realism. In the intellectual and political mainstream, solutions by governmental action are clearly "out" and the age of entrepreneurship and individual achievement is "in." Similarly, "the kinds of speculative thinking most in vogue among present-day cultural theorists are such as to leave them little room for genuine, effective engagement with matters of real-world ethical and political concern," Christopher Norris writes. "More specifically: the turn toward post-structuralist, postmodernist and neo-pragmatist doctrines of discourse and representation is one that can only lend support to prevailing (consensus) notions of reality and truth by making it strictly *unthinkable* that anyone could offer good arguments—or factual counter-evidence—against the effective self-images of the age, or ideas of what is (currently and contingently) 'good in the way of belief'."[2] In this vapid political and intellectual context it was perhaps inevitable that, on the one hand, many postmodernists should abandon politics altogether, and that, on the other hand, a new and pathetic strand of "populism" should emerge to demonstrate that ordinary individuals have power and can triumph, not just Bill Gates, Ted Turner, and Rupert Murdoch.

But pessimism and disillusionment are not only "symptoms of political defeat," in Eagleton's words;[3] they have also led some to a further retreat, to an abandonment of the desire as well as the hope for progressive change, and to a celebration of the status quo and the options it affords the individual. The postmodern celebration of popular culture as the locus of subversion and resistance ignores its increasing integration into the lifestyle of the shopping-mall world and takes the domination of consumer capitalism as a given. Some of the active audience analysts have become almost as fond of the market as Chicago School economists—the market is "an expansive popular system" for Angela McRobbie, and an arena in which workers struggle with bosses on not grossly unequal terms, as in media-audience interactions, for John Fiske. This is why, as Eagleton explains, postmodernism's questioning of the existence of "such concepts as truth has alarmed the bishops and charmed the business executives, just as its compulsion to place words like 'reality' in scare quotes unsettles the pious *Burger* in the bosom of his family but is music to his ears in his advertising agency."[4]

In an academic context, the focus on individual responses and micro-issues of language, text interpretation, and ethnic and gender identity is politically safe and holds forth the possibility of endless deconstructions of small points in a growing framework of technical jargon. The process has been a longstanding one in economics, where mathematics opened up opportunities to build complex gothic structures on the foundation of very unrealistic assumptions. These models have slight application to reality, but conveniently tend to reaffirm the marvels of the free market, given their simple assumptions of perfect knowledge, competition, rationality, and minimal (or no) time lags in adjustment to equilibrium. Mathematical models could be usefully designed to figure out risk-return tradeoffs in complex market environments, helpful to arbitrageurs, and therefore valuable to the model-maker as a salable service. Such returns are not available to postmodernists, although those who say the right things about feminist excesses and the fallacies of theories of cultural imperialism (which have ignored differences in audience readings of TV programs such as "Dallas") will benefit from generous media publicity and book sales.

Notes on Active Audience Analyses

In active audience analyses it is standard practice to assail critics of TV culture for excessive and elitist negativism and an undue preoccupation with the substance of programming and theoretical foregone alternatives, rather than to observe the pleasure viewers get from existing fare, how they adapt TV messages, and how effectively they are empowered in the viewing process. Because of their ability to switch stations, TV viewers can virtually self-program, which increases their independence, brings families together, and provides materials for conversation, etc.

The methodology employed is "field investigations" of TV viewers, which give great weight to what a tiny sample of viewers say about their perspectives on TV. The positive gloss that viewers commonly place on their own viewing practices is fitted into a framework that takes the existing programmatic offerings as a given, and of necessity yields positive findings on effects. Active audience analysts stress that viewers "use" the TV instrument. The possibilities that the viewer may be used by others, or that there might be alternative programming, or that the cumulative effects on the viewer and his or her community of the particular options offered may be important, are outside their framework of thought.[5] Some of the defenses of the TV culture against "elitist" media critics (specifically, Dorothy Hobson's writing about soap operas) led William Seaman to remark that precisely parallel defenses could be made for a retreat to religious fanaticism or valium addiction, but "such an 'understanding' does not take into account the brutally restricted *range* of options within which this particular choice is seen as rational and 'free' (and, indeed, defiant)."[6]

Active audience guru John Fiske regularly uses the word "interaction" to describe the relationship between audience and TV station/network owners and programmers. He contends that, unlike ordinary commodities, TV programs are "co-produced" by the supplier and the viewers, the latter having the "semiotic power" to inflect meaning, which "liberates them" from program constraints and even allows them to "promote" their own interests. "The production of meaning/pleasure is finally the responsibility of the consumer and is only undertaken in his/her interests."[7] What is important for social change, therefore, is not program diversity and who controls programs, but diversity of readings by the active audience. And Fiske contends that it is in the financial interest of TV stations and network owners "to serve and promote the diverse and often oppositional interests of its audiences" because audience size means profits, so that "the cultural economy drives the financial in a dialectic force that counters the power of capital. . . . Far from being the agent of the dominant classes, it is the prime site where the dominant have to recognize the insecurity of their power."[8]

In short, program control is of no importance because the controllers will have to give the audience what it wants or fail, and viewers read programs as they see fit and thereby "promote" their interests anyway. The first line of argument is identical with a long-standing industry rationale for the steady decline of public service programming and the parallel growth of entertainment-cum-violence—namely, that owners are democratically serving popular demand. This line of defense glosses over the importance of consumer sovereignty, as opposed to mere freedom of consumer choice. Audiences do not have sovereignty—they have no direct say in what will be offered, suppressed, and edited out of programs, for reasons that are helpful only to the ownership interest. The sovereign media proprietors derive their revenue mainly from "selling eyeballs" to advertisers, so that not only the owners but the advertisers as well must approve the offerings before the audience is given the opportunity to promote their own interests.

Because of global marketing considerations, sex and violence have been pushed by the media, and because of the interests of owners, advertisers, and global corporations, public service programs have been displaced by entertainment and liberal-radical ideas have been excluded altogether. For many years these dominant interests have pushed consumerist values, the Cold War and the arms race, nuclear power, and private ownership, and these therefore became the dominant ideology of programming and ads (described brilliantly in Erik Barnouw's *The Sponsor*). The audience has not participated in or even known about these sovereign infusions of ideology and limits on its menu of choices.

Will the active audience be sufficiently aware of the steady stream of Cold War and consumerist messages to be able to resist them and develop or sustain counter-ideologies? Not likely, not plausible, and it hasn't happened. Active audience methodology, which involves asking people their opinions at a point of time, is completely inappropriate for dealing with ideologically structured programming over time. Viewers can switch stations, but the stations may all follow the same market imperatives, and the corporate and political establishment can try and try again, using formulas based on polls and studies of points of audience vulnerability. Viewers may resist and some of them may be very hard to manage, but some will be persuaded, others will be confused, and still more will be depoliticized by the barrage of entertainment and the replacement of the public sphere of debate with propaganda. Media commercialization and concentration entails serious "disempowerment," which must be fought by means beyond individual resistance.

Active Audience Protection of the Empire

It was noted earlier that studies of the differences in audience readings of "Dallas" abroad caused the active audience analysts to question whether U.S. domination of the global movie-TV regime had any ideological impact. The new style analysis allowed an intellectual response to what Ien Ang has called "a stubborn fixation on the threat of 'American cultural imperialism'."[9] Tamar Liebes, Robyn Penman, Elihu Katz, Michael Tracy, and John Fiske all share Ien Ang's methodological principle that the "real question" is "what happens in the process of watching Dallas."[10] In Herbert Schiller's words, "With Ang as with the others, the production of meaning is an individual act, in which the program/text is no more influential than what the viewer/reader makes of it."[11] As Ang puts it, despite worries about about susceptibility to American media products by inhabitants of ivory towers and "guardians of the 'national culture' . . . the issue is rather one of pleasure."[12] Or as Tamar Liebes expressed it to the sympathetic Thomas Friedman in the *New York Times*, varying readings of a text show that "The idea of a simple 'American` message imposing itself in the same way on viewers all over the world is simply not valid."[13] But nobody has claimed such a simple relationship, and once again, the possibility that deeper consumerist, neoliberal, and other political messages may have a cumulative impact is outside the orbit of active audience methodology and thought.

Schiller notes that the emergence of the active audience perspective "corresponds nicely with the creation of the movement for a new international information order in 1976 at Nairobi. This was the time, too, of the beginning of the U.S. counteroffensive against the New International

Information Order, culminating in the U.S. withdrawal from UNESCO in 1984."[14] In short, the active audience intellectuals have been as useful to the cause of the "free flow" of information as the mainstream economists have been in helping along "free trade."

Notes

1   Terry Eagleton, "Where Do Postmodernists Come From?," *Monthly Review* (July/ August 1995), 66.

2   Christopher Norris, *Uncritical Theory: Postmodernism, Intellectuals, and the Gulf War* (Amherst: University of Massachusetts Press, 1992), 93.

3   Eagleton, "Where Do Postmodernists Come From?," 68.

4   Terry Eagleton, *The Illusion of Postmodernism* (Oxford, UK: Blackwell Publishers, 1996), 28.

5   Dave Morley, who has done outstanding critical work that frequently conflicts with active audience theory, displays some of its weaknesses in his book *Family Television: Cultural Power and Domestic Leisure* (London: Comedia, 1986), and is criticized for this by William Seaman in "Active audience theory: pointless populism," *Media, Culture & Society* (April 1992), 308.

6   Seaman, "Active audience theory: pointless populism," 308.

7   John Fiske, *Television Culture* (London: Methuen, 1987), 317.

8   Ibid., 326.

9   Ien Ang, *Watching Dallas* (London: Methuen, 1985), 3.

10 Ibid., 10.

11 Schiller, *Culture, Inc.*, 150.

12 Ang, *Watching Dallas*, 3.

13 Thomas Friedman, "J.R.'s Message? As Varied As Kibbutz And Bazaar," *New York Times*, 1 April 1986. Thomas Friedman saw that Liebes, in her doctoral dissertation at Hebrew University, had a message worthy of inclusion in the *Times*. By contrast, the veteran and distinguished communication analyst Herbert Schiller, who has a different message than Liebes, has never had a book reviewed or op ed column in that paper and Thomas Friedman has never cited his work.

14 Schiller, *Culture Inc.*, 151.

Chapter 20

Word Tricks and Propaganda

The mainstream media carry out their propaganda service on behalf of the corporate and political establishment in many ways: by choice of topics addressed (government rather than corporate abuses, welfare rather than Pentagon waste, Khadaffi rather than Guatemalan state terrorism), by their framing of issues (GDP growth rather than distribution, Federal Reserve policy effects on inflation and security prices rather than on unemployment), by their choice of sources of information (a heavy reliance on government officials and think tank flacks), and by their use of language, among other practices.

I want to focus here on the tricks of language that serve propaganda ends, although it should be recognized that biased word usage is closely tied to the other modes of bias. Heavy reliance on officals allows the officials to frame the issues and to use words in ways that serve their agenda. The word "terrorist" is applied to the target enemy (Iran), or the enemy of our friend (Hamas, the PLO, the Kurdish PKK), not the "constructively engaged" governments of Colombia, Israel, Turkey or, back in the 1980s, Savimbi and the apartheid government of South Africa. The examples below will show how story framing and word usage are essentially two aspects of a single process.

The Struggle Over Words

The integration of word usage, framing, and source selection points up the fact that language is an arena of conflict and struggle. Word meanings, connotations, and applications are fluid and change in the course of struggle. For example, labor has long fought to have the word "strike" mean a legitimate labor tactic and part of the institution of collective bargaining, whereas management has always tried to get the word to symbolize labor violence, inconvenience to the community, and damage to the GDP and to the balance of payments. Management has been pretty successful in getting the word interpreted with negative connotations. Similarly, "welfare" has taken on negative connotations as part of the 25 year long corporate and right-wing attack on the welfare state. This same campaign has seen the word "government" become a word of derogation. Politicians run against "Washington" and "government." At the same time, interestingly, because the rightwingers are fond of the military establishment, they have succeeded in making the word government applicable only to the government in its civil functions; in denouncing the "government," they do not denounce the Pentagon.

Words are regularly transformed in the service of the powerful. "Terrorism," originally used to describe state violence, as in the French Revolution era's "reign of terror," has evolved in modern times to focus mainly on antigovernment, anti-establishment forms of political violence. "Political correctness," originally an ironical leftist term for the standards of comrades prone to sectarianism, was seized by establishment spokespersons for a broad-brush castigation of the academic left. "Freedom" has been subtly transformed in the New World Order from political to economic liberty (including liberty for General Electric, General Motors, Exxon, and Royal Dutch Shell), just as "democracy" has lost its substantive qualities in favor of adherence to electoral forms. "Entitlement" has taken on negative connotations because the dominant class has succeeded in identifying it with claims of the weak, as in "Social Security entitlements" (there are no military-industrial complex "entitlements," only "procurement," service contracts, and occasionally acknowledged "subsidies").

"Reform" is the classic of word revisionism in the service of those in power, transformed from meaning institutional and policy changes that help the afflicted and weak to moves away from the welfare state and toward free markets, thus helping the afflictors and strong. In an Orwellian twist, "reform" that frees the poor and weak of their "entitlements"— pushing them into a labor market kept loose by Alan Greenspan—is referred to as "empowerment"!

Dossier of Word Tricks

Let us review some of the common word tricks of the servants of power in the media and think tank-academic community, taking examples from recent press usage.

Purring

Purr words are those with positive and warming overtones that create an aura of decency and virtue. Reform, responsible, accountability, transparency, choice, jobs, growth, modernization, flexibility, cost-benefit analysis, national security, stability, and efficiency are all prime purr words. The "reformers" are always having their "patience tested," but they never test the patience of others.[1] And reformers are invariably moderate, centrist, courageous, daring, and proud. The *New York Times*'s Leslie Gelb spoke of Les Aspin, Stephen Solarz, and Al Gore as "courageous" for having broken ranks and supported George Bush's decision to bomb Iraq rather than pursue any less violent course of action.[2] A *New York Times* headline of April 11, 1997, reads "Proud But Cornered, Mobutu Can Only Hope." Mobutu was one of the great thieves and scoundrels of modern times, but because he was installed by the CIA and protected by the West until 1997, even now he is accorded the purr word "proud," which the paper would never apply to Kim Il Sung or Saddam Hussein.

We can make a long list of purr words from names of congressional bills, always designed to express positive values, even if in substance they threaten enormous pain: New Jersey's "Family Development Initiative Act" (stripping benefits from the poor); the "National Security Revitalization Act" (more boondoggle money); the August 1996 "Personal Responsibility and Work Opportunity Reconciliation Act" (which includes five purr words in a single Orwellian classic of doublespeak for a law that ended the federal commitment to help poor people). Republican pollster and deception manager Frank Luntz carefully tested the "resonance" of words in advising Gingrich and company on the language to be used in the Contract With America. He quite openly sought and used purr words that misrepresented intent, which yielded the deception masterpiece "Job Creation and Wage Enhancement Act," for a proposal whose core content was sizable cuts in capital gains taxes.

The use of "flexibility" in "Democrats Show Flexibility On Capital Gains Tax Cut,"[3] illustrates how word usage and framing are integrated—"flexibility" gives a positive resonance and tacit approval within a framework that stresses political compromise. The paper could have used words like "cave in" or "weakening" and framed the issue as one of Democratic acceptance of a further regression in the tax structure.

For the *New York Times*, spokespersons for the military-industrial complex like senators Sam Nunn (Georgia, Lockheed) and Henry Jackson (Washington, Boeing), and the recently retired Republican Senator

Alan Simpson are "moderates" and automatically get words that express approval—an article by Claudia Dreifus about Simpson is titled "Exit Reasonable Right," and in an interview she allows Simpson uncontested justifications for his "rough" usage of Anita Hill and his assault on Peter Arnett's Gulf War reporting as traitorous.[4] A column on Jeane Kirkpatrick by Barbara Crossette was titled "A Warrior, A Mother, A Scholar, A Mystery."[5] Kirkpatrick was most memorable as a "scholar" for her view that "totalitarian" regimes like those in the Soviet bloc can never open up; and as a humanist she was perhaps best known for alleging that the four American nuns raped and murdered in El Salvador in 1980 had asked for it.

For the *Times*, the Arab world is "split into a clearly moderate, pro-Western camp led by Egypt . . . and a fiercely nationalistic anti-Western coalition gathered around Iran."[6] Moderate and pro-Western are synonymous and sources of "stability," as in "In Uneasy Time, Saudi Prince Provides a Hope of Stability."[7] Pro-Western moderates like Saudi princes, or Suharto, are never "tyrants" like Fidel Castro, and if they are not explicitly tagged moderates, approval is expressed by references to their economic accomplishments in "growth"—as regards Suharto, for example, "even his critics [unnamed] acknowledge that he has brought growth and prosperity to this country of 190 million people."[8]

A moderate program is one approved by the Western establishment, whatever its impact on the underlying population, as in "Jose Maria Aznar was appointed prime minister [of Spain] on a moderate platform, promising strict austerity to put the economic house in order."[9] As noted earlier, those who implement approved programs are accorded other purr words— they are bold and courageous, they are realists, they slay ogres, and they do things "quietly," never noisily and recklessly.[10] These purr words often not only express approval but mislead as to substance. Thus, James Sterngold says that "NAFTA is all about corporate efficiency,"[11] which is false—it is about corporate bargaining power, corporate rights to invest abroad, etc. If "moderates" carrying out neoliberal programs do so in violation of election promises, this is seen as courageous and meritorious to the dominant Western media. Politicians must "not flinch," "stay the course," and avoid "pandering to fears" (i.e., do what the electorate wants),[12] which displays the triumph of media class bias over the nominal commitment to democratic processes.

Snarling

Snarl words are those that induce negative reactions and feelings of anger and rejection, such as extremist, terrorist, dictator, dependency, welfare, reckless, outlaw, and "snarling" itself. Moderates never snarl, nor can they be outlaws, terrorists, dictators, or reckless. Established institutions like the Pentagon and large corporations don't suffer from "dependency" or receive "welfare payments." There is "waste" in social budgets, so assassins of the welfare state pretend that that is what they seek to contain in budget cuts (along with "dependency" and immorality). They can count on the mainstream media not to make comparisons of waste in social and military budgets.

Fidel Castro runs an "outdated police state."[13] Leslie Gelb spoke of the "vicious dictator" of North Korea in an article entitled "The Next Renegade State."[14] To the mainstream media, there is no "outdated police state" or "vicious dictator," let alone renegade, among the "commercially engaged" countries of the world. The *Times* has never used "vicious dictator" to describe the leader of Saudi Arabia, Pinochet, or the Argentinian generals of 1976 to 1983 who, in the words of an Argentinian truth commission, brought to Argentina a terrorism "infinitely worse" than the terror they were allegedly combatting.

Environmental "extremists" who use "junk science" are now frequently encountered in the mainstream media, especially with the numerous industry mouthpieces like ABC reporter John Stossel, Gina Kolata of the *New York Times*, and the editors of the *Wall Street Journal*. This reflects the intensified corporate assault on environmental regulation, which feeds into the media through corporate public relations and corporate-funded think tanks.[15]

The industry-think tank-media complex uses words like extremism and junk science to characterize oppositional positions and data. There is a struggle over who perpetrates junk science, but as described in chapter 17, the monied interests have a strong edge in defining the terms of the debate and word usage in the mainstream media.

Putdowns
These are less aggressive words of denigration that chide rather than snarl. Leftists are "noisy,"[16] whereas those who pursue neoliberal ends like Mexico's Zedillo, as noted, are "quiet." Leftists are victims of dogmas,[17] whereas those pursuing neoliberalism are showing courage and realism in advancing what by implication are true principles. And when leftists are not noisy but recognize their setbacks and need to adapt, they are "chastened."[18] That they might be chastened by systematic state terror that decimates their ranks need not be mentioned.

Playing Down Violence

Economic "reforms" are "tough" and toughening; Latins are "Toughened by experience."[19] Our own managers of terror abroad are "tough,"[20] and our client state leaders who kill and torture are not ruthless killers and torturers but also "tough" or merely "forceful" in their pursuit of "security."[21] Their massacres are muted into the use of "disproportionate" force or "repressive tactics" ("Mr. Clinton made the requisite complaints about Indonesia's repressive tactics in East Timor");[22] their torture is the use of "physical force" or "harsh interrogation."[23] After each Israeli invasion of Lebanon—referred to as an "incursion"—the *Times* refocuses attention away from the killed, wounded, and dispossessed victims to the "new opportunities" for diplomacy [24]

Back in 1982, U.S. officials brought to the United States a Nicaraguan officer allegedly captured in El Salvador who "confessed" that Nicaragua and Cuba were aiding the Salvadoran rebels. In a press conference in Washington, he declared that his confession had been extracted under torture. The *New York Times* article describing this was entitled "Recanter's Tale: Lesson in Humility for the U.S." (April 2, 1982). The use of "humility" allowed the story to be framed around U.S. official embarrassment at the failure to properly assess the Nicaraguan's shrewdness and ability to "hoodwink" us, and away from the fact that our clients torture people. We should be "humble" in expecting torture payoffs.

Obscuring Appeasement of Client State Terror

Key phrases that serve this function include "quiet diplomacy," "commercial diplomacy," and "constructive engagement," which are intended to suggest that the appeasing administration is really bargaining hard for human rights rather than putting a public relations face on its appeasement. We also "delink" commerce and human rights, which implies that we merely separate the two rather than that we attend to the former and ignore the latter. With commercially important client states it is notable how often relations are "complex" and negotiations with them "delicate" ("The American relationship with Saudi Arabia is complex and delicate," NYT, ed., Jan. 29, 1997), in contrast with our dealings with, say, Cuba, where words and action can be "rough." This language covers over the fact that material interest causes us to appease and even aggressively protect regimes that grossly exploit and deny basic rights to their populations.

Facilitating Innuendo

Words and phrases like "linked" and "it is reported" and "officials claim" permit connections and actions to be presented without verifiable evidence. The headline "Link to Iran suspected in Saudi blast" (*Philadelphia Inquirer*, August 3, 1996) illustrates an important mode of disseminating propaganda; and the more the allegation fits existing biases the easier it is to pass it along without supporting evidence. Only the powerful can play this game on a regular basis.

The way this system manifests bias can be seen by comparing Eric Schmitt's "Few Links in Church Fires, Panel Is Told: Official Sees Racism but No Sign of Conspiracy in Firebombings" (*New York Times*, May 22, 1996), and William Broad's "Unabom Case Is Linked to Antiwar Tumult on U.S. Campuses in 1960s" (*New York Times*, June 1, 1996). The *Times* has always treated the 1960s resistance with hostility, so here Broad "links" the accused Unabomber Theodore Kaczyinski to the antiwar movement simply because some of his teachers and fellow students opposed the Vietnam War and urged peaceful resistance, even though Broad admits that "by all accounts he was cool to the antiwar unrest." Broad could have "linked" Kaczynski's alleged violent acts to the *actual* violence of the war itself, which was the source of the peaceful protests that he "links" to Kaczynski. Broad also could have said there is no evidence tying Kaczynski to any groups that advocate violence, but that would have precluded making use of the thin and even ludicrous link that allows him to trash the 60s antiwar movement once again.

In the case of the church bombings, the *Times* chose to play down the linking possibilities. It is evident from the subhead given above that the paper could have "linked" the church-bombings to racism, but instead it chose to deny a link to a "conspiracy." This makes the bombings sound less ominous and pernicious than if they were "linked" to something. The bombings of the black churches didn't offer the paper any links they were eager to make, as in the case of the Unabomber.

Personification and Use of Collective Words

Personification of groups and nations and the use of collective words are other devices commonly employed to get across preferred positions that are not supported by evidence. The use of "Brazil" in "Faith in reform buoys Brazil" (*Financial Times*, February 24, 1997) is based entirely on attitudes expressed by Brazilian bankers and securities market professionals, who constitute less than 1 percent of the Brazilian people.

A classic of this genre was David Sanger's "Jittery Asia Has Visions of a Nuclear North Korea" (*New York Times*, April 7, 1991); the generalization to Asia was apparently based on statements of three individuals, two of them officials, one Japanese, the other South Korean. David Rosenbaum's "The Tax Break America Couldn't Give Up" (*New York*

Times, October 8, 1989) illustrates the use of a collective term to confuse an issue. He claims a generalized feeling among Americans that they are overtaxed, but this overlooks class differences in attitudes toward specific taxes. It is possible that ordinary Americans feel overtaxed but would be pleased to see higher taxes on the affluent and corporations. "America" could not give up these tax breaks because ordinary citizens have little weight in national policy making. Rosenbaum effectively obscures such consideration by his use of "Americans."

Falsely Imputing Benevolent Motives

Among my favorites are "risk" and "gamble," as they were applied to the savage welfare "reform" bill of August 1996. The *Philadelphia Inquirer* asserted that "Congress and Clinton are gambling that many poor Americans won't need a safety net to land on their feet" (August 4, 1996). The *New York Times* editorialized on the "gamble," and their house economist Peter Passell quoted a think tank analyst that the bill was taking a "risk" that the people thrown off welfare might not find jobs (August 8, 1996). The use of these words implies that Clay Shaw, Newt Gingrich, David McIntosh, and Bill Clinton were really concerned about those poor folks being pushed out on the streets and that they no doubt weighed the costs and benefits in some kind of humanistic calculus. This is apologetic nonsense. These politicians weren't taking any risks or gambles; they were serving their own political ends and/or completely unconcerned, if not actually pleased, about any pain that the victims would suffer.

It is of course standard media practice to assume that their own country has good intentions as it ravages in its backyard or other parts of the world (e.g., in the Persian Gulf or Indochina). In the media's characterization of geopolitical events, we always strive for "democracy" and resist somebody else's aggression, but never commit aggression ourselves. Even when we have destroyed a democracy, as in Guatemala in 1954, the U.S. mainstream media uniformly found this justifiable in view of "the threat of communism," which was a conveniently internalized cover for the pursuit of the interests of United Fruit Company and a determination to get rid of a reformist leadership that wouldn't take orders. The power of media rationalization of U.S. aggression reached its height during the Vietnam War when, despite the U.S.'s exclusive reliance on force, and the official recognition that our agents could not compete with the "enemy" politically, in James Reston's classic of apologetics we were in Vietnam to establish the principle "that no state shall use military force or the threat of military force to achieve its objectives."[25] With a "liberal media" that can serve state policy so egregiously, there has not been much in the way of constraint on external aggression that comes from the media itself.

Removing Agency

When we or our allies have done terrible things, watch for the resort to the passive voice and other modes of removing agency. Thus the *New York Times* subhead for the article on the ending of the Guatemalan civil war (December 30, 1996) is "After 100,000 dead, the peace ceremony is more solemn than celebratory." Actually, the numbers were well above 100,000 dead, but note the failure of the *Times* to say who did virtually all the killing or what government in 1954 displaced a nonkilling elected regime with the regime of terror whose violence is supposedly now ending. In its Indonesia reporting, also, the *Times* has trouble identifying an agent: "More than 500,000 Indonesians are estimated to have died in a purge of leftists in 1965, the year Mr. Suharto came to power" (April 8, 1997). Actually, the "purge" went well beyond "leftists," and included several hundred thousand peasant farmers; and there is no doubt who did the purging and what great power that supported the purge viewed it as a "gleam of light" in Asia.[26]

Concluding Note

These are just some of the modes by which words are manipulated to serve bias and propaganda. In many cases the process entails simply passing along the word usage and frame of the originating source. But the media claim to seek truth and serve the public (not corporate and elite) interest. That should be the standard by which we evaluate and criticize them as we seek to shrink the immense gap between their own proclaimed ideal and their actual performance.

Notes

1   "Labour costs test patience at US Airways," *Financial Times*, 14 April 1997.

2   Leslie Gelb, "A Party Derided," *New York Times*, 10 March 1991.

3   Richard Stevenson, "Democrats Show Some Flexibility On Capital Gains," *New York Times*, 23 February 1997.

4   Claudia Dreifus, "Exit Reasonable Right," *New York Times*, 1 June 1996.

5   Barbara Crossette, "A Warrior, A Mother, A Scholar, A Mystery," *New York Times*, 17 August 1994.

6   Youssef Ibrahim, "The Split Among Arabs Unleashes a People's Anger," *New York Times*, 12 August 1990.

7   Douglas Jehl, "In Uneasy Time, Saudi Prince Provides a Hope of Stability," *New York Times*, 19 January 1996.

8   Seth Mydans, "Protesters Angered by Raid Battle Police in Indonesia," *New York Times*, 28 July 1996. For an analysis of the character of, and beneficiaries from, Indonesian growth, see chapter 16.

9   Andres Wolberg-Stok, "Conservative prime minister brings Spain's socialist era to a close," *Philadelphia Inquirer*, 5 April 1996.

10 David Pilling, "Argentina slays ogre of inflation," *Financial Times*, 16 December 1996; Thomas Friedman, "Mexico's Quiet Revolution," *New York Times*, 17 December 1995.

11 James Sterngold, "Nafta Trade-Off: Some Jobs Lost, Others Gained," *New York Times*, 9 October 1995.

12 Editorial, "Why Poland Can't Flinch," *New York Times*, 17 October 1991.

13 Bill Keller, "Soviet Press Snaps Back at Castro, Painting an Outdated Police State," *New York Times*, 8 March 1990.

14 Leslie Gelb, "The Next Renegade State," *New York Times*, 10 April 1991.

15 See Sheldon Rampton and John Stauber, *Toxic Sludge Is Good for You* (Monroe, ME: Common Courage Press, 1996); Dan Fagin and Marianne Lavelle, *Toxic Deception* (Secaucus, NJ: Birch Lane Press, 1996); "A Million For Your Thoughts: The Industry-funded Campaign Against the FDA by Conservative Think Tanks," Public Citizen (1996).

16 Thomas Vogel and Matt Moffett, "Latin Leftists Make a Noisy Comeback," *Wall Street Journal*, 2 January 1997.

17   Wolfgang Munchau, "German unions dump left-wing dogmas," *Financial Times*, 16–17 November 1996.

18   Larry Rohter, "A Chastened Latin Left Puts Its Hope in Ballots," *New York Times*, 29 July 1996.

19   Virginia March and Kevin Done, "Tough reforms bring rewards," *Financial Times*, 16 December 1996; Stephen Fidler, "Toughened by experience," *Financial Times*, 10 February 1997.

20   Philip Shenon, "'Tough' Guy For Latin Job" [Elliott Abrams], *New York Times*, 1 May 1985,

21   Argentinian General Robert Viola was described as "tough," though a "populist figure," by Edward Schumacher in the *New York Times*, 6 October 1980; see also, "Sharon, the Forceful General Intent on Security for Israel," *New York Times*, 11 February 1983 (no byline).

22   Lionel Barber, "EU criticises Israel's use of disproportionate force," *Financial Times*, 2 October 1996; the Clinton quote is from David Sanger, "Real Politics: Why Suharto Is In and Castro Is Out," *New York Times*, 31 October 1995.

23   Serge Schmemann, "Israel Allows Use of Physical Force in Arab's Interrogation," *New York Times*, 16 November 1996; Joel Greenberg, "Israel Is Permitting Harsher Interrogation of Muslim Militants," *New York Times*, 17 November 1994.

24   Bernard Gwertzman, "Shock of War Could Improve Opportunities For Diplomacy," *New York Times*, 11 July 1982; Leslie Gelb, "U.S. Sees Opportunities and Risks In Mideast After War in Lebanon," *New York Times*, 31 October 1982.

25   James Reston, "The Guiding Principle in Vietnam," *New York Times*, 26 February 1965.

26   James Reston, "Washington: A Gleam of Light," *New York Times*, 19 June 1966. Many more illustrations of the *Times*'s playing down of the Indonesian killings are given in chapter 16.

Chapter 21

Toward a Democratic Media

A democratic media is a primary condition of popular rule, hence of a genuine political democracy. Where the media are controlled by a powerful and privileged elite, whether it be by government leaders and bureaucrats or those from the private sector, democratic political forms and some kind of limited political democracy may exist, but not genuine democracy. The public will not be participants in the media; instead, they will be consumers of facts and opinions distributed to them from above. The media will, of structural necessity, select news and organize debate supportive of agendas and programs of the privileged. They will not provide the unbiased information and opinion that would permit the public to make choices in accord with its own best interests. Their job will be to show that what is good for the elites is good for everybody, and that other options are either bad or do not exist.

Media Sovereignty and Freedom of Choice

Economists have long distinguished between "consumer sovereignty" and "freedom of consumer choice." The former requires that consumers participate in deciding what is to be offered in the first place; the latter requires only that consumers be free to select among the options chosen for them by producers. Freedom of choice is better than no freedom of choice, and the market may provide a substantial array of options. But it may not. Before the foreign car invasion in the 1960s, U.S. car manufacturers chose not to offer small cars because the profit margin on small cars is small. It was better to have choices among four or five manufacturers than only one, but the options were constrained by producer interest. Only the entry of foreign competition made small cars available to U.S. buyers. Freedom of choice prevailed in both cases, but consumer sovereignty did not. The cost of *producer* sovereignty was also manifest in the policy of General Motors Corporation, in cahoots with rubber and oil interests, of buying up public transit lines and converting them to GM buses or liquidating them.[1] The consumers of transportation services, if fully informed, might well have chosen to preserve and subsidize the electric transit option, but this sovereign decision was not open to them.

This distinction between sovereignty and free choice has important applications to both national politics and the mass media. In each case, the general population has some kind of free choice, but lacks sovereignty. The public—actually, a shrinking fraction of the public—goes to the polls every few years to pull a lever for slates of candidates chosen for them by political parties that are heavily dependent on funding by powerful elite interests. The public has "freedom of choice" only among a very restricted set of what we might call "effective" candidates, effectiveness being defined by the ability of candidates to attract the funding necessary to make a credible showing.

At the level of mass communication as well, the dominant media with large audiences are owned by an overlapping set of powerful elite interests. There is a fringe media with very limited outreach that might support "ineffective" candidates, but because of their marginal status they and the candidates they support can be easily ignored. As with the candidates, the populace has "freedom of choice" among the dominant set of mainstream media, but it lacks sovereignty except in a legalistic and formal sense (we are each legally free to start our own newspaper or buy our own paper or TV network).[2] The elite-dominated mass media, not surprisingly, find the political system admirable, and while they sometimes express regret at the quality of candidates, they never seriously question the absence of citizen sovereignty in decisions about the effective options.

Naturally, also, the mass media hardly mention the undemocratic underpinning of the political process in the media itself. In fact, one of the most disquieting features of propaganda systems of the constrained democracies of advanced capitalism is that the consolidation of mass media power has closed down discussion of the need for radical restructuring of the media. It has also pushed such changes off the political agenda. As the "gatekeepers," the mass media have been in the enviable position of being able to protect themselves from debate or political acts that threaten their interests, which illustrates the deeply undemocratic character of *their* role.

The last great fight over structural change in the mass media was in 1934, when the FCC was created and broadcasting policy was fixed. At that time, an important lobbying effort pressed for the reservation of 25 percent of air channels for nonprofit operations. This was defeated by the power of the commercial lobby and by their assurance that they would service public interest needs.[3] As advertising grew, however, and entertainment and "noncontroversial" programming proved more profitable than public affairs and educational children's programming, the latter were gradually abandoned—but all on the quiet, as the gatekeepers determined, without any public debate or public decision.

Occasionally, issues like TV violence have aroused public opinion and caused the Congress to hold hearings and assail the TV networks, but the whole business has always been settled by appeals to corporate responsibility and self-regulation, and the media barons' assurance of their deepest concern and commitment to rectifying the situation. In 1977, however, an unusually aggressive and naive congressional subcommittee actually drafted a report that called for investigation of the structure of the TV industry, as a necessary step toward attacking the violence problem at its source. As George Gerbner described the sequel:

> When the draft mentioning industry structure was leaked to the networks, all hell broke loose. Members of the subcommittee told me that they had never before been subject to such relentless lobbying and pressure. Campaign contributors were contacted. The report was delayed for months. The subcommittee staffer who wrote the draft was summarily fired. The day before the final vote was to be taken, a new version drafted by a broadcast lobbyist was substituted. It ignored the evidence of the hearings and gutted the report, shifting the source of the problem from network structure to the parents of America. When the network-dictated draft came to a vote, members of the full committee (including those who had never attended hearings) were mobilized, and the watered down version won by one vote.[4]

In short, the power of the highly undemocratic mass media is enormous.

What Would A Democratic Media Look Like?

A democratic media can be identified by its structure and functions. In terms of structure, it would be organized and controlled by ordinary citizens or their grassroots organizations. This could involve individuals or bodies that serve local or larger political, minority, or other groups in the social and political arena. Media fitting these structural conditions would be bound to articulate demands of the general population because they are either part of it or instruments created to serve its needs.

In the mainstream system, the mass media are large organizations owned by other large organizations or shareholders and controlled by members of a privileged business elite. The ownership structure puts them at a distance from ordinary people. They are funded by advertising, and advertisers have to be convinced that the programs meet their needs. Thus in terms of fundamental structure the mainstream media are not agents serving the general public: the first responsibility of their managers by law is to stockholders seeking profits; and as advertisers are the principal source of revenue, their needs come second. There is no legal responsibility to audiences at all; consumers must be persuaded to watch or buy, by any means the gatekeeper chooses, within the limits of law and conventional standards of morality.

As regards function, a democratic media will aim first and foremost to serve the informational, cultural, and other communications needs of the members of the public that the media institutions comprise or represent. The users would determine their own needs and fix the menu of choices either directly or through their closely controlled agents, and debate would not be limited to selected voices chosen by corporate or governmental gatekeepers. The sovereign listeners would not only participate in choosing programs and issues to be addressed, they would *be* the voices heard, and they would be involved in continuous interchanges with other listeners. There would be a horizontal flow of communication, in both directions, instead of a vertical flow from officials and experts to the passive population of consumers.

At the same time, a democratic media would recognize and encourage diversity. It would allow and encourage minorities to express their views and build their own communities' solidarity within the larger community. This would follow from the democratic idea of recognizing and encouraging individual differences and letting all such flowers bloom irrespective of financial capability and institutional power. This is also consistent with the ideal of pluralism, which is part of mainstream orthodox doctrine but is poorly realized in mainstream practice. The commercial media serve minority constituencies badly; they tend to repeat homogenizing mainstream cultural and market themes and ignore groups entirely when they are really poor. In Hungary, for example, the new commercial media, "have a radio programme for tourists from German-speaking countries, but none for hundreds of thousands of gypsies living in Hungary (7 percent of the population)."[5] The same criticism often applies to state controlled media.[6]

A democratic media would encourage people to know and understand their neighbors and to participate in social and political life. This is likely to occur where media structures are democratic, as such media will be open to neighbors who want to communicate views on problems and their possible communal resolution. Commercial media aim to entertain and divert, and tied in as they are to the dominant institutions, they serve the dominant elites and status quo, and avoid controversial messages of people who want to initiate change. The commercial and state media treat the citizenry as passive recipients of entertainment and information that are offered from above. The media are not agents of a democratic citizenry, but of a business and state elite.

Talk Shows: Phony Populism, Phony Democracy
The talk show radio and TV "revolution" in the United States offers the facade of something democratic, but not much of the substance. The interaction of talk show hosts with the public is carefully controlled by screening out undesired questions, and there are very limited exchanges between hosts and a "statistically insignificant" proportion of the listening audience.[7] Rush Limbaugh, for example, has a sizable audience of proudly self-styled "ditto heads," but they are entertained in pseudo postmodern monologues with a minimum of genuine interaction. There is a kind of quasi-community built among the followers, who listen, meet together, buy and discuss the master's (and other recommended) books, but the community has a cultish quality, and the master's discourse is no more democratic than was Father Charles Coughlin's radio talk show back in the 1930s. The community is led by a leader who possesses, and guides the followers to, the truth.

As is well-known, many of the talk show hosts are right-wing populists, who claim concern over the distress of ordinary citizens but never succeed in finding the sources of that distress in the workings of corporate capital and its impact on politics, unemployment, wage levels, and economic insecurity. They focus on symptoms and scapegoats, like crime, black welfare mothers, enivronmental extremists, and "family values" issues. Their service is comparable to that of the Nazi movement during the Weimar Republic years in Germany in the 1920s in that they divert attention from real causes of distress, and by obfuscating issues and stirring up the forces of irrationality they serve to weaken any threat of meaningful organization and protest from below.

Routes to Democratizing the Media

There are two main routes to democratizing the media. One route is to try to influence the mainstream media to give more room to now-excluded ideas and groups. This could be done by persuasion, pressure, or by legislation compelling greater access. The second route is to create and support an alternative structure of media closer to ordinary people and grassroots organizations that would replace, or at least offer an important alternative to, the mainstream media. This could be done, in principle, by private and popular initiative, by legislative action, or by a combination of the two.

The first route is of limited value as a long-run solution to the problem precisely because it fails to attack the structural roots of the media's lack of democracy. If function follows from structure, then the gains from pursuit of the first route are likely to be modest and transitory. These small gains may also lead both activists and ordinary citizens to conclude that the mainstream media are really open to dissent, when in fact dissent is securely kept in a nonthreatening position. And it may divert energy from the task of building an alternative media. On the other hand, the limited access obtained by pursuit of the first route may have disproportionate and catalyzing effects on elite opinion. This route may also be the only one that appeals to many media activists, and there is no assurance that the long run strategy of pursuing structural change will work.

The second route to democratization of the media is the only one that can yield a truly democratic media, and it is this route that I will discuss in greater detail. Without a democratic structure, the media will serve a democratic function inadequately at best, and very possibly even perversely, by working as agents of the *real* (dominant corporate) "special interests" to confuse and divert the public. The struggle for a democratic media structure is also of increasing urgency because the media have become less democratic in recent decades with the decline in relative importance of the public and nonprofit broadcasting spheres, increased commercialization and integration of the mass media into the market, conglomeration, and internationalization. In important respects the main ongoing struggle has been to prevent further attrition of democratic elements in the media.

This has been very evident in Western Europe, where powerful systems of public broadcasting as well as non-profit local radio stations have been under relentless attack by commercial and conservative political interests that have become increasingly influential in state policy. These changes have threatened diversity, quality, and relatively democratic organizational arrangements. In the former Soviet bloc, where state controlled media institutions are being rapidly dismantled, there is a dire threat that an undemocratic system of government control will be replaced by an equally undemocratic system of commercial domination. The same is true of Third World nations, which, while presenting a mixed picture of a government sector, private/commercial sector, and a sometimes important civic sector, have increasingly been brought within the orbit of a globalizing commercial media.

It is obvious that a thoroughgoing democratization of the media can only occur in connection with a drastic alteration in the structure of power and political revolution. Democratizing a national media would be very difficult in a large and complex society like the United States even with unlimited structural options, just as organizing a democratic polity here would be a bit more tricky than in a tiny Greek city-state or an autonomous New England town. An important step toward a democratic media would be a move back to the Articles of Confederation and beyond—to really small units within which people can interact on a personal level. For larger political units personal interaction is more difficult; efficiency and market considerations make for a centralization of national and international news gathering, processing, and distribution, and of cultural and entertainment productions as well. Funding would have to be insulated from business and government, but it could not be completely insulated from democratic decision-making processes. Maintaining involvement and control by ordinary citizens, while allowing a necessary degree of specialization and centralization, and permitting artistic autonomy as well, would present a serious challenge to democratic organization. As this is not on the immediate agenda, however, I will not try to spell out here the machinery and arrangements whereby these conflicting ends can be accomplished.

Some partial guidelines for the pursuit of democratic structural change in the media here can be derived from the current debates and struggles in Europe, where the democratic forces are trying to hold the line (in Western Europe) and prevent wholesale commercialization (in the East). The democrats have stressed the deadly effects of privatization and commercialization on a democratic polity and culture and have urged the importance of preserving and enlarging the *public* and *civic* sectors of the media. The public sector is the government-sponsored sector, which is far more important in Western Europe than it is in this country. It is funded by direct governmental grants, license fees, and to an increasing but controlled extent, advertising. This sector is designed to be and is responsible for serving the public interest in news, public affairs, educational, children's, and other cultural programming. It is assumed in Europe that the commercial sector will pursue large audiences with entertainment (movies, sitcoms, cowboy and crime stories) and that its long-term trend toward abandonment of nonentertainment values will continue.[8]

The civic sector comprises the media that are noncommercial but also not government sponsored, and that arise by individual or grassroots initiatives. This includes some mainly local newspapers and journals, independent movie and TV producers, and radio broadcasters. The civic sector has virtually no TV presence in Europe, but radio broadcasting by nonprofit organizations is still fairly important, sufficiently so to have produced a European Federation of Community Radios (FERL) to exchange ideas and coordinate educational and lobbying efforts to advance their ideals and protect their interests.

FERL has been lobbying throughout Europe for explicit recognition of the important role of the noncommercial, and especially the civic, sector in governmental and intergovernmental policy-making. It has urged the preservation and enlargement of this sector by policy choice. In France, the civic sector actually gets some funding from the state through a tax on commercial advertising revenues. This is a model that could be emulated elsewhere. It should be noted, however, that in the conservative political environment of the past decade, the policies of the French regulatory authority, the Higher Broadcasting Council, have reduced the number of nonprofit radio stations from 1,000 to under 300, and have also discriminated heavily in favor of religious and right-wing broadcasters.

Democratizing the U.S. Media

Democratizing the U.S. media is an even more formidable task than that faced by Europeans. In Western Europe, public broadcasting is important, even if it is under siege, and community radio is a more important force there than it is in the United States. In Eastern Europe the old government-dominated systems are crumbling, so that there are options and an ongoing struggle for control. In the United States, commercial systems are more powerfully entrenched; the public sector is weak and has been subject to steady right-wing attack for years; and the civic sector, although it is alive and bustling, is small, mainly local, and undernourished. The question is, what is to be done?

Funding
An extremely important problem for those who want to democratize the media is that the commercial sector is self-funding, with large resources obtained from advertising, whereas the public and civic sectors are chronically starved. This gives the commercial media an overwhelming advantage in technical quality, polish, price, publicity, and distribution. An im-

portant part of a democratic media strategy must consist of figuring out how to obtain sizable and more stable resources for the public and civic sectors. The two promising sources are taxes on commercial media revenues and direct government grants. Commercial radio and TV are getting the free use of the spectrum and satellite paths, which are a public resource, to turn a private profit, and there is an important record of commitments to public service made by commercial broadcasters and the FCC in 1934 and 1946 that have been quietly sloughed off.[9] These considerations make a franchise or spectrum use tax, with the revenues turned over to the public and civic sectors that have taken on those abandoned responsibilities, completely justifiable. We could also properly extend a tax on spectrum use to cellular and other telephone transmission, which also use public airwaves, possibly placing the tax revenue into a fund to help extend telephone service as well as other communications infrastructure to Third World areas at home and abroad.

The funding of the public and civic sectors from general tax revenues and/or license fees on receiving sets is also easily defended, given the great importance of these sectors in educational, childrens', minority group, and public affairs programming. These services are important to the cultivation of a democratic citizenry, among other aims.

In sum, local, regional, and national groups that are interested in democratizing the media should give high priority to organization, education, and lobbying designed to sharply increase and stabilize the funding of the financially strapped public and civic sectors. Success in these endeavors will depend in large measure on the general political climate.[10]

The Commercial Sector
The commercial sector of the media does provide some small degree of diversity, insofar as individual proprietors may allow it and advertisers can be mobilized in niche markets of liberal and progressive bent (such as *The New Yorker*, the *Village Voice*, and the urban alternative press). But this diversity is within narrow bounds, and rarely if ever extends to support for policies that involve fundamental change. Furthermore, the main drift of commercial markets is absolutely antithetic to democratic media service, and although we may welcome offbeat and progressive commercial media institutions, we should recognize the inherent tendencies of the commercial media.[11]

It will still be desirable to oppose further consolidation, conglomeration, cross-ownership of the mainstream media, and discriminatory exclusions of outsiders, not only because they make the media less democratic, but also because they help further centralize power and make progressive change in the media and elsewhere more difficult.[12] I also favor "fairness doctrine" and quantitative requirements for local, public affairs, and children's programs for commercial radio and TV broadcasters. Part of the reason for this is straightforward: it is an outrage that they have abandoned public service in their quest for profit. A more devious reason is this: pressing the commercial broadcasters, and describing in detail how they have abandoned children and public service for "light fare," will strengthen the case for taxing them and funding the public and civic sectors.

In Europe, commercial broadcasters are sometimes obligated by law, or by contract arrangements that were made when spectrum rights were given, to provide a certain amount of time to quality children's programs at prime time, or to give blocks of broadcasting time to various groups such as labor organizations, church groups, and political parties in proportion to their membership size (not their money). In Europe and elsewhere, also, broadcasters are obligated to give significant blocks of free time to political parties and candidates in election periods. These are all desirable, and should be on the agenda here in the United States. They are not being considered because the media would suffer economic costs, so that the public is not even allowed to know about and debate these options.[13]

Various groups have been formed in this country to lobby and threaten the media, the most important and effective of which are those on the right.[14] Notable among those that represent a broader public interest was Action For Children's Television (ACT), which was organized in 1968 to fight the commercial media's degradation of children's programming.[15] Also worthy of special mention is Fairness and Accuracy in Reporting (FAIR), a media monitoring group that has published numerous special studies of media bias as well as an ongoing monitoring review, *EXTRA!* FAIR also produces a weekly half-hour radio program, "Counterspin," heard on over 115 (mostly public, community, and college) stations, that provides media criticism and alternative news analysis.

The Public Sector
The Corporation for Public Broadcasting was brought into existence in 1967, with the acquiescence of the commercial broadcasters, who were pleased to transfer public interest responsibilities elsewhere as long as they were funded by taxpayers. Over the years, public radio and public TV have been more open to dissent and minority voices than the com-

mercial broadcasting media, partly a result of original design, but also because, despite their ties to government, they have proven to be somewhat more independent of government and tolerant of the controversial than the commercial broadcasters.[16]

The independence and quality of the public sector depends heavily on the political environment. As long as it is kept on a short financial leash, underfunded, and worried mainly about attacks from the right, it will feature a William Buckley and a John McLaughlin, with Mark Shields on "the left," and offer mainly bland and cautious news and commentary along with noncontroversial nature programs and cultural events.[17] Not surprisingly, public broadcasting went into serious decline in the Reagan-Bush years. It needs a lot more money, longer funding periods, more autonomy, and less continuous threatening pressure from the right-wing to perform well. There is an important role for the public sector in a system of democratic media, and its rehabilitation should definitely be on the democratic media agenda.

The Civic Sector
For real progress in democratizing the media a much larger place must be carved out for the civic sector. This is the nonprofit sector organized by individuals or grassroots organizations to serve the communications interests and needs of the general population (as opposed to the corporate community and the government). The building of a media civic sector is important as part of community-building and the democratic process itself. Democratic media analysts stress that the public must *participate* in the media, and in the public sphere in which public opinion is formed, if they are to participate in public life.[18]

Alternative Press. There is an alternative local press in many cities in the United States, usually distributed without charge and funded by advertising, that provides a small but shrinking opening for dissent and debate. This alternative press has a national Association of Alternative News Weeklies with 113 members and a readership of over six million, but there may be as many more nonmember alternative papers. Most of its members came into existence in the 1970s and 1980s as businesses, targeting a young, affluent audience and advertisers of fashion, food, movies and popular music. As David Armstrong points out, this press was a "depoliticized successor" to the highly committed underground press of the 1960s, and it "is looking less 'alternative' all the time, becoming in subtle degrees safer and softer, emphasizing more entertainment coverage and lifestyle journalism."[19] It has been integrated even more closely into the market system through a merger movement that has absorbed a quarter or more of the alternative papers into chains, with New Times and Stern Publishing in the vanguard.[20] This has further weakened the alternative press as a force for dissent and diversity.

Although it is possible to depend on advertising and still maintain press substance, the costs of serious dissent may be heavy and the sorry evolution of the alternative news weeklies is not encouraging. Nevertheless, the *Village Voice* has provided a small quantum of dissent in the huge market of New York City. Even more interesting is the *Anderson Valley Advertiser* (*AVA*) of Boonville, California, a local paper that has survived in a small town despite the radical perspectives of its editor. It has been subjected to advertising boycotts and is avoided regularly by some advertisers on political grounds, but its advertising penalties are partially offset by the wider readership generated by its exciting quality and vigor. *AVA* is a model of democratic newspaper work in its good local news coverage, its exceptional openness to letters and petitions, and the continuous and sometimes furious debates among readers and between readers and editors that constitute a kind of town meeting on paper. A host of local issues are addressed, and national and global issues are debated in columns and letters, although no attempt is made to provide national and international news coverage. A thousand papers like *AVA* would make this a much more democratic country.

With the demise of the New York *Guardian* in 1992, the only national alternative newspaper is the biweekly *In These Times*, with a circulation of only 15,000, despite its high quality and avoidance of the doctrinaire. Even this one publication struggles each year for reader and other subventions to keep afloat. It deserves support, and its continued existence and growth, and the addition of other alternative national papers, is important in a democratic media project.

Alternative Journals. There are a fair number of liberal and left alternative journals in the United States, including *The Nation, Z Magazine, The Progressive, Mother Jones, Dollars and Sense, Monthly Review, MS Magazine, The Texas Observer, CovertAction Quarterly, EXTRA!*, and others. Apart from *Mother Jones*, which has sometimes crossed the quarter million mark in circulation, based on large promotional campaigns, *The Nation* has the largest readership, with about 100,000. Most of the alternative journals have circulations between 2,000 and 30,000, and have chronic financial problems. By contrast, *Time* has a circulation of some four million and *Reader's Digest* 15 million in North America alone (both have large sales overseas as well). Some of the alternative journals could expand circulation with aggressive and large-scale publicity and higher quality copy, but this would cost a lot of money. Not many of the 189 U.S. billionaires are inclined to set up trust funds to help enlarge the circulation of alternative journals.[21] Advertisers are also not bending over backwards to throw business their way.

Alternative Radio. Radio may be a more promising avenue for growth and greater outreach of alternative media than the print media. More people are prone to listen to radio and watch TV than read journals, or even newspapers, which are harder to get into the hands of audiences. Radio broadcasting facilities are not expensive. Community radio grew rapidly in the early 1970s, but its growth then tapered off, in part a result of the shortage of additional frequencies in the larger markets. Of the roughly 1,500 noncommercial radio licenses outstanding, half are allocated to religious broadcasters. Many of the remaining 750 are college and university linked, and Larry Soley estimates that fewer than 150 licenses are held by community organizations.[22]

Many of the community stations have languished for want of continuity of programming and spotty quality. Discrete and sporadic programs do not command large audiences; building substantial audiences requires that many people know that particular types of programs are going to be there, day after day, at a certain time period. (This is why stations become "all news," or have talk shows all morning and rock music all afternoon.) There are also the usual problems of funding and threats to licenses by more powerful commercial interests who are seeking to enlarge their domains. Nonetheless, these stations are precious in their pluralism in programming and diversity among staff and volunteers, and they meet the democratic standard of community involvement and serious public debate. Noam Chomsky "has observed that when he speaks in a town or city that has an alternative radio station, people tend to be more informed and aware of what is going on."[23]

Pacifica's five-station network and News Service have done yeoman work in providing alternative and high-quality radio programming and in developing a sizable and loyal listenership. Under constant right-wing attack and threat, and suffering even more from a centralization and abuse of top management power in the late 1990s, it is in constant turmoil and its important dissident role has been put in jeopardy. Radio Zinzine in Forcalquier, a small town of Upper Provence in France, provides an important model of constructive use of radio. Organized by the members of the progressive cooperative Longo Mai, Radio Zinzine has given the local farmers and townspeople a more vigorous and action-oriented form of local news (as well as broader news coverage and entertainment), but also an avenue for communication among formerly isolated and consequently somewhat apathetic people. It has energized the local population, encouraged its participation, and made it more of a genuine community.

In a dramatic example of how democratic media come into existence out of the needs of ordinary people who want to speak and encourage others to communicate, M'Banna Kantako, a 31-year-old black, blind, unemployed public housing resident in Springfield, Illinois, organized Black Liberation Radio in 1986, out of frustration with the failure of the major media to provide news and entertainment of interest to the black community. Operating illegally on a one-watt transmitter with a range of one mile, Kantako provides a genuine alternative to the black community. Kantako was ignored by the FCC and dominant media till he broadcast a series of interviews with blacks who had been brutalized by the local police. Soon thereafter the FCC tried to get him off the air and a court order was issued to close him down, but it remains unenforced. Undefended by the local media, Kantako has gotten considerable national publicity and support. Grass roots organizers and student groups from practically every state and a number of foreign countries have contacted him, and numerous other similar "micro-radio" stations have gone on the air.[24] As Soley says, free radio broadcasting "has emerged as a major tool for circumventing government restrictions on free expression,"[25] and it is a genuinely democratic media. But it remains under steady FCC attack and threat, even as the FCC approves gigantic media mergers that increase concentration and weaken the public sphere.[26]

Another important model is David Barsamian's Alternative Radio, which has produced and distributed a weekly one-hour public affairs program since 1986, using rented space on a satellite channel to provide solid alternative programming to U.S. stations interconnected with the satellite. Alternative Radio uses a one-on-one interview format, and has focused on "the media, U.S. foreign policy, racism, the environment, NAFTA/GATT and economic issues, and other topics," with guests like Elaine Bernard (Canadian labor activist, speaking on Creating a New Party), Juliet Schor (author of *The Overworked American*), Charles Kernaghan (speaking on the Global Factory: Kathie Lee, The Gap and Disney), John Stauber (on Lies, Damn Lies and Public Relations), and Vandana Shiva (on Biopiracy: The Plunder of Nature and Knowledge).[27] These are quality offerings of unusual depth and commentators of high merit rarely encountered in the mainstream media. Some 400 stations have a capacity to receive Alternative Radio's offerings; foreign stations in

Canada, Australia, and elsewhere have to be reached by tapes that are mailed.

Alternative TV. The mainstreaming and commercialization of public TV led to the entry of several new public TV stations in the 1980s that were designed to service the public interest function abandoned by the dominant PBS stations. In an embarrassing episode for PBS, an internal PBS research study found that the new applicants and entrants would not be competing much with the older stations, as the older ones had moved to serve an upscale audience.[28] Meanwhile, the older stations have lobbied aggressively to prevent the new ones from sharing in government funding slotted for public TV stations. It goes without saying that the new stations deserve support as a democratizing force, although the older ones should not be written off—rather, they need reorganization and regeneration to allow them to throw off the Reagan-Bush era incubus and better serve a public function. This renewal has not taken place in the Clinton era, during which time the line has barely been held against further erosion.

The growth of cable opened up democratic options, partly in the greater numbers of channels and potentially enlarged diversity of commercial cable, but more importantly in the frequent obligation of cable systems to provide public access channels and facilities. First imposed as a requirement by the FCC in 1972, partly as an impediment to cable growth by an FCC that was still serving the commercial broadcasters' interests, the public access movement was eventually institutionalized as part of negotiated agreements between cable companies seeking franchises and community negotiators. In many cases the contracts called for cable companies to provide facilities and training to public access users, and in some instances a percentage of cable revenues (1 to 5 percent) was contracted to be set aside to fund the access operations.[29]

This important development offers a resource and opportunity that demands far more attention from media activists than it has gotten. Spokespersons for the public access movement call attention to the fact that there are over 1,200 public, educational, and governmental access organizations and local origination services where TV production takes place for access on cable, and that more than 20,000 hours of original material is transmitted over public access channels per week to an unknown but probably fairly sizable audience. The problems here, as with community radio, lie in the spotty quality of original programming, the frequent absence of the continuity that makes for regular watching, and the lack of promotional resources. The existing levels of participation are valuable, but public access remains marginal and has been under increasing attack from cable owners who no longer need public access supporters as allies and have been trying hard to throw off any public access responsibilities. Although important for a democratic media—along with community radio, this *is* democratic media—public access is under threat; the relevant cable contracts are up for renewal over the next few years and cable access needs to be used, enlarged, and protected from attrition.

A strenuous effort has been made by some media democrats to fill the programming gap with centrally assembled or produced materials that are made available through network pools of video-tapes and by transmission of fresh materials through satellites. Paper Tiger TV has been providing weekly programs on Manhattan Cable for years, and has been making these programs available to public access stations and movement groups who want to use them in meetings.[30] An affiliated organization, Deep Dish Network, has tried to provide something like a mainstream network equivalent for public access stations, assembling and producing quality programs that are publicized in advance and transmitted via satellite to alerted individual dish owners, groups, and university and public access stations able to downlink the programs. There are some 3 million home satellite dish owners in North America who can receive Deep Dish offerings, and it is programmed on more than 300 cable systems and by many individual TV stations.

In addition to its notable ten-part Gulf Project series, which provided an alternative to mainstream TV's promotional coverage of the Persian Gulf War, Deep Dish has had a six part program on Latino issues (immigration, work exploitation and struggles, history, etc.), and during 1992, counter-celebratory programs on Columbus's conquest of the New World. On December 1, 1991, it transmitted an hour-long live program by Kitchen Center professional artists in conjunction with Visual AIDS, entitled "Day Without Art," as part of a day of action and mourning in response to the AIDS crisis. Although the program was performed in New York City, live audiences received the program in eight cities, and a much wider audience call-in operation was organized as part of the program. Group viewings and cable showings were encouraged in advance. Deep Dish has also broadcast a series on "Beyond Censorship: The Assault on Civil Liberties," a program on "Staking a Claim in Cyberspace," a twelve-part series on the U.S. healthcare system entitled "Sick and Tired of Being Sick and Tired," and most recently, two series on the U.S. prison system and the prison-industrial complex ("Bars and Stripes," and "Lockdown USA").

Deep Dish has tried to use its productions as an organizing tool and has worked with community groups to help them tell their stories and to get them to mobilize their constituencies to become aware of access and other media issues. This is extremely valuable, but Deep Dish suffers from the sporadic nature of its offerings, which harks back to the basic problem of funding. An excellent case can be made for funding Deep Dish and similar services to the civic sector out of franchise taxes on the commercial stations or from general tax revenues.

Internet

The Internet affords a new mode of communication that opens some possibilities for democratizing communications. It allows very rapid communication locally, nationally, and beyond national borders; it is relatively cheap to send messages to a potentially wide audience; and up to this point it is not completely dominated by advertisers, governments, or any other establishment institutions. This and related forms of relatively uncontrollable communication were important in bringing about the collapse of the Soviet Union; the Internet allowed dissident forces to maintain close contact and helped keep foreign allies abreast of events. It has also been important in the Chiapas revolt in Mexico and its aftermath; it enabled the Zapatista rebels to get out their messages at home and abroad quickly, and interfered with government attempts to crush the rebellion quietly, in the traditional manner.[31] This caused Rand Corporation analyst David Ronfeldt to speak of "netwar" and a prospective problem of "ungovernability" in Mexico that followed in part from this uncontrollable media.[32] This recalls Samuel Huntington's and the Trilateral Commission's fears of ungovernability in the United States and other Western countries based on the loss of apathy of the unimportant people in the 1960s. In short, the new media-based "threat" of ungovernability is establishment code language for an inability of government to manipulate and repress at will, or an increase in democracy.

However, it is important to recognize the limitations of the Internet as a form of democratic media, both currently and in the more uncertain future. Access to the Internet is not free; it requires a powerful computer, programs, the price of access, and some moderate degree of technical know-how. Business interests are making very rapid advances into the Internet, so that problems of more difficult and expensive access and domination and saturation by an advertising-linked system is a real possibility. Furthermore, the Internet is an individualized system, with connections between individuals that require prior knowledge of common interests, direct and indirect routes to interchanges and shared information, and the buildup of information pools. It is well geared toward efficient communication among knowledgeable and sophisticated elites and elite groups, but its potential for reaching mass audiences seems unpromising. This is extremely important, as constructive change is not likely to come about unless supported by a mass movement, built on a rational understanding of social forces, and with a coherent vision of an alternative set of institutions and policies. Otherwise, those in command of access to mass audiences (and military forces) will eventually restore "law and order" in a more repressive environment, with business institutions and priorities intact.

Technological Change

More generally, the sharp reductions in price and increased availability of VCRs, camcorders, FAX machines, computers, modems, e-mail, the Internet, and desktop publishing have made possible easier communication among individuals, the low cost production of journals and books, and new possibilities for TV production and programming. Of course, the telephone, mimeograph, offset printing, and photocopying machines had the same potential earlier and were put to good use, but they never put the establishment up against the wall. When significant technological changes occur, those with money and power tend to guide innovation and use the new technologies first, and frequently have moved on to something better by the time these innovations reach ordinary citizens. Camcorders do not solve the problem of producing really attractive TV programs, let alone getting them shown and widely distributed. Although books may be produced more cheaply with new desktop facilities, changes in commercial distribution—blockbusters, saturation advertising, deals with the increasingly concentrated distribution networks—may easily keep dissident books as marginalized as ever. It remains to be seen whether the Internet produces an exception to this tradition of commercial domination.

In perhaps the most dramatic illustration of the problem of catch-up, the new communications technologies in the possession of the Pentagon and mainstream media during the Persian Gulf War—video, satellite, and computer—conferred a new and enormous power to mold images, block out history and context, and make instant history. John M. Phelan summarized his analysis of the new, centrally controlled communications technology with the title "Image Industry Erodes Political Space."[33] And George Gerbner pointed out that "past, present and future can now be packaged, witnessed, and frozen into memorable moving imagery of instant history—scripted, directed, and produced by the winners."[34]

The point is, it is important for democratic media advance that democratic participants be alert to and take advantage of every technological innovation. The growth of common dissident carriers like EcoNet, LBBS, and PeaceNet has been an important source of tools for education, research, and a means of alerting and communicating among activists.[35] But the challenge of reaching large audiences, as compared to the relative ease with which democratic activists can communicate within and between small groups, remains severe.

Concluding Note

The trend of media evolution is paradoxical: On the one hand, there is an ongoing trend in the West toward increasing media centralization and commercialization and a corresponding weakening of the public sector. On the other hand, the civic sphere of nongovernmental and noncommercial media and computer networks linked to grassroots organizations and minority groups has displayed considerable vitality; and even though it has been pressed to defend its relative position overall, it has a greater potential than ever for coordinating actions and keeping activists at home and abroad informed.

It has been argued in this chapter that the civic sector is the locus of the truly democratic media and that genuine democratization in Western societies will be contingent on its great enlargement. Those actively seeking the democratization of the media should seek first to enlarge the civic sphere by every possible avenue, to strengthen the public sector by increasing its autonomy and funding, and lastly to contain or shrink the commercial sector and work to tap its revenue for the civic sector. Funding this sector properly will require government subvention. Media democrats should be preparing the moral and political environment for such financial support as they do their utmost to advance the cause of existing democratic media.

Notes

1   R.B. Du Boff, *Accumulation and Power* (Armonk, NY: M. E. Sharpe, 1989), 103.

2   There is a wider array of choices on the fringe, but a large fraction of the population doesn't even know these fringe publications exist.

3   See Robert McChesney, "The Battle for the U.S. Airwaves, 1928–1935," *Journal of Communication* (Autumn 1990), 29–57.

4   George Gerbner, "Science or Ritual Dance? A Revisionist View of Television Effects Research," *Journal of Communication* (Spring 1984), 170.

5   European Federation of Community Radios, *Final Report*, 3rd Congress (May 16–20, 1991), 5.

6   The state-owned radio station RAI does not provide programming in Friulian, a language spoken by two-thirds of the population of the northern Italian province of Friuli. A community radio station, Radio Onde Furlane, now serves this 5 million person audience. See ibid.

7   "Factor in the prevalence of repeat callers, and it's clear that the caller pool [on radio talk shows] represents a statistically insignificant slice of the electorate." Jon Keller, "'Hi, I'm Bill, a first-time caller'," *Boston Globe*, 30 April 1995.

8   A major spokesperson for this form of critique and analysis has been Karol Jakubowicz, an official in the General Secretariat of Polish Radio and Television. See his background paper, "Post-Communist Central and Eastern Europe: Promoting the Emergence of Open and Plural Media Systems," 3rd European Ministerial Conference on Mass Media Policy, Cyprus, Oct. 9–10, 1991. Similar views are common among members of European Federal of Community Radios. See text below and document cited in note 5 above.

9   See chapter 3 at note 3.

10   The victory of Gingrich and company in the national elections of 1994 was a setback for democratic broadcasting, among many other matters; Gingrich immediately began a campaign to defund PBS entirely. This has been a longtime aim of Reed Irvine of Accuracy in Media and the extreme right in general, who are opposed to any independent broadcasting and prefer the air waves to be under the protective control of commercial interests. President Clinton and the dominant Democrats have helped PBS survive, but have not done more than that.

11   See chapter 3, and Edward Herman and Robert McChesney, *The Global Media* (London: Cassell, 1997), chaps. 5 and 6.

12   For example, John Malone's and Tele-Communications Inc.'s destructive treat-
      ment of the only fulltime liberal TV network, The 90s Channel, in 1995. See the
      Introduction.

13   A variant of the European system of allocation of time to citizens groups was
      proposed by Ralph Nader in espousing an "audience network." This would be a
      national membership institution of viewers and listeners that would be granted a
      congressional charter as a nonprofit corporation and would also be given 60
      minutes of prime radio and TV time each day to air programs of its choice.
      Audience member contributions would be the prime source of funding; members
      would vote for a governing board, which would decide on programs. Apart from
      its extreme political unrealism, both at the level of legislative possibilities and the
      potential of democratic organization and participation involving something as
      amorphous as an "audience," the proposal would not change the structure of the
      media; it would only insert an hour of noncommercial time in the midst of 23
      hours of commercial programming. The proposal has never gotten off the ground.
      See Ralph Nader, "The Audience Network: Time for the People," (undated, pro-
      vided by the Nader-related Audience Network Coalition); also, Ralph Nader and
      Claire Riley, "Oh Say Can You See: A Broadcast Network for the Audience,"
      Virginia Law Review (Fall 1988).

14   See Herman and Chomsky, *Manufacturing Consent*, 26–28.

15   See chap. 3, 8–9.

16   Many illustrations are provided in Erik Barnouw, *The Sponsor*. (New York: Ox-
      ford University Press, 1978).

17   For history and analysis, see Ralph Engelman, *Public Radio and Television in
      America: A Political History*, (Thousand Oaks, CA: Sage, 1996); William Hoynes,
      Public Television for Sale (Boulder: Westview, 1994); "The Broken Promise of
      Public Television," *EXTRA!* (September/October 1993); "Tilting Right," *EXTRA!*
      (April/May 1993).

18   Robert H. Devine, "The Future of a Public," *Community Television Review*
      (April 1992), 8–9.

19   David Armstrong, "Alternative, Inc.," *In These Times*, 21 August 1995.

20   Eric Fredericksen, "Merger madness in newsweekly biz," *In These Times*, 16
      June 1997.

21   They are, of course, lavish in funding right-wing journals and TV programs that
      propound market-friendly messages. See John Saloma III, *Ominous Politics: The
      New Conservative Labyrinth* (New York: Farrar, Straus and Giroux, 1984). In
      1995 billionaire Rupert Murdoch committed $3 million to help fund *The Stan-
      dard*, to fill a perceived niche in the lineup of right-wing journals.

22   Larry Soley, *Free Radio: Electronic Civil Disobedience* (Boulder, CO: Westview
      Press, 1999), 34.

23 David Barsamian, "Audio Combat," *Z Papers* (October/December 1993), 12.

24 Micropower station Free Radio Berkeley, which has so far fended off attempts by the FCC to shut it down, claims that micropower stations are now able to broadcast to 60 countries via a shortwave radio station in Costa Rica. It reports that excerpts from broadcasts of microwave stations Anarchy Radio, Radio Free Detroit, San Francisco Liberation Radio, and its own station have been relayed through Costa Rica. Free Radio Berkeley and the Free Communications Coalition puts out a newsletter, "Reclaiming the Airwaves," available from Free Radio Berkeley, 1442 A Walnut Street #406, Berkeley CA 94709 (510) 464-3041.

25 Soley, *Free Radio*, 4.

26 For an account of the FCC's attack on micro-radio, ibid., chaps. 7–9.

27 See Barsamian, "Audio Combat," 11.

28 John Fuller and Sue Bomzer, "Friendly (and Not So Friendly) Competition in the PTV Overlapped Markets," PBS Meeting Presentation, PBS Research Department (June 19, 1990).

29 For details on this process, see Diana Agosta, et al., *The Participate Report: A Case Study of Public Access Cable Television in New York State* (New York: Participate/AMIC, 1990).

30 *Roar: The Paper Tiger Television Guide to Media Activism*, published in 1991 by Paper Tiger and the Wexner Center for Arts of Ohio State University, provides a short history of Paper Tiger plus other materials, including an excellent bibliography on the media and media activism.

31 See DeeDee Halleck, "Zapatistas On-Line," *NACLA Report on the Americas* (September/October 1994), 30–32.

32 Ronfeldt's views are summarized in "Netwar Could Make Mexico Ungovernable," a Pacific News Service report dated March 20, 1995.

33 *Media Development* (Fall 1991), 6–8.

34 "Persian Gulf War: The Movie," in Hamid Mowlana et al., eds., *Triumph of the Image* (Boulder: Westview, 1992), chap. 20.

35 LBBS, a community bulletin board system initiated by Z Magazine, began offering a "Left on Line School" in January 1995, with courses given by Barbara Ehrenreich, Holly Sklar, Noam Chomsky, and others.

Name Index

Subject Index

MEDIA AND CULTURE

Sut Jhally & Justin Lewis
General Editors

This series will be publishing works in media and culture, focusing on research embracing a variety of critical perspectives. The series is particularly interested in promoting theoretically informed empirical work using both quantitative and qualitative approaches. Although the focus is on scholarly research, the series aims to speak beyond a narrow, specialist audience.

For additional information about this series or for the submission of manuscripts, please contact:

Dr. Sut Jhally
Dr. Justin Lewis
University of Massachusetts at Amherst
Machmer Hall
Amherst, MA 01003

To order other books in this series, please contact our Customer Service Department at:

800-770-LANG (within the U.S.)
(212) 647-7706 (outside the U.S.)
(212) 647-7707 FAX

or browse online by series at:

WWW.PETERLANG.COM